ADVANCE

A Parent's Guide to

"Laurie LeComer's book provides ‹
they need to observe and assess the
mation provided in the book suppc
provides information on what asses
Helplessness turns into action and
—Larry Silver, M.D., author of *Th*
Understanding and Coping With You

"An operating manual for troublesl
ioral, sensory, educational, and dev
children's healthy, normal developr
Delays is an invaluable resource for
—Sam Goldstein, Ph.D., author of
and *Raising Resilient Children*

A PARENT'S GUIDE TO
Developmental Delays

Recognizing and Coping
with Missed Milestones
in Speech, Movement, Learning,
and Other Areas

Laurie LeComer, M.Ed.

A Perigee Book

THE BERKLEY PUBLISHING GROUP
Published by the Penguin Group
Penguin Group (USA) Inc.
375 Hudson Street, New York, New York 10014, USA
PenguinGroup (Canada), 90 Eglinton Avenue East, Suite 700, Toronto, Ontario M4P 2Y3, Canada
(a division of Pearson Penguin Canada Inc.)
Penguin Books Ltd., 80 Strand, London WC2R 0RL, England
Penguin Group Ireland, 25 St. Stephen's Green, Dublin 2, Ireland (a division of Penguin Books Ltd.)
Penguin Group (Australia), 250 Camberwell Road, Camberwell, Victoria 3124, Australia
(a division of Pearson Australia Group Pty. Ltd.)
Penguin Books India Pvt. Ltd., 11 Community Centre, Panchsheel Park, New Delhi—110 017, India
Penguin Group (NZ), cnr. Airborne and Rosedale Roads, Albany, Auckland 1310, New Zealand
(a division of Pearson New Zealand Ltd.)
Penguin Books (South Africa) (Pty.) Ltd., 24 Sturdee Avenue, Rosebank, Johannesburg 2196,
South Africa
Penguin Books Ltd., Registered Offices: 80 Strand, London WC2R 0RL, England

Copyright © 2006 by Laurie Fivozinsky LeComer
Text design by Kristin del Rosario
Cover design by Jack Ribik

This publication is designed to provide accurate and authoritative information in regard to the subject matter covered. It is sold with the understanding that the publisher is not engaged in rendering legal, medical, or other professional services. If you require legal or medical advice, or other expert assistance, you should seek the services of a competent professional.

PRINTING HISTORY
Perigee trade paperback edition / January 2006

PERIGEE is a registered trademark of Penguin Group (USA) Inc.
The "P" design is a trademark belonging to Penguin Group (USA) Inc.

Library of Congress Cataloging-in-Publication Data

LeComer, Laurie.
   A parent's guide to developmental delays : recognizing and coping with missed milestones
in speech, movement, learning, and other areas / by Laurie LeComer.
      p.   cm.
   ISBN 0-399-53231-5
      1. Developmentally disabled children. 2. Child development deviations. 3. Child
development deviations—Treatment. I. Title.

HV891.L43 2006
649'.152—dc22

                                                                        2005050902

PRINTED IN THE UNITED STATES OF AMERICA

10 9 8 7 6 5 4 3 2 1

To Victor, and my children.

And in loving memory of my mother,
Marilyn.

Contents

Acknowledgments

Words alone cannot express the gratitude and heartfelt thanks I have for the people I am listing here, and who stood alongside me during the book writing process.

I owe so much to my husband, who held down the fort for hours upon hours during the past year. You were my solid rock to lean on, and I could not have done this without you. Thank you for your love and support, Victor. (It definitely came in handy . . . living with a computer god, too!)

And thank you to my kids, who were patient and tolerant, and who heard the phrase, "I have to work on my book," far too many times. Thanks, guys, for helping me in so many special ways, and for trying to have fun with me even when I was, let's say, a little bit tense.

I owe so much to my agent extraordinaire, Judith Riven, who looked, checked, and took the leap. I hope to never have to sell a book without you. You are a pleasure to work with, and it is a wonderful feeling to be contractually attached to someone I trust completely.

Thanks so much to my editor, Marian Lizzi, whose guidance, directness, and sharp intelligence were a gift throughout the process, and thanks to Sheila Curry Oakes for her belief in and support of this project. It was an honor for this book to have landed at Perigee. I am also grateful to Laurie Cedilnik, for her assistance and warmth, Brian Phair, for his careful and meticulous copyediting, and Charles Björklund for the wonderful cover art. To Kim Koren and Colleen Barrett, I thank you for your in-house work on this book. And thank you, Adrienne Schultz. You were truly helpful and made an uncertain transition completely painless.

A special thanks to Douglas Rushkoff, for your respect of my idea and your encouragement in the beginning. You have been my "blood brother" through a couple of my big projects, and I can't wait to see what you and your amazing mind will do next.

Thanks to Kate Kelly for teaching me that a proposal is like a poem; Kitsey Canaan, for holding my hand through the first two chapters, and giving me a good dose of confidence to just move on solo; and thanks to Deborah Herman, who taught me to be mindful and careful about inadvertently making a parent feel "blamed," even within the pages of a book.

Thank you to Ellen Talley Lotsky and Melinda Stickel for great discussions, true friendship, and support. Also, thanks to Joan Villegas and Andrea Timchak for conversations that I treasure; your support has helped me to multitask throughout this year. Thank you to Ann Friedman, M.A., CCC-SLP; Kerry Knop, PT; June Gold; Audrey Barrette; Fionnuala Browning; and Jeffrey Tomlinson for their help and expertise. Thank you to the American Occupational Therapy Association and the Occupational Therapy Associations of the states of California, New York, and Massachusetts.

To Julie Russell Seen, OTR/L, a huge thanks for our friendship and conversations. I was so happy to have had the opportunity to work with and treat kids with you. Our conversations over the years definitely had an impact on what was written in this book.

To my Dad, Sherman, and also Carol, Karen, and Jon, thank you for being behind me, and for your excitement with all of the LeComer family endeavors.

I owe a lot to Carol Sissala and Easter Seal Treatment Center, for my early success with autistic children. And thank you to United Cerebral Palsy, Georgetown University Hospital, the University of Maryland, Tufts University, Lesley University, Scarsdale Public Schools, and Greenwich Public Schools.

A special thank-you to the families who have trusted me with their children, and to the children who let me challenge them.

Introduction

As a professional special educator, I work directly with children who have special needs, and their families. I work one-on-one with kids, run special groups, consult with teachers and therapists, and oversee many caseloads by monitoring programs and measuring progress. Along with teams of child professionals, I evaluate and diagnose disabilities.

As a consultant for developmental and behavioral issues, I help doctors, parents, and child organizations understand the importance of diagnosing developmental delays and differences early, as well as the diverse daily struggles faced by children with developmental delays, autism, cerebral palsy, learning disabilities, and a host of other difficulties. I also help parents learn new ways to approach everyday tasks with their children, and I help them understand that the little things they do daily will help their children learn and make progress. I work with doctors to correctly diagnose children, because many pediatricians only see kids for a short "snapshot in time." I observe, spend time with, and get down on the floor with many kids to help discern confusing and look-alike symptoms.

As a mother of three, I have experienced my share of fear and concern over my own kids' development. I remember when it became apparent that my second child, a toddler at the time, was having difficulty coordinating his motor movements and forming sounds. Although *I* could usually understand him, other family members and friends would constantly look to my husband and me for clarification. Through my work, I was practiced at keeping an objective distance when working with other people's children, but seeing *my* child struggle left me emotionally out of sorts. I remember my son trying his best to communicate with others, and how fiercely protective I became when people pointed out his difficulties. I was beside myself with worry. I felt that if I didn't do something to help him right away, I would be failing him.

When I raised these issues at my son's next well-baby visit, the pediatrician brushed off my concerns. He even suggested with a condescending chuckle that my profession was making me paranoid. I've since discovered it is all too common for pediatricians to respond to parents' legitimate concerns and questions by simply saying "Children will develop at their own rates," or "You shouldn't compare your children." While these are true statements, they unfairly and unwisely discredit the intimate knowledge parents have of their children.

Despite the doctor's comment, I knew something was not right in my son's development. Trusting my instincts, I began looking for information about my son's symptoms. Scouring dozens of books and websites, I found descriptions of disorders that matched some of my observations of my child, but no one book or description specifically defined what I was seeing. I discovered many definitions of disorders that included deficits that clearly did not pertain to my child. I found that popular child development books give good information on the typical milestones babies and children should reach, but they left many questions unanswered. There was no one book that addressed multiple types of symptoms.

I later learned that, like me, many concerned parents pour over numerous books trying to answer questions such as:

- What do I do if my child isn't reaching typical milestones?

- Is my child's behavior abnormal?

- When is the right time to worry?

- Am I being overly sensitive?

- Will my child have a learning disability or be a special education child?

A Parent's Guide to Developmental Delays is the book I wish I had had. Whether you are a parent or caregiver, this book will help you identify atypical or late development early. You will gain the knowledge you need about what developmental differences may look like and how they may play out. The following chapters will shed light on the "gray areas" of your child's development and will clearly describe what behaviors at what age should be viewed with careful scrutiny. Behaviors of concern may relate to one or several different areas of development including:

- cognition

- speech and language

- social and emotional skills

- gross and fine motor skills

- sensory integration and sensory processing

It is important for you to know that *not every developmental difference or delay leads to a disability.* When caught early, many developmental differences can be remedied. That's why it is so important for you to *trust your instincts* if something about your child doesn't seem right. When diagnosed and treated early, children can make tremendous gains in developmentally weak or delayed areas. After early intervention, many children catch up to their peers and cannot even be identified by an outsider as having had a delay. When a child does not receive help before school age, however, it is more likely the child's progress will be slower and more likely he or she will be labeled as having a disability. Early detection of potential developmental delays will allow you to partner with qualified professions for a plan of strategic interventions that can make a huge difference in your child's life. This book will show you how to do this.

As parents, it is easy for us to fear for our children, and it is easy for those fears to grow to huge proportions as we worry about our children's futures. Our fears for our children come from not knowing what is wrong. For many of you, this book will allay your fears, as you learn that what you are seeing is actually within the range of what is considered "typical" or "age-appropriate." In the early years almost all parents have a concern about their child's development. In fact, fewer than a third of these concerns will turn out to be a true developmental delay or disorder.

This book will honestly and simply address your questions about your child's development. It will provide a clear roadmap from your first moment of concern through all the steps necessary to meet your child's needs. This book will empower you to help your child.

Part I will address your questions about normal and atypical development. It will explain how to know if your child is or is not developing typically or on time. Checklists and exercises will be provided to help you pinpoint and clarify your concerns. Also, I will describe the roles of the child professionals you may encounter, including doctors, therapists, and teachers. You will learn what questions to ask them, and a script will be provided so that you can approach and talk with these professionals confidently.

Part II covers the different categories of development and the disorders associated with each one. In this section, you will find information that will directly illuminate your individual concerns. Children that I have worked with will be described, providing you with a window into other children's true lives, difficulties, and treatments. These examples will help you gain new insights into what the different types of developmental challenges look like. You will learn about how normal growth progresses in each area, as well as learn some of the factors that can negatively affect normal growth. You will learn how to formulate your own at-home intervention plan, called "The Test of Three." Using this technique, you will be able to discern whether your child's difficulties may be related to outside or environmental factors, or whether they may truly be related to developmental or biological factors. Checklists for Red Flags of Atypical Development are provided so that you may gain information on developmental warning signs, and special exercises for each developmental category can be found at the end of each chapter, so that you can identify potential problems and begin to stimulate development in your child right away.

Part III offers plans for taking action and getting help. You will learn about the evaluation process and what testing may be like for your child. You will learn how delays and disorders are treated, and the different plans that address them. You will "see" what actual therapy sessions are like, and you will be able to use an Early Help Checklist as a guide for moving forward. Creative solutions and other parents' suggestions will inspire you, and you will learn that children *do* often progress.

The case studies, examples, and checklists in this book are truly meant to help guide you in researching and addressing your own child's unique symptoms and situation.

This book has been a labor of love. It is my way of reaching out to all parents who love and worry about their children. Many of you have phoned and e-mailed me with your questions. This book is the best answer I can give you.

PART I

Unsettling Questions

Am I Overreacting?

I'm worried that my baby isn't crawling yet. She can't hold her bottle very well either. Our doctor said to wait and see if she's doing better at her next well-baby visit. She's a good baby. It's probably nothing, but how do I know for sure?

My three-year-old son seems different to me than the other kids. He refuses to join in many activities at his preschool and will scream uncontrollably if his teachers try to force him to participate. His teachers are concerned, and so are my husband and I. A lot of the time it seems as if he doesn't hear or understand what I say to him. Our pediatrician told us to wait and see if another year of preschool will help him develop better skills. Am I overreacting?

The many parents I have heard from over the years have told me uncannily similar stories. Typically a parent becomes aware of a behavior or an inability in her baby or child that doesn't seem quite right. Family and friends begin to comment and compare. "Shouldn't he be talking by now?" "Isn't that kind of tantrum unusual for a child her age?" All parents have moments of worry for their children. How are you to know when your worries merit real concern?

The first thing I want to tell you when you suspect your child is not developing normally is to *trust your intuition*. Your instincts and your uneasiness about your child's development are meaningful tools. Over and over again, I have found that parents can be trusted to know when something about their child is not right. Though there is the rare parent who is needlessly convinced that the child's behaviors are abnormal, most parental concerns are not unfounded. In almost every case, it is in your child's best interest to be overly vigilant rather than ignore a possible developmental problem.

We parents, however, tend to second-guess ourselves even when in our hearts we know that no one knows our children as well as we do. We love our children and feel an enormous responsibility to care for them. With this responsibility often comes the fear of making the wrong move. Consequently, when you feel concern about your child's development, it is often the not-knowing that causes the deepest worry. Do I see what I think I see? What am I supposed to do about it? What could it mean about my child's future? These questions can cause you enormous fear and distress, and sometimes even panic. You might feel sad and isolated. Often we feel helpless or blame ourselves when we witness our children being overly reactive or unable to perform certain skills others their age do with ease.

When family members, doctors, or friends brush off your concerns for your child, or when they don't validate what you see, your confusion and stress can increase. You might feel doubt, hopelessness, or even anger. But remember, these people probably don't spend as much time with your child as you do and may not be around to witness the day-to-day behaviors or interactions your child has. If you are concerned about your child's behavior or abilities, *trust your judgment*. If you pursue the issue and discover that your child is progressing normally, you will have gained a better understanding of child development and of *your* child, which will only help make you a better parent. Many parents who are vigilant early quickly educate themselves and ascertain that their child will be just fine. However, because early intervention makes a huge difference in the outcome of children with developmental differences and disorders, your vigilance is key.

Developmental concerns should always be addressed with attention and respect. If it turns out that your suspicions were justified, you will be doing your child an invaluable service by intervening early.

Four Children with Puzzling Behavior

When Diana was twenty months old she stopped using words she had previously known quite well. She also began to resist being held by her mother. Instead of showing interest in other children or a desire to play, Diana would quietly walk to her bedroom closet and crouch there, all the while fluttering her tiny fingers in front of her eyes. "It took me a while to believe that what I thought was happening was really happening," her mother reported. "I could not fathom that my daughter could actually lose words and even personality traits that were so much a part of her." Diana became obsessed with the household lights and would beckon for help so that she could flip the switches on and off repeatedly. Her mother let her because it became one of the few times Diana sought out interaction. Terrified, her mother brought her to their pediatrician, only to be told it was "too early to tell" if there were problems with her daughter. "After that, I called the pediatrician almost daily to describe new unusual behaviors I was seeing in Diana. I think they thought I was losing my mind."

When a trusted professional discounts what you see, it can almost feel as if you *are* losing your mind. Sadly, many pediatricians and other professionals fail to recognize the early signs of developmental difficulties. Because parents often assume the family doctor is the final authority on their children's health, they often mistakenly accept advice to "wait and see."

Seth, a three-and-a-half-year-old, had violent tantrums. He would throw things, and kick and bite people around him. Though Seth was generally a quiet child, his tantrums and explosiveness were unpredictable. Sometimes simply receiving a compliment or being asked to do something would set him off. Though his teachers thought Seth was bright, his tantrums were so uncontrollable they were actually afraid of him. When the director of his preschool asked his parents to find another school, Seth's parents were ready to get help. They, too, thought something was not quite right. When they brought Seth to their family doctor, his response was to advise them to be firmer with their parenting.

No doubt some children do behave inappropriately because of lax parenting. But when a child has a real disability, blaming the parents, in effect, for the child's behavior only increases the parents' feelings of guilt and the stress the family is under. Even worse in Seth's case was that stricter parenting did not help him cope with his disability.

David, almost five, was extremely uncoordinated. He had a hard time throwing and kicking balls, and during games it was hard for him to keep track of what was happening. His peers frequently teased him. David's walk was unusual, too, and his teachers reported that he always ran his hand along the walls when walking down hallways. Though David seemed willing to play with and help his peers, children tended to avoid him, and he had no real friends. When David's parents asked their doctor for the name of a child psychologist, the doctor told them they were in danger of giving their child a lifelong complex if they sent him to therapy because he's lousy at sports.

This is another sad example of unhelpful advice. The physician failed to see that David's weak areas needed remediation, and he made a psychological judgment ("giving him a complex") for which he had no training. Reactions like these often stop parents from getting help for their children.

None of the children in the examples had an obvious syndrome or physical disability at birth. All reached many typical milestones as infants. As they grew, however, there were things about them that did not seem quite right, problems that could be signs of atypical development. While their parents were aware of the problems, they were not equipped with the information they needed to make informed choices for their children.

Often when parents voice concerns, they are told "No two children develop alike" or "you're overreacting" or "just wait and see." Even when the parent thinks something is wrong, such a comment can be comforting because it's often what parents hope to hear.

For some children, the problems will indeed go away over time. But if a child does have a real delay or disability, parents who take the "wait and see" route later express deep regret they did not intervene sooner. All the evidence shows that the earlier a delay or disability is diagnosed and treated, the better the outcome for the child.

There are many well-trained and attentive doctors and therapists who handle developmental difficulties superbly. Many physicians do make accurate diagnoses and referrals for our children. However, it's important for parents to remember that not all pediatricians notice the nuances of developmental difficulties in the brief periods they see children. In the medical and educational communities, there continue to be frequent oversights in noticing early warning signs that a child's development may not be on track. This ignorance causes parents needless pain and confusion, and worse, it deprives children of the early help they need and deserve. Perhaps this is why studies show that fewer than half of children with developmental and behavioral problems are identified before they enter school.

What Causes a Disability?

A child's development begins before a baby is born—much sooner than most of us realize—and sometimes developmental anomalies have already made their marks long before we gain any knowledge of their presence. Prior to birth, some parents learn of syndromes and malformations from prenatal testing. Parents who give birth to seemingly "perfect" babies may not know of or see developmental difficulties until they become more visible in the course of time.

When parents discover a possible delay or disability in their children, they often spend sleepless nights reviewing the pregnancy. "Could the fish I ate have had too much mercury?" "I must have damaged the baby when

I took that ibuprofen before I knew I was pregnant!" "I should not have gone on the plane because of the radiation." Before you start blaming yourself, remember that most experts believe that abnormal development is due to a combination of hereditary factors, environmental influences, and random or unknown factors.

Some sort of injury to the brain is one cause of abnormal development. Oxygen deprivation during pregnancy or labor can cause subtle to severe brain damage, as can alcoholism and drug use. Children born to alcoholics or drug addicts have a very high risk for atypical development. If a pregnant woman contracts fifth disease or measles there is a risk of brain injury to the fetus. Children born prematurely also have a statistically higher risk of brain injury. Accidental brain injuries, such as from near-drowning or choking experiences, can also severely impede development.

While we can identify biological factors and environmental risk factors for some delays and disabilities, we still do not know precisely what causes most of them. Delays and disabilities may be caused by chemical imbalances and/or genetic factors. Chemical imbalances have been implicated in disabilities such as ADHD and bipolar disorder. Medications are used at times to correct faulty biochemical levels.

Certain genes, whether acquired through heredity or mutation, can also cause abnormal development. For example, Down Syndrome and other chromosomal abnormalities are known to cause severe disabilities in children. ADHD, learning disabilities, and dyslexia seem to be expressions of inherited brain wiring; it has been demonstrated that these disabilities appear in succeeding generations of some families. But before you start blaming yourself or your dyslexic grandfather, remember that genetic factors alone do not determine whether or not a child will have a given disorder. Sometimes these disorders come forth, but sometimes they don't. As for the factors that make this difference, scientists are still looking.

The currently available guidelines for the risk of children with developmental delays or disabilities include:

- Pregnant mothers who are age thirty-five or older.

- Pregnant mothers who ingest or are exposed to drugs, alcohol, or toxins.

- Parents who have a biological child with a chromosomal abnormality.

- Parents who themselves have a developmental disability.

- Parents who have a family history for a certain disability or birth defect.

- Parents who may carry certain genes known to cause disabilities in certain ethnic groups.

Child Development

An infant's brain grows from the early stages of pregnancy, but at birth it is still not fully developed. During infancy and childhood, the brain grows rapidly, generating millions of brain cells and connections. Inside the brain, there are distinct areas that house the many different potentials for skills we need to properly function. One area of the brain may house the potential for the development of language. Another area may house the potential for vision, and another, the potential for coordinated movement. For each of these areas there is a period of time in infancy or early childhood when it is optimally plastic or malleable, that is, when the opportunity for neurological growth is at its highest. Therefore, for each area of development there is a unique window of opportunity when the neurological "wiring" of the brain can be affected by external experience and dramatic leaps in learning are possible.

When a healthy child is cared for, her brain grows rapidly, resulting in a rapid growth of skills. Studies in child development have documented infants' and children's growth and acquisition of skills so that we know on average what milestones children typically reach month to month and year to year. But even some healthy babies and children do not fall neatly into the typical patterns. Some may lag and then have a growth spurt, while other babies' brains may grow too fast, possibly resulting in autistic-like symptoms.

Significantly, if a healthy child's environment does not provide the opportunity to practice skills, her brain will not be stimulated and her growth will be delayed. For example, a mother I know was very worried about her baby's motor skills. He was not crawling or pulling up to a stand at the time the child development charts said he ought to be able to. Eventually she realized that her day care provider kept the baby in an exersaucer most of the day. He was not getting the opportunity to explore or to exercise his body. With a change in day care, the baby quickly acquired new motor skills and caught up to the typical developmental timeframe.

Many families who adopt children from overseas report that their children have developmental delays. Children who spend their first years in orphanages often lack opportunities to physically explore or to develop emotional attachments. For example, babies who are always kept in cribs may not learn to walk, or even to sit up, at the usual age. If they have insufficient interaction with adults, or insufficient exposure to language, they may not learn to speak. With appropriate therapy in early childhood, however, most parents report that many of these children progress rapidly, many catching up to their peers.

The science of the growth of a child's brain is of great importance for children who have atypical development. When an infant or child receives help early, the child's brain can actually be stimulated and changed for the better because it is in the stage of rapid growth. Over time, however, the brain's rate of growth slows down. Most of the "windows of opportunity" for the acquisition of skills begin early and end early. Many of these windows close before a child reaches seven or eight. This is why you may hear many child professionals speak of a child's early years as an overall window of opportunity. After this age, therapeutic interventions tend to be far less effective simply because the growth rate of the child's brain is so much slower.

Many, but not all, delays and disabilities originate in the brain. If neural or chemical connections break down in one part of the brain, information flow is interrupted. This may not only affect the breakdown area but other areas as well that would have put the "stopped" information to use.

The Difference Between Developmental Delays and Disabilities

A developmental delay and a disability (also called a developmental disability) are two different things. The term *developmental delay* describes a significant lag in functioning in one or more areas, as compared to what is expected for a child that age. A developmental delay is not considered to be a lifelong condition. In many cases developmental delays are considered to be curable with appropriate therapy. Occasionally, however, what parents or professionals originally believe to be a developmental delay may ultimately turn out to be a symptom of a disability.

A *disability* (also called a developmental disability) is a lifelong condition that results in major impairments and requires services indefinitely. Though a person with a disability may learn and progress, by definition, he will have the disability for the rest of his life. For example, a person with dyslexia who receives appropriate therapy may learn to read, but he will always be dyslexic and will always need accommodations (such as oral instructions or extra time for reading assignments).

The Confusing Nature of Diagnoses

Children who are diagnosed with a disability are presumed to have a lifelong condition. However, because of human fallibility, the ongoing research into disabilities, and the political realities of school bureaucracies, this is not always the case. Sometimes children are misdiagnosed. Sometimes new research changes our understanding of a disability and its treatment. Sometimes parents lobby for a specific diagnosis for a child because they believe that is their only means of obtaining the services the child needs, and in some cases it may well be. For example, a child might have Nonverbal Learning Disorder (NLD), but the parents insist on a diagnosis of Asperger Syndrome because the school district won't provide services for NLD.

Of course many children are properly evaluated and accurately diagnosed, but I have seen questionable evaluative procedures in both the medical and educational communities. Therefore, I advise you to educate yourself as much as you can. If you are ever uncomfortable with a professional's opinion or diagnosis, get a second opinion.

Will My Child Be Labeled?

If your child is significantly lagging behind in one or more developmental areas when he enters kindergarten, there is a good chance he will be labeled as having a disability or a learning disability. In most states the law requires schools to provide special services (such as special education, therapy, or classroom accommodations) for a child *only if* he has that label. (Some states allow a child to use the label "developmentally delayed" until age eight.) While this kind of labeling is unfortunate in that it can stigmatize a child, given the way the laws are now written, it may be the only way children can obtain the help they need to succeed.

Some children are very weak in certain areas but are not what most would call disabled. Forward-thinking school systems sometimes provide "building level" services without requiring a diagnosis and a label so that these children can get the help they need. I believe this is an excellent idea that helps to keep many kids from being diagnosed with a disability.

The Importance of Early Intervention

Whenever I am about to take on a new case, my first question is, "How old is he/she?" As I discussed above, science has shown that there is a window of opportunity in the child's early years when the rapidly growing brain is most receptive to outside stimuli. My own experience in working with children bears this out: *the earlier a delay or disability gets treated, the better.* Dramatic progress can be made when a child's difficulties are addressed early, especially before school age. Sometimes, developmental delays can be completely taken care of by the time the child enters kindergarten. In the case of a disability, treating it early can make a tremendous difference in how it affects the child's life.

If you wait until the child is older, her progress can be slower and more laborious. Certainly a child can still be helped after she has started school, but the older the child, the slower her progress will be. Older children also generally experience far more emotional frustration in trying to catch up to their peers.

When I work with delayed and disabled kids, I have a constant feeling of racing against time. The race is one well worth winning because I know that the more I can do for them early, the better their lives will be.

If your child has a delay or disability, it is in his best interest to begin interventions as early as possible. The sooner difficulties are supported and the sooner remediation is received, the better the outcome for the child. Although some doctors state that disabilities may not show up until a child has to perform classroom tasks, I have never known a disability to suddenly appear when the child enters school (with the exception of extremely rare degenerative syndromes). There are always early signs in the child's skills or behavior. In the best case, an alert parent will notice these signs early on and seek help.

Most parents understand the importance of the decisions they make for their children. Granted, decisions about interventions are not always easy to make. I have seen many parents become paralyzed by the sudden involvement of professionals expressing opinions about their child. I have seen parents become overwhelmed with information and the sheer weight of anxiety. In these circumstances it can be very difficult for parents to know what to do for their child. Some parents respond by halting all action. While this is understandable, in my experience, it's a poor choice for the child.

These two boys were very much alike when I first saw them, but their parents made very different choices for their children.

Cameron was evaluated at three years, five months, at the recommendation of his preschool teacher and a school administrator. His frequent tantrums, hand-flapping, and limited eye contact and speech made him stand out from the other children. Cameron's teacher reported that the other children shunned him and that she felt unsure about how to deal with him. The other classroom teacher also stated that she and the other children felt unsafe with Cameron around. Cameron's parents decided that Cameron was not ready for social situations and that he needed more time to be with Mom and to develop at home. They decided against sending Cameron to a special education preschool where he would have received special help and services.

Enrique was evaluated at three years, seven months, due to parent concerns about his inability to relate to others. Enrique used little speech, flapped his hands and arms when excited or agitated, and at times would bite his wrist. Enrique had poor eye contact and would frequently have a tantrum or drop to the floor when guided to a new location or when interrupted from an activity. Enrique's parents were nervous but relieved when their son was placed in a special education preschool that would provide special services. His parents chose to be in close contact with the professionals who worked with him so they would know what they could do with him at home.

Currently, Cameron and Enrique are first graders. Cameron is in a self-contained classroom for children with severe special needs. Cameron's teacher reports that she feels he is bright, but that it is almost impossible to get him to do any academic work. She says he has huge tantrums, but that his aide handles them well. Enrique is currently in a regular first grade classroom. With the support of a classroom aide, he does regular first grade work. He has some special classroom tools to help keep him organized, such as his own schedule and a reinforcement plan designed especially for him. He works on social skills with the school psychologist. He has a friend and enjoys play dates with that friend.

Early intervention and remediation can make a big difference for children with developmental delays and disabilities. Noticing and doing something about developmental difficulties early can prevent problems later. Engaging your child and being vigilant about his or her development can be one of the greatest gifts you give your child. I applaud you for looking further, for checking, and for wanting to find out more. Your child doesn't know it yet, but you have embarked on a journey that will help him or her succeed.

TWO

What Do I Do If I Suspect My Child Is Not Developing Normally?

"I'm tired of being told that this is nothing, and that he'll grow out of it!"

"This is my third child, and I know something isn't right!"

"Everyone says to wait and see if she'll start to do all of these things, but how long am I supposed to wait?"

"None of the child development books seem to apply to my child."

You're concerned that your child is not developing normally, and you want to find out for sure if something is wrong. How do you go about it? Who are the professionals you should talk to? How do you discuss your concerns?

For many parents (myself included), it takes time to feel comfortable talking about what may be going on with your child. It may be hard to even explain what you are seeing. Describing a child's general demeanor can be extremely difficult, especially when it strikes you as unusual.

So how does a parent begin to clearly define their concerns, or know whether help is needed? Friends and family may be discreetly or not-so-discreetly hinting that you should get help, and you may be receiving all sorts of conflicting opinions and suggestions. To know whether your child will indeed need help, you must first develop a critical eye and ear. You must begin to watch the behaviors or inabilities of concern carefully and often. When observing the child, keep in mind that each behavior has a purpose. Notice whether the behaviors or inabilities happen at certain times of the day or in certain places. Notice whether they are sporadic or constant.

In order for you to get an accurate assessment of your child's difficulties, you need to be able to describe your concerns to professionals such as physicians, therapists, and psychologists. Because these professionals have individual areas of expertise, and because each profession tends to use a particular jargon, it's important for you to learn how to talk about what you see in your child using clear, specific observations. The better you are able to describe your child, the more likely it is that the professionals will get an accurate picture of her issues.

We are going to begin to define what you are seeing. I will give you a simple and easy way to do this, but please do not underestimate the importance of this first step.

Divide a piece of paper in two, and write "strengths" at the top of one side and "concerns" at the top of the other side. Begin to think about your child's strengths. Ask yourself, what does my child do well? What do I love about my child? List your child's positive traits and abilities under the heading, "strengths." Next, think about what truly concerns you about your child. Ask yourself, where is my child struggling? What do I feel my child should be better at right now? What scares me about my child? What does my child do that seems "not quite right?" List your thoughts, and what you feel are your child's difficulties under the heading, "concerns."

Make your lists in both columns as long as necessary. Don't leave anything out, whether it is an obvious behavior that only happens once in a while, or a subtle behavior that happens every day. Not only will the entries under "concerns" help define your child's difficulties, your entries in the "strengths" column will provide you, and the professionals who might help, clues to the best "ways in" to your child, so that they can help your child to progress.

Now take a close look at your completed lists. Do your lists reflect the parts of your child that you find wonderful and appealing? Do your lists thoroughly reflect the difficulties he is having? Many parents find that this simple exercise helps them to clarify their true concerns. Parents also find that this exercise reminds them of how many wonderful things there are about their child, which can be overlooked when the possibility of a developmental problem looms overhead.

Once you've made your list, the next step is to flesh it out with specific documentation and examples. While some may be able to complete this next step quickly, others will find that it may take a few days of observing and thinking about their child. Take the time you need to ensure your examples are accurate and representative of your situation.

Let's now define your concerns even further. For each item under concerns, complete the following by placing one concern into the blank and providing specific examples.

My child shows that he/she _____ when he/she:

1. _____

2. _____

3. _____

Let's say in my "concerns" column I have written: "He's uncoordinated, I can't understand him when he's saying something, and he gets dizzy far too easily." Now I will enter each one of my concerns into the phrase above and come up with three different specific examples that demonstrate the weakness or concern. I will do this step separately with each concern that I have or weakness I am seeing in my child. This is what I would have after completing the sentence blank for my first concern:

My child shows that he is uncoordinated when he:

1. _can't figure out how to get his body to kick a ball_

2. _trips over his own feet_

3. _frequently bumps into people_

Here is my second concern:

My child shows that he is not understandable when he:

1. _tries to tell you something and he can't pronounce the words_

2. _points and grunts instead of using words_

3. _gives up in frustration when people don't understand him_

I now have some specific illustrations of the types of difficulties I am seeing in my child. The longer the list you can generate of real-life incidents, the more clues you and child professionals will have to work with when looking into what may be happening with your child. It will help therapists, doctors, and child professionals to know these specific examples.

Now it's your turn to complete the phrases with your child's concerns. Do this for each item listed in the concern column. You may fill in the page here or do this on your own paper.

My child shows that he/she _____ when he/she:

1. _____

2. _____

3. _____

My child shows that he/she _____ when he/she:

1. _____

2. _____

3. _____

My child shows that he/she _____ when he/she:

1. _____

2. _____

3. _____

You will use these specific examples that you have listed when you speak with the child professionals that can help your child. But first, you can now use them to gain clarity on which areas of development need to be investigated further.

The Different Areas of Development

When developmental delays or disabilities are suspected in children, the professionals who evaluate children's difficulties look carefully at the different areas of development. Within these areas are varied skills. Through testing and observation, professionals can determine how well a child is performing these skills in comparison to same-age typical peers. Investigating suspected developmental problems is usually a team effort involving several child professionals. Through testing, interacting with, and observing the child, professionals try to pinpoint specific areas of need or "deficit areas."

In this section we will look at each category and the professionals who treat deficits in that area. Below each description you will find a "categories of concern checklist." This checklist is meant to help you decipher which areas of development your child may need help in and/or the areas of development you need to know more about. The examples of concerns within each list are common concerns for children of several different ages, and are meant to give you a general idea of the typical skills in each catagory of development. I will also explain which professionals work with children whose behaviors may look similar to your child's behaviors. After reading through each category description, check off any concern that relates to or is similar to the concerns you have for your child. You can then find more specific and detailed information in the following chapters extremely helpful and beneficial. A separate chapter is devoted to each category of development to help make your research quick and easy.

Cognitive Development

Cognitive development refers to a child's abstract thinking, reasoning ability, and ability to retain and apply new information. Attending and problem-solving are also cognitive skills.

Cognitive functioning and development are evaluated by special education specialists, neurologists and psychologists. Cognitive deficits and delays are usually treated by special educators. These teachers help children learn concepts and use individually tailored strategies to help children learn. Here are some cognitive concerns:

_____ He/she seems to act much younger than other children the same age.

_____ He/she has an unbelievably short attention span and can't seem to concentrate.

_____ He/she does not recognize family or friends.

_____ He/she can't seem to remember simple songs or games.

_____ He/she does not seem interested in or inquisitive about toys.

_____ He/she does not recognize when objects, books, or toys are upside down or right side up.

_____ He/she has an "out of sight, out of mind" attitude about his or her favorite toys, food, and people.

_____ He/she seems unusually docile.

_____ He/she seems really slow to learn anything new.

_____ He/she cannot remember numbers or letters even though we work on them every day.

_____ He/she has no concept of "tomorrow."

_____ He/she cannot tell me his or her name nor age.

_____ He/she needs me to constantly reshow him or her, over and over again, how to do things.

Speech and Language Development

Speech and language refers to the child's ability to form speech sounds, the ability to express and receive communications, and the child's auditory processing and processing of information. Speech and language pathologists are specialists who are trained to evaluate and treat speech and language difficulties. They help children with different types of communication issues, from language processing to articulation errors. Here are some common speech and language concerns:

_____ He/she is extremely hard to understand.

_____ He/she has continual difficulties with feedings.

_____ He/she will only eat soft foods and/or will not chew.

_____ He/she does not babble or try to imitate words like I see other children my child's age doing.

_____ He/she does not remember very common words.

_____ His/her voice sounds unusual.

_____ He/she struggles to get words out.

_____ He/she is not using real words yet.

_____ He/she seems to have his/her own language.

_____ He/she does not seem to understand or remember my directions.

_____ He/she does not seem able to express him/herself.

Social and Emotional Development

Social and emotional development are evaluated by psychiatrists, psychologists, or social workers. These specialists look at whether a child is socially competent in his or her interactions with others, and whether the child has the ability to cope with different types of situations. They will also look at whether the child has appropriate adaptive and play behaviors, and how the child sees him or herself. Psychiatrists, psychologists, and social workers can help children develop better social skills and teach strategies for improving attention and behavioral difficulties. Here are some common social and emotional concerns:

_____ He/she is unable to stay focused on an activity.

_____ He/she will inappropriately focus on an object for a long period of time, or will repeat an action over and over again.

_____ He/she does not show a need for love and interaction.

_____ He/she loses control and becomes explosive or aggressive frequently.

_____ He/she will "lose it" over unusual reasons that most wouldn't even think of.

_____ He/she does not make frequent eye contact.

_____ He/she does not show interest in playing with other children.

_____ He/she does not seem to fear anything.

_____ He/she seems anxious and fearful about something almost daily.

Gross Motor and Fine Motor Development

Gross motor skill development refers to the child's use of his or her large muscle groups. Skills such as rolling over, sitting up, and walking require gross motor skills. Physical therapists help children who are having difficulty with mobility and large muscle movements. Fine motor skills use the small muscles of the arms and hands, allowing children to grasp tiny objects, write, or lift utensils such as spoons to their mouths. Occupational therapists help children who are having difficulties with fine motor movements. Here are some common gross and fine motor concerns:

_____ He/she is completely unable to hold his/her head up.

_____ He/she isn't walking yet and should be, I believe.

_____ He/she likes to sit in one place most of the time.

_____ He/she usually only uses one side of his/her body.

_____ He/she seems much floppier than other children his/her age.

_____ It appears that his/her arm(s) or leg(s) is (are) stiff.

_____ He/she is unable to feed him/herself.

_____ He/she still scribbles when his/her classmates are already drawing.

_____ He/she walks on his/her toes.

_____ He/she is constantly dropping things out of his/her hands.

Sensory Processing and Sensory Integration

Sensory processing is a less well-known area of development. It refers to how well the child's sensory systems (feelings of touch, spatial awareness, sensitivity to noise, light, movement) work together. Some children over-register sensory information and may be extremely sensitive or overly reactive, while other children may under-register sensory information, causing a compromised awareness of sensations, or sensory seeking behaviors. Children with sensory processing difficulties may not understand how their bodies relate to people or objects around them. Sensory processing and sensory integration issues are treated by occupational therapists. Here are some common sensory processing concerns:

_____ He/she is unable to get the hang of toilet training.

_____ He/she is extremely sensitive to loud noises.

_____ He/she will not keep his/her clothes on.

_____ He/she grinds his/her teeth every night.

_____ He/she will only eat certain foods with similar textures.

_____ He/she seems to be extremely uncoordinated.

_____ He/she gets tired extremely easily.

_____ He/she bumps into people and furniture frequently.

_____ He/she gets dizzy very easily.

_____ He/she can spin and spin and will not get dizzy.

_____ He/she does not like to be touched.

_____ He/she seems to want to be inappropriately close to people and tends to be "touchy" too much.

In children, a delay or disability in a certain area of development may affect other areas of development. For instance, a child's inability to attend or focus may make it difficult for him to make cognitive connections and understand new information. A child's slow motor development may also hinder learning new cognitive skills because exploration may be limited. Therefore, when children present with difficulties in seemingly one area of development, other areas of development may be evaluated, too. For instance, if a child appears to be having difficulty grasping cognitive skills or concepts, there is a good chance the child's language skills will be looked at and evaluated as well. Sometimes a child's language processing difficulties make the child appear as if he or she is unable to understand new cognitive or academic skills. Cognition and language are closely related, and deficits in one area can affect the other.

Now that you have completed the categories of concern checklist, make a list of the areas of development you are concerned about for your child.

Finding a category of concern can be empowering, but it also may leave you feeling anxious about your child's situation. Take a moment to congratulate yourself on completing this important step. Then, before we move on, I suggest the following exercise to help you get even more clarity and focus on why this process is important to you. Fill in the following phrase:

It is important to me that my child be able to improve and move forward because:

_____

_____

_____

List as many reasons as you can think of. Maybe you don't want your child to stand out or be teased. Maybe you know how important it will be for your child to be able to play with other children and make friends. You may feel your child will need to learn to cope with his sensitivities so that he can enjoy everyday experiences. Possibly you want your child to be able to communicate much more skillfully so that she can show how much she knows. You probably want your child to feel proud of herself and confident.

The purpose of this exercise is to remind yourself *why* you are taking these steps for your child. You have your own personal reasons, and every one of them is important.

Keep the list in a place where you can refer to it as you travel with your child through the coming months. Look back at the list in your moments of unease, fear, or frustration. It will empower you to keep going and finding out more.

Once you've made your lists, you may be ready to approach your family physician, or you may want to continue to educate yourself. You may want to read further in this book, or browse online (See Appendix II: Resources). You can help yourself help your child by learning as much as possible. Remember first, trust your instinct, learn to describe what you are seeing, and then begin to educate yourself on delays or disabilities you think your child may have symptoms of. Talk with other parents about concerns, and with parents who have gone through early interventions or testing with their children. Ask questions. Ask your pediatrician or local school district questions you may have about how certain situations may be handled.

You may be pleasantly surprised if you find that the symptoms of your "worst scenario" are very different than your child's or much more extreme than what you are seeing. I know one mother who was convinced her child was autistic. After some research, however, and after observing a class for autistic preschool children, she realized that her son's symptoms were much less severe than the children she observed. Her son was much more communicative, independent, and would interact with other children to a much larger degree than the autistic children. She left relieved but eager to find out more about her own son's more subtle symptoms.

When you are ready—and I urge you not to delay—make an appointment with your family physician. He or she may be able to give you an accurate diagnosis or may need to refer you to other professionals. If you're not satisfied with the outcome, you may need to do more research on your own.

Some parents are comfortable talking to physicians, clinicians, and other professionals. Others of us find ourselves easily intimidated by people, experts, or people in authority. Remember, however, that you know your child better than anyone else, and you care about your child more. So do your best to put aside shyness or insecurity and speak up. Say what you know or suspect, and say it as clearly as you can.

To help you talk with your doctor or with child professionals, you can use these phrases:

My child has difficulty _____.

He/she doesn't seem to be able to _____.

He/she doesn't show interest in _____.

My child becomes very frustrated when he/she tries to _____.

Or you can try using this script:

My child may need extra help with his/her _____, because when he/she tries to _____, he/she ends up _____. Also, he/she sometimes _____. Do you see these problems often with kids you work with? I'm not sure what to do to help him/her.

Here is an example, using my concerns from an earlier exercise:

My child may need extra help with his speech and language because when he tries to tell me something, he can't pronounce the words. Also, he will point and grunt instead of using words, and he will give up in frustration if people don't understand him. Do you see these problems often with kids you work with? I'm not sure what to do to help him.

What's in Your Child's History?

Most professionals who diagnose developmental delays and disorders will want to know your family history. Biological and environmental factors can play large roles in a child's growth and development. A family history, including any significant events during pregnancy, infancy, or early childhood, can sometimes shed light on a child's deficits.

When a child is evaluated for developmental delays or disabilities, usu-ally a member of a team of professionals evaluating the child will interview you to record information about your pregnancy and your child's infancy and first years. Some evaluation teams will give parents questionnaires to fill out that ask the same questions about the family's developmental his-tory. This information is a very important part of the evaluation process. However, for some, this process can be unnerving and even feel like a per-sonal intrusion. It is hard to look at your family members in a way that you may not have before. It is unsettling to have to speculate as to whether your uncle's refusal to read to you may have been a reading disability, or you may not know about certain family members or remember specific details of your child's infancy. Just try to be honest and as accurate as you can be. Possibly you will be able to talk with other family members and learn a lit-tle more. Research has shown that there are genetic connections for cer-tain delays and disabilities, and since certain child difficulties are related to fetal and birth occurrences and exposures, taking a developmental history has become an important piece of a thorough evaluation process.

When professionals want to know your family's history, they are looking for:

- Information that may show a genetic predisposition to certain types of disabilities.

- Evidence of lifestyles that may help explain the presence of inabilities.

- Bilingual or trilingual families, a different language spoken at home with a parent or nanny—children may be slow to develop proper syntax (correct word ordering) in one or all of their languages.

- Information about the ages your child reached certain milestones. When did your child sit up? When did your child begin to walk? When did your child speak his or her first word?

Getting a Diagnosis

Many parents—and educators, too—are uncomfortable with the idea of diagnosing and labeling a child with a delay or disability. You and I know that a child is so much more than a label, that each child is a precious, unique individual. For some, the thought of their child having a diagnosis is stressful. For others, getting a diagnosis is a welcomed event, for help and resources will be at hand.

When a parent I know took her daughter to have an evaluation at a major university, the results validated what the parents had suspected all along. Their daughter had ADHD (Attention Deficit Hyperactivity Disorder). The mother said, "It was such a relief to not be a parent crying wolf anymore, and to have our daughter recognized as a child who truly needs help!"

Sometimes parents are completely surprised by a diagnosis they did not expect. One couple felt very confident that their daughter was autistic. Many of their daughter's symptoms such as her lack of communication and her seeming to be in her own world matched the symptoms they read about in their research on autism. Doctors also agreed with the possibility of autism. Later, a full auditory evaluation found their daughter to have a severe hearing impairment. She was not autistic. The approach to their child's learning was substantially altered to help the little girl find a functional mode of communication. She immediately began to blossom, and this change, as well as new knowledge about their daughter's disability, had a wonderful and inspiring effect on the whole family. Having their daughter evaluated by qualified child professionals truly made a huge difference in their lives.

It is common for parents to fear discovering information that could have prevented the child's current situation ("If we had only known . . ."). Many parents find themselves developing defensive and antagonistic feelings toward the professionals who are helping their child. Many also find that the anxiety and guilt about their child's situation make their way into personal relationships, especially their relationship with their spouse. So it is imperative to take time to regroup, unwind, and honestly share your feelings about your concerns. Some parents fearfully wonder if their child will have a disability and lifelong hardship. Some wonder whether they will be able to love and support their child in the way he or she needs. By knowing more, you will be able to do more. By learning more about developmental difficulties, the choices you make for your child will be focused and precise.

Next, let's take a more detailed look at the different areas of development that are so important for your child's overall growth and well-being. You may want to turn to a specific chapter on an area of development that you know concerns you, or you may want to educate yourself fully by delving into the information on all of the different areas of development.

Specific *red flags of atypical development* will be provided at the end of each chapter. Use these lists as tools in helping you to define your child's unique and individual symptoms. If you find yourself checking one or more red flags, take note of the symptoms and even write them down. Share them with your doctor and use "The Test of Three" to determine if your child may need outside or additional help. Also, use the exercises at the end of each chapter to help stimulate development right away. Most important, remember that children can and do progress. Developmental red flags can be helped.

PART II

The Search for Answers

"She's having trouble learning"

THREE

The Development and Disorders of Cognition

"My daughter's preschool teacher called us with concerns about her progress. She can't seem to do what the other kids are doing. She's not remembering what's taught. All the other kids have moved on to harder things. She is very social and has friends. Should I be worried?"

To this day I get an uneasy feeling when I hear child professionals tell parents, "His cognition appears to be intact" or "Her cognition does not appear to be intact." It almost seems disrespectful to describe such an awesome combination of processes in eight words or less. "Cognitively, she's okay," many a relieved parent will hear. But what does it look like when a child is not cognitively okay? The thought of a child whose cognition is "not intact" brings forth pictures of children with severe disabilities, such as Down Syndrome. Interestingly, children who have severe disabilities have many different ranges of cognitive ability. A severely handicapped child who has cerebral palsy may in fact be intellectually gifted, and a child with Down Syndrome may be much more academically able then most would ever expect.

When you think of *cognitive development*, think of building a "base," or a foundation of information that you know and understand, and can then build upon without losing any understanding of the lower parts. What would happen if you were unable to remember the "base" information? The structure would collapse, wouldn't it? You would have to start at square one again and rebuild your base. And what would happen if building your "base" were so strenuous and difficult that you wanted to give up? You really would not be able to move on to higher information without a solid base. This inability to build an informational "base" or keep an informational structure standing is, in a way, the essence of cognitive difficulties in young children.

Some of the basic components of cognitive development involve *perceiving*, that is, taking in information from our environments; *assigning meaning*, which involves processing and understanding that information, *remembering*, which allows us to "hold" the information so that we may learn more and build upon what we know, and *using*, which allows us to outwardly use and express known information through communication or performance.

To get a better idea of the types of difficulties a child with cognitive deficits may encounter, let's take a look at a five-year-old little girl named Kim.

Kim Can't Count

Kim, a kindergartener, is working hard to dress for school. She slowly pulls on her socks and holds up her pants to try to tell the front from the back. She turns them again and again, but she is unable to tell which way they go. Finally, she puts them on backward. Her mom peeks in the doorway, and with frustration, pulls Kim's pants down and off. Kim stands on one foot and then the other as her mother pushes her pants on correctly and helps her with her shoes and jacket. They hurry to the car, and upon arriving at school, Kim is met by an assistant. When Kim enters her kindergarten classroom, she wants to play house in the house corner and immediately starts to walk in that direction. "Good morning, Kim. Hang up your jacket," the teacher says. Kim, hearing her name, turns around and looks at the teacher. "I said 'hang up your jacket,'" the teacher emphasizes. Kim leaves the house corner and walks to her hook. She gets her jacket off and tries to hook it. It falls down on the floor. She raises it again to the hook. Her jacket falls again. A nearby boy starts to laugh. Kim's eyes fill with tears. She hides her face in her hands. The teacher quickly walks over. "Do it like this." Kim's teacher takes the jacket and hangs it up. She then takes Kim's hand and leads her to the rug while Kim still hides her face with her other hand. "We are going to work on counting to twenty today. Everyone, please come sit on the rug." The children move to the rug and sit down. The teacher sits in a large chair in front of them. The boy who had laughed near the jacket hook sits down next to Kim. Kim looks at him. "Leave me alone!" she yells. The teacher, startled, says, "Kim, nobody is bothering you! Apologize, please!" "Sor-rEE!" Kim says angrily. The teacher asks the children to count with her while she points to the numbers on a large counting chart. "One, two, three, four . . ." Kim tries to say the numbers with the teacher. Kim counts to ten, but isn't able to remember the numbers past ten. She looks around at the other kids. Kim watches as a boy named David stands up next to the teacher. "Count how many bears I have," says the teacher. Kim watches as David counts little plastic bears. He counts to twenty, and does something with the bears when he's counting. Kim watches Phyllis and Taj count, too. They, too, can count to twenty and put down the plastic bears when they count. "Kim, your turn," says the teacher. Kim stands up and takes the little pile of plastic bears from the teacher. She looks down into her hands and looks at the bears. "One, two, three, four, five, six . . ." Kim starts to forget which bears she has already counted, and begins to count bears over again, saying numbers "nine" and "ten" again and again. Some of the other children begin to laugh, and Kim's eyes tear up. "Who will help Kim count these bears?" she hears the teacher say. Kim sees David, the boy who knew how to do something with the bears when he counted, moving toward her. Kim quickly tries to put the bears on the floor like David had done, as if she were about to try by herself again. "No, Kim, give the bears to David and let him help you," the teacher says. Kim hides her eyes in her hands and cries. One child says, "Why is Kim crying?" Another says, "Kim can't count."

Cognitive Difficulties

Kim is showing some "red flag" behaviors that would warrant some investigation by a special education teacher and a psychologist. You probably noticed some of Kim's difficulties and inabilities to perform the simple math activity in class. You may have also noticed subtle difficulties with her adaptive skills (skills needed for everyday tasks and everyday interactions). Some professionals may reason that Kim's inability to perform in a quicker, more aware way may be due to her lack of attention and focus. Let's see how you did in assessing the situation. Here are some of the behaviors of concern:

- Kim appears to be "slow" with simple tasks. She was slow to put her socks on and could not readily tell the front from the back of her pants.

- She appears to need reminders to complete simple tasks. Kim's teacher had to remind her to hang up her jacket.

- Kim does not appear to readily catch the meanings of verbalized instructions. Possibly she does not readily process language.

- Kim also seems unaware of "the big picture." She seemed unaware of the daily routine when she entered her classroom and headed straight for the house corner upon arrival with her jacket still on.

- Kim struggled with adaptive skills needed for dressing and undressing, and for appropriate social interactions in daily situations. Though she did respond to the little boy who laughed at her, her response was delayed and after the fact, and therefore seemed out of context.

- She had difficulty remembering and sequencing numbers. She was unable to count to twenty even after hearing the numbers to twenty several times.

- Kim has difficulty making sense out of what she sees. Even though she saw several children using a "technique" to be able to count the many plastic bears, she was unable to "understand" what the children were doing and why.

An observant parent, teacher, or professional would also notice Kim's strengths and would use them to help support her weaknesses. Here are some of the positive behaviors and skills that Kim displayed:

- Kim appears to want to be independent. She was cooperative and attempted to do many tasks on her own.

- Kim shows an attraction to an activity in class (the house corner) and may be attracted to "hands on" and more active activities in general.

- Kim showed some reasoning ability when she continued to count because she knew there were more than ten bears in her hands. She knew the pile in her hands had more than ten items.

- Kim could remember a visual process. When she saw David and others use a "technique" to count the bears, she tried to reproduce the technique, even though she did not get a chance to try again.

- Kim is a willing participant in activities she does not fully understand, and she clearly wants to learn.

These strengths are very important because the teachers and professionals who might help Kim can use these strengths to develop strategies that can help her learn.

Child professionals can speak with Kim's parents and encourage them to plan more time around tasks she needs to complete independently, such as dressing. Kim may do very well with some of these tasks if she were allowed more time to think them through. It would also be helpful for Kim's teacher to allow her more time to complete tasks independently, and the teacher could advise other students to "wait" and listen so that Kim can think through what was said and think of what she would want to say in return.

Kim's teacher may want to make her a visual reminder schedule of the daily tasks that have to be done and the correct way to do them. For instance, the teacher could take a picture of Kim hanging up her jacket while her hands hold the jacket correctly at the hood and as she hangs it on the hook. This picture could be first on her daily picture schedule.

In addition, when the teacher feels the class may be learning something that will be hard for Kim to "pick up," she can preview material with Kim before it is presented in class. Kim could also practice the material at home with a parent. This would give Kim a greater sense of comfort when participating in her classroom learning activities. Kim's teacher could also check with Kim to see if she had heard and understood directions that were given.

Without help, questionable patterns of cognition can be very frustrating for children and their families. Difficulties with intellectual skills and learning can affect a child's self-esteem and attitude toward trying any new skill. Frequent failure and disapproval from parents and teachers can make for an angry and confused child. It is important to investigate any cognitive concern early. Early detection of cognitive difficulties and learning disabilities can allow for early help to make a child's learning experiences more comfortable and successful.

Defining a Concern: Learning Disability? Mental Retardation? Or Interfering Condition?

When parents and caregivers have concerns about a child's cognitive skills, it is important to take a close look at not only the child's performance and ability, but also the child's environment, developmental history, and developmental status in other areas. It is helpful to look at the varied types of cognitive difficulties in separate categories. The categories are as follows: *learning disabilities, mental retardation,* and *interfering conditions.*

Learning disabilities is a vague term that refers to any one or combination of specific learning problems. For instance, a child may have a specific reading disability such as dyslexia, or a specific learning disability in math. These learning disabilities become apparent in children when they fail to learn and perform as most of their same-age peers. Children who have specific learning disabilities are often typical children who have a harder time learning, remembering, or using certain academic skills than their peers. You would not be able to pick out a learning-disabled child on the playground, at a party, or at a social event, because the kids truly are regular kids who happen to have difficulty learning and performing in school. Sometimes learning-disabled kids are extremely socially adept and well liked by peers. Intellectually disabled children, such as children with mental retardation, are easier to pick out of a crowd.

When a child has **mental retardation**, the cognitive difficulties affect most, if not all, areas of his life. One of the telltale signs of mental retardation is an inability to learn or perform adaptive skills. Remember, adaptive skills are skills needed to independently care for oneself and relate to others. Children with mental retardation function poorly on their own and need support throughout their day.

Interfering conditions are disabilities that can interfere with learning. There are many professionals who consider any interfering conditions to be learning disabilities simply for this reason, but conditions such as ADHD and Sensory Processing Disorder are truly conditions with their own symptoms and treatments. Cognition may be completely fine in these children, but children who are dealing with different types of symptoms and discomforts find it hard to attend and concentrate when symptoms are prevalent.

Pervasive or global interfering conditions are disabilities that can truly and wholly interfere with not only learning, but also the adaptive skills needed for self-care and successful interactions with others. These might include autism, Asperger Syndrome, and Nonverbal Learning Disorder. Because these children present with their own set of symptoms (and in many cases, above-average IQ scores), they are not considered to have a learning disability or mental retardation.

We will discuss each of these cognitive categories in more detail, but first it is important to have an understanding of how cognition develops in the brains of our children.

The Typical Patterns of Cognitive Development

Have you ever noticed the way babies explore objects? They look intently at them, feel them and move them with their hands, smell them, and of course, taste them. Exploring in this way gives babies information about the objects and information about their world. Babies' perceiving information from the environment and the budding ability to form an understanding of their world will get better as they grow and as they continue to investigate their surroundings. A newborn's cognitive development will depend upon the physical growth of his brain and his experiences within his environment.

So how does the mind begin to think? Where does intelligence come from? Fetuses, still in the womb, seem to show some early processing of information from the environment. Research has shown that fetuses will startle at the sound of an unexpected noise, but when the noise is repeated over and over, the reactions lessen and dissipate. Some fetuses wouldn't react at all after repeatedly hearing the sound. This "getting used to" an environmental stimulus is one of the first emerging signs of learning.

Cognition in newborn babies is apparent very early. Newborns definitely show that they have an awareness of events happening around them. A change in temperature, a wet diaper, or hunger, frequently leads them to cry, fuss, and express their discomfort. What they receive in response to their newly emerging expressions will help them learn and perceive information about their world.

A child's brain grows rapidly in the early years of his life. Surprisingly, a child's brain will just about reach its full size by the time he is five years old. At this time, the physical hardware and connections between the many working centers in the brain are just about ready to solidify. The child's learning, varied experiences, and use of his perceptions about the environ-ment up to this point will have an important influence on his future ability.

The processing speed of a child's brain will also affect whether he will be deemed "intelligent," or "cognitively intact." Faster brains are now con-sidered to be more "intelligent" brains. The faster a child's brain processes information, the faster the child can perceive, make judgments, and learn. Experts reason that greater brain speed is a hallmark of highly efficient brains. A child who has a highly efficient brain will be a child who learns quickly, has talents, and scores highly on intelligence tests.

Babies use their sight very early and show great interest in colorful pat-terns, faces, and facial expressions. They show burgeoning cognition and intelligence with their ability to imitate facial expressions. To imitate a facial expression, a new baby needs to perceive the expression visually, and then somehow coordinate a motor reaction and send it to the correct place, his face. Certainly, this is an impressive feat for a newborn brain.

Older babies show cognitive growth with new emerging abilities. One of these is the ability to understand that an object is itself whether it is right side up, upside down, turned sideways, or turned backward. Some scien-tists believe that a child younger than four months old may experience his mother as "several mothers" due to the different visual experiences of his mother. A little later, at about one year of age, a child will also develop the understanding or knowing that an object still exists even though she can-not see it. For instance, a baby will understand that his favorite bear is in his crib, even though he cannot see his bear from his present position or location. The baby will also realize his mother is in the house, even though he may not see her in the room. He may now call out instead of fret or cry.

As babies grow into toddlers, the connections between the centers of the brain work together more quickly and efficiently than ever before. A child's language begins to develop more fully, and self-awareness begins to develop. A child will now contemplate more difficult concepts, physi-cally, intellectually, and emotionally. He may try to aim his kick, figure out how to reach the cookie jar that is out of his reach, and he may possibly begin to become fearful about certain situations.

When a child reaches her fourth year, an important intellectual dis-tinction commonly takes place (for some, this may take place a little later).

The child begins to judge what she is seeing not only by appearance. She begins to apply prior knowledge and understanding about the world to her perceptions and expressions. You may have already heard of the water and glass trick. A grown-up has two identical glasses with the exact same amounts of water in both. The grown-up asks the child which has more? The child replies, "they have the same." The grown-up then pours one of the glasses of water into a tall, very thin glass, and the water rises up high in this glass. The grown-up asks the child again, "Which glass has more water?" If the child is over four-years-old, there is a good chance she will respond, "they have the same," demonstrating a knowledge of reality over just appearance. A child younger than four will likely say the tall, thin glass has more water.

It is amazing to watch a child's cognition and understanding of the world develop. But sometimes, something happens along the way and one infant, toddler, or preschooler develops differently from the typical pattern.

Cognitive Disorders

Let's take a look at some disorders associated with atypical cognition. Maybe you will see shades of your own child reflected in the stories of the children described here, or maybe you will feel that your child's difficulties are much more subtle and less worrisome than the children described.

Disorders that affect cognition may be present before birth, as in genetic abnormalities, or may appear later in a child's life, for instance, after a bout with a severe illness. Sometimes a child has trouble learning and processing information without any clear physical abnormality or event to point to.

Remember, the disorders that affect children's abilities to learn and successfully navigate their world independently usually fall into three categories:

- Learning Disabilities
- Mental Retardation
- Interfering Conditions

LEARNING DISABILITIES

Learning disabilities are inabilities to understand or successfully perform academic concepts and tasks. They interfere with a child's achievement in one or more subjects at school. They may also interfere with a child's ability to carry through with tasks at home. The causes of learning disabilities are not well known, though the genetic link with many different types of learning difficulties lead many experts to believe that families can actually "pass down" a certain pattern of brain wiring. These brain wiring differences may cause learning differences that in turn may end up as learning disabilities in the affected family members. The pattern of brain wiring and learning differences may be typical within the particular family.

A child may receive a diagnosis of **Learning Disabled** (LD) if he is unable to perform age-appropriate academic skills, or if his academic performance is extremely poor for his intellectual ability. Most learning-disabled children have average to superior intelligence and it is estimated that as many as one in five children have a learning disability. Child professionals may say, "he has a learning disability in reading" or "he has a writing learning disability" or "he has a severe math-learning disability." Often, the true culprits causing the academic difficulties are severe weaknesses in visual perception, auditory perception, memory, or language. Visual perception can affect how a child sees symbols, and a weakness in this area can interfere with skills needed for reading, writing, and math. Children with visual perception difficulties will frequently reverse letters and numbers because they are unable to discern the differences between the visually similar symbols. Children with auditory perception difficulties may find it difficult to catch directions and explanations in class, and may find it difficult to concentrate with any sort of background noise. A child with auditory perception difficulties may find it difficult to tell the difference between the sounds that correspond to letters of the alphabet, especially sounds that are similar. Sounds such as /a/ as in *apple* and /e/ as in *egg* can be very difficult for children with auditory perceptual problems. It is hard for these children to perceive any difference in the sounds when heard. Memory is essential for children to hold information long enough to make sense out of it. Many children who have learning disabilities have difficulties with their short-term memories. Frequent repetition is often needed to help these children remember new concepts and skills.

Visual Perception

An example of typical visual perception:

The first-grade teacher points to a word and tells Emily to give her the sound for the first letter. The word is *pet*. Emily correctly responds, "/p/."

An example of atypical visual perception:

The first-grade teacher then points to another word and asks Angela to tell her the sound of the first letter. The word is *dad*. Angela incorrectly responds, "/b/."

Angela shows a typical reversal that occurs with children who have visual perceptual difficulties. Reversing letters and mistaking visually similar letters and numbers is a common symptom of a learning disability called *dyslexia*. There are many visually similar symbols, and this type of problem can make learning to read, spell, and perform mathematical calculations very difficult.

Another example of typical visual perception:

A first-grade class just finished reading a list of words, all from a particular "word family." The words were: *cat, mat, sat, pat,* and *rat*. The teacher then passes out a sheet with a story on it to all of the students. The story has all of the words they just practiced in it. The teacher asks DeWayne to read the first paragraph. He had read all of the words on the list perfectly. DeWayne reads the first paragraph with ease and is able to correctly read the words *mat* and *cat*.

Another example of atypical visual perception:

In the first-grade class, Lana also read the word-family list correctly. She was able to read: *cat*, *mat*, *sat*, *pat*, and *rat*. The teacher asked Lana to read the second paragraph of the story that had been passed out. Lana, feeling confident, starts to read. Something isn't working, though. She can't see where to start, and her friend next to her shows her. When Lana begins, the words look like they are everywhere and blending together. It is hard for her to keep her eyes on one word at a time. Her trying to keep her place, see each word, think of what she is reading, and sound out at the same time is just too much. "I don't want to read," Lana says.

Auditory Perception

An example of typical auditory perception:

A first-grade teacher has the word *red* on the blackboard. "This is the word *red*," she says. "Let's think of another word that has the same 'eh' sound in the middle." Carlos raises his hand and correctly suggests the word *bed*.

An example of atypical auditory perception:

The first-grade teacher has the word *red* on the blackboard. "I'd like another word that has the sound 'eh' in the middle." Brent raises his hand and incorrectly suggests the word *mad*. "Brent, I need the 'eh' sound in the middle, *mad* has the sound 'aah' in the middle. Say the sound 'eh' with me." "Aah, ah," Brent says as he tries to match the teacher's sound. "Say 'eh,' Brent," the teacher says again. "I did!" Brent replies.

Children with poor auditory perception find it very difficult to hear the differences between similar sounds. The sounds of the short vowels, *a, e, i, o*, and *u* are very similar, and knowledge of sound/letter relationships is important for learning early reading skills. Poor auditory perception can affect a child's ability to understand phonics (phonemic awareness) and correctly hear as well as sound out words.

Memory

An example of typical short-term memory:

The kindergarten teacher calls Mimi to her desk to do a subtraction problem and "take away." The teacher shows her how to start with a certain number of manipulatives, and then take some away. Mimi does two problems by herself, and then later on at her home, does the class subtraction homework correctly, just like the teacher had showed her.

An example of atypical short-term memory:

The kindergarten teacher sits with Nadia to show her how to "take away." Nadia does three problems with the teacher. She seems to "get it" and returns to her seat. When the teacher notices Nadia talking with children at her table, she asks Nadia if she finished the subtraction problems. "Yes," Nadia replies. The teacher looks at her paper and sees that Nadia had correctly subtracted the first row, but she had added the remaining two rows. It looked as if she had completely forgotten what she was doing.

Poor short-term memory can make it difficult for a child to remember and "hold in their minds" directions, a process, and any new learned information. Repetition and visual examples to have at hand are very important for these children.

Children with learning disabilities may also find tasks involving reasoning, sequencing, categorization, or the understanding of abstract concepts quite difficult. Reasoning involves understanding cause and effect, and the "why" and "how" behind an action or event. A child with reasoning skills would use what she has learned through experience to help her relate to and make sense out of new situations. Many children with learning disabilities find this to be very difficult. *Sequencing* involves using a known order as a base of information. For instance, a child may learn the order of the letters in the alphabet and the months of the year, and may use this knowledge to put words into alphabetical order or let a teacher know the month that comes after March. In school, children are also expected to be able to sequence events in a story and tell the events of a story in order from beginning to end. Children with sequencing difficulties may be able to hold the different pieces of information in their memories, but the information is not held "in order," and this can lead to frustration and confusion.

Categorization involves being able to recognize a difference, or recognize an object or group of objects as "different" from one another. To categorize, a child must also be aware of characteristics that are "similar" or "alike." Children who are unaware of differences may suffer severe learning difficulties, as will children who are unable to understand abstract concepts. An infant can typically recognize by sight an object that he has explored with his hands and mouth but never seen before.

The ability to form an understanding of or form a picture of an object or idea is a very important skill for learning. Every time we come to a door and need to open it, we do not search, think through, and have to experiment with the doorknob to open and walk through the door. We learned long ago to turn the knob and open the door, and then generalized this knowledge to every door and knob we later encountered. When a child does not readily generalize learned information, learning can be quite a struggle.

The term *learning disability* is often attached to a wide range of difficulties and disorders, and many respected professionals disagree on the different problems that should or should not be included in this category. Some professionals categorize fine motor difficulties, where a child may have difficulty holding a pencil or crayon, as a learning disability, where others do not. Some professionals categorize ADHD (Attention Deficit Hyperactivity Disorder) as a learning disability, and many do not. Many times, each situation and each child will be carefully considered, for every child, and every child's experience with hardship, is unique. Children who have learning disabilities usually have the age-appropriate adaptive skills that children with mental retardation lack.

Dos and Don'ts

If you believe your child may have a learning disability,

Do:

- Celebrate and frequently praise your child's strengths.

- Praise any work effort in areas of difficulty.

- Have your child participate in social and active learning activities.

- Try to model organization and good planning.

- Keep surprise situations, events, or activities to a minimum.

- Help your child to organize multistep tasks into smaller doable chunks.

- Try to remain calm when your child feels anxious or frustrated.

Don't:

- Don't use participation in social or recreational activities as rewards for academic performance. Encourage social success and special talents, even if your child's academic performance may be lacking in areas.

- Don't criticize your child if you think your child can perform better. Praise your child's efforts and help your child practice difficult skills.

- Don't assume your child knows how to behave or react appropriately in various situations. If you must stop an inappropriate act or behavior, tell your child the appropriate thing he/she needs to do instead.

- Don't panic. Children with learning disabilities can succeed.

MENTAL RETARDATION

Mental retardation can affect a child's performance in all areas of his life. Children are diagnosed as having mental retardation when they have a combination of low IQ scores and an inability to pick up the adaptive skills that same-age peers can perform with ease. A child with mental retardation will be slow to learn, and may never master certain skills. Almost three percent of our entire population in the United States has mental retardation, and most of these disabilities are considered to be mild.

The causes of mental retardation are truly numerous, ranging from genetic disorders, to illness, accidents, and even neglect. The most common genetic culprits are Fragile X Syndrome, which is an abnormality of the X sex chromosome, and Down Syndrome, which is caused by having one extra chromosome. Giving birth to a child with these genetic conditions can be devastating for parents, but children who have these conditions have a wide range of intellectual ability, with some children being surprisingly intellectually able.

There are several genetic conditions that can cause mental retardation in children if they remain undetected or are left untreated. Examples of these are phenylketonuria (PKU) and hypothyroidism. When treated quickly and properly, a child with these conditions can grow normally without negative effects on their growth and cognitive development.

Factors and events that affect a fetus still in its mother's uterus can also cause mental retardation in children. Fetal alcohol syndrome has become a well-known preventable cause. Consistent cigarette smoking, or a pregnant woman's use of drugs, can also cause mental retardation.

A pregnant mother's contracting of certain diseases can also cause damage to the growing fetus, which can in turn result in the child having mental retardation. Rubella, toxoplasmosis, and fifth disease are examples of illnesses pregnant women should avoid being exposed to. Cat lovers need to beware of toxoplasmosis because it is contracted by coming in contact with cat feces. Mothers who play with their small children at parks or sandboxes need to exhibit caution because they could inadvertently come into contact with infected cat feces.

Birth complications and untreated childhood diseases can also cause mental retardation. Parents need to be especially vigilant and immediately get medical help if their child has symptoms of the chicken pox, whooping cough, or meningitis, to name a few.

A baby or young child with mental retardation will frequently be delayed in several areas of development, and may not reach many typical milestones in the usual time periods.

Dos and Don'ts

If you believe your child may have mental retardation,

Do:

- Encourage your child to be independent, and praise any effort you see your child making in this regard.

- Give your child jobs or chores that he can be successful at completing.

- Look for opportunities for activities in your school system or community that would help your child to interact socially.

- Plan to teach manners, safety, game rules, and other important, helpful information in little lessons, or small chunks.

Don't:

- Don't do for your child what he could do for himself, because it is faster or feels easier.

- Don't rush your child if he is working on completing a task.

- Don't criticize if a task is not done as well as you would like. Try to help teach better skills by saying, "Next time, I would love it if you would also _____. Would you like me to show you how?"

INTERFERING CONDITIONS

Interfering conditions hinder cognition because of their effect on the process of learning. They cause difficulties with organization, sensory processing, executive function, and attention. Interfering conditions usually are considered "in their own category" with symptoms that range from mild to severe. Some interfering conditions are well known, such as ADHD and autism. Others are less known, such as Nonverbal Learning Disorder. Interfering conditions make children less "available" for learning, as you will see with Mari and Sean.

Mari was described by her parents as a social butterfly. She had a lot of friends in her first-grade class, and though an excellent reader, she was not completing tasks and not performing well, especially when it came to working independently. Her parents believed she was concentrating too much on her friends and not paying enough attention to her work. Upon being observed in her classroom, though, this did not appear to be the case. Mari appeared to pay close attention to directions and could answer questions that showed her knowledge of the subjects taught. She appeared to have a problem when it came to starting independent tasks and gathering the tools needed. She did not appear to know where to start or what to do first. Mari was obviously a bright girl, but she was having difficulty organizing steps into a logical sequence. Since Mari was not organized from the inside out, we needed to organize her from the outside in, and we assisted the teacher in posting lists of the sequential steps needed to complete independent assignments, so that Mari would not have to think through the steps completely independently. Large tasks that may have seemed overwhelming to her were broken down into small chunks to be completed one by one. These adaptations helped her to perform at a level commensurate with her intellectual ability.

Difficulties with executive function, which include skills with organizing, carrying out tasks, and orderly thinking (what many professionals call "higher-order thinking skills") can affect a child's ability to perform at her full intellectual capacity.

Sean's parents had always been amazed by their son's verbal prowess. From the age of two, he was speaking with complex, compound sentences and asking questions that were quite unusual for his age ("What is combining?"). At first, Sean's mother felt his difficulty getting along with other kids was due to Sean's being so intellectually ahead of his peers, but by midyear in his second year in preschool, both peers and teachers seemed to avoid him. Both Sean's mother and father were noticing oddities in the way he would interact at home and at school. Suddenly his "giftedness" felt like "differentness." It got to the point where he was irritable and confused almost all the time, and he was a kind child who always tried to do the right thing, but things just never seemed to work out well for him. Sean was taken to a major university child-development center for an evaluation, and through this process, the family learned about NLD. "We learned that Sean needed tasks spelled out step by step, and that he may have to learn how to get along socially through lessons and examples. We have changed the way we handle situations at home, and his teachers are putting much more effort into helping him at school, so things are going much better for him now."

Nonverbal Learning Disorder is an interfering condition marked by a lack of understanding of abstract concepts and underlying meaning, both in social situations and in academics. Frequently, a child with NLD will be extremely bright and able, with an excellent vocabulary and an ability to verbalize with advanced word orders. Unfortunately, children with NLD have great difficulty noticing the social rules and social cues that typical children pick up and use naturally. NLD kids have trouble understanding the attached gestures and the communications that are nonverbal. This difficulty with skills that are nonverbal gave birth to the name of this condition, yet the title "Nonverbal Learning Disorder" is widely criticized for naming a disability by what it's not.

Dos and Don'ts

Interfering conditions each have their own unique and varied symptoms. So if you believe your child may have an interfering condition that is hindering your child's learning,

Do:

- Research your child's suspected condition at the library and on the Internet.

- Try to structure your child's day into a predictable pattern, and warn your child ahead of time if a certain day's schedule will be very different.

- Be consistent with your child about expected behaviors, rewards, and consequences.

- Try to model calm and patience when confronting challenging situations.

- Encourage activities that can help to develop your child's social skills.

Don't:

- Don't overlook or ignore inappropriate behaviors your child may display out of guilt. Calmly and firmly let your child know what you believe to be appropriate.

- Don't overwhelm your child with events that may be stressful for him. Plan ahead. For instance, if holiday company is coming, let your child know where a "quiet room" in the house will be, and let him know that he may go there at any time.

The information you've just read may have illuminated exactly what was worrying you, or you may still feel a bit puzzled. If you're not sure whether your concern warrants further investigation, then use the *Test of Three*.

Important Considerations Before Diagnosis

Before a final diagnosis of a learning disability or mental retardation is given, several considerations should be taken into account. Diagnosis related to intellectual and cognitive disorders can be very tricky due to issues

The Test of Three

Use this technique to assess whether your child may need professional intervention or specialized help regarding cognitive functioning.

Write down *three* characteristics that concern you. Examples would be:

"He can't remember how to dress himself."

"He has not learned the letters in the alphabet."

"He can't seem to figure out a simple shape toy."

Decide to "intervene" with *three* ideas to help your concern. For example:

• I will make him a picture chart to show step by step how I would like him to dress himself.

• I will use repetitive alphabet songs and games with movement, along with a colorful alphabet chart to review daily the alphabet with him.

• I will play with and model how to play with the shape toy, and do it together with him until he seems to understand that he needs to look at the different shapes. I will take his finger and have him trace the different shapes with his finger. We will also look at different shapes around the house.

Work on your interventions daily for *three* weeks, or if you are unable to do this, work on them intermittently for *three* months. Either way, write down specific characteristics that you see. Do not be afraid to critically watch your child's development over a three-month period. Some children develop in uneven spurts, so you might observe big leaps in skills, or you might continue to see a lag in skills, which would warrant further assessment.

At the end of the chosen time period, write down what you see. Write down how your child performs in the specific areas of concern. Compare your notes with the notes you took in the beginning. Are there any differences? Has there been progress? If you have chosen to work on your interventions daily, you should see some progress in three weeks. If the additional and focused stimulation is only scratching the surface of the difficulties, and your child has not shown obvious progress, it may be time to look into getting further help. After three months, your child has had time to grow, develop, and interact in many different types of situations. How is he doing? Did he have a developmental growth spurt? Or is reaching milestones still a struggle, slow and incremental? If it is the latter, he may need help.

related to the "nature versus nurture" debate. Lack of exposure and lack of ability can look very similar, and it is imperative that skilled professionals take great care in gathering information when conducting observations and testing on children with suspected cognitive problems. Professionals also argue at times that "slow" performance does not mean "inaccurate" or "impaired" performance.

Also, language skills and cognitive skills are closely related and children who are experiencing difficulties with their speech and language skills are sometimes cognitively misdiagnosed. (Please see Chapter 4 for information on Speech and Language disorders.)

A Word on Learning Disabilities and the Intelligence Quotient

While intellectual disabilities are diagnosed from a combination of a low IQ score and poor adaptive skills, learning disabilities are diagnosed differently. Learning disabilities are diagnosed by looking at a child's intellectual ability (from the IQ score), and by then comparing this ability (score) to the child's performance on a verbal IQ test, as well as tests of specific academic skills. Professionals look for a discrepancy between the child's IQ and a child's academic performance. For instance, if a child is found to have an IQ score in the superior range, and that child has extremely poor performance when it comes to reading skills, this child might be considered to have a reading disability. Although if a child is found to have a very low IQ score and is performing poorly in reading, this would not be "discrepant" in the eyes of the professionals, and would not be considered to be a learning disability.

Cognitive difficulties in young children are very hard to test because the tests available, including the tests that measure IQ, include activities that are affected by prior exposure. For instance, if a child were able to practice test-like activities for one week, the child's IQ score may be higher. Children who have had preschool experience frequently score higher than children who have not been exposed to academic-like activities or requests. Another difficulty that arises when testing for cognitive deficits is whether difficulties in performance are actually cognitive or language-based. Is the child simply not understanding the request of the teacher? Would the child be able to perform the skill if the child was given a visual example or cue as opposed to a verbal direction? Sadly, children with language deficits may appear to be less intelligent than they really are.

Red Flags of Atypical Cognitive Development

Red flags can act as warning signals that development may not be progressing as it should. Below, you will find a list of characteristics that commonly accompany cognitive difficulties. Don't panic if you check one or more; there is no way to "score" your child here. Simply use the list as a tool that will assist you in defining and gauging your child's vulnerabilities, so that you can find him the help he may need.

Birth to Three Months

_____ Baby does not wake him/herself to feed.

_____ Baby does not look around at people or objects in the environment.

Three to Twelve Months

_____ At five months old, baby does not reach for objects.

_____ At twelve months, baby does not demonstrate through play a basic understanding of tool use (such as how one uses a crayon to draw, a spoon to eat, or how one holds a telephone to one's ear).

Twelve to Twenty-four Months

_____ At eighteen months, he/she is not showing some imitative play.

_____ At eighteen months, he/she is not gesturing, and using some beginning words to indicate her needs.

_____ At eighteen months, he/she is not exploring his/her environment.

_____ At twenty-four months, he/she is unable to understand and carry out a simple one-step direction.

_____ At twenty-four months, he/she seems unable to concentrate and moves from toy to toy impulsively without truly "playing" with or exploring any of the toys.

_____ At twenty-four months, he/she does not imitate everyday grooming actions, such as brushing, combing, and washing actions (adaptive skills).

_____ At twenty-four months, he/she is unable to hold a cup or use a spoon independently (adaptive skills).

Twenty-four to Thirty-six Months

_____ At thirty months, he/she is unable to stay with an activity for six to seven minutes.

_____ At thirty months, he/she is unable to hold a book in its correct orientation (right side up).

_____ At thirty-four months, he/she is unable to understand any time concepts, such as, "after dinner" or "tomorrow."

_____ At thirty-four months, he/she is unable to join in singing simple songs or saying simple rhymes that are familiar to him/her.

_____ At thirty-four months, he/she is unable to match simple shapes or colors.

_____ At thirty-four months, he/she is unable to tell or show how old he/she is.

_____ At thirty-six months, he/she is unable to hang a coat onto an accessible hook (adaptive skill).

_____ At thirty-six months, he/she is unable to use a napkin, or pour from a small container or cup independently (adaptive skills).

Three to Four Years Old

_____ At thirty-six months, he/she is unable to decipher whether he/she is a girl or a boy.

_____ At thirty-eight months, he/she is unable to answer a simple "Why do . . ." question, such as, "Why do we use toothpaste?"

_____ At forty-two months, he/she is unable to learn to count to five.

_____ At forty-five months, he/she is unable to answer a simple, "What do you do when . . ." question, such as, "What do you do when you are sleepy?"

_____ At forty-eight months, he/she is unable to understand "empty" or "all gone."

_____ At forty-eight months, he/she is unable to select "the one that is different" or "the one that is not like the others."

_____ At forty-eight months, he/she is unable to discriminate between the fronts and backs of clothing (adaptive skill).

_____ At forty-eight months, he/she is unable to eat a meal independently, and in a relatively socially way (adaptive skill).

Four to Five Years Old

_____ At four, he/she is unable to match objects or pictures.

_____ At four, he/she is unable to learn to count to ten.

_____ At four and a half, he/she is unable to respond to simple "How do you . . ." questions, such as, "How do you put on your shoes?"

_____ At four and a half, he/she is unable to recall one or two things that happened in a story.

_____ At four and a half, he/she is unable to sing a simple familiar song.

_____ At five, he/she is unable to independently clean up a spill (adaptive skill).

_____ At five, he/she is unable to dress independently, button and unbutton (adaptive skill).

Five to Six Years Old

_____ At five, he/she is unable to learn to count to twenty.

_____ At five, he/she is unable to recall events that happened in the past, such as "yesterday" or "last week."

_____ At five, he/she is unable to hand you a correct number of objects when asked (up to ten).

_____ At five, he/she is unable to tell you how old he/she was last year.

_____ At five and a half, he/she is unable to recognize a simple repeating pattern and/or continue it.

_____ At five and a half, he/she does not talk about or ask questions about future events.

_____ At six, he/she is unable to completely dress independently, including putting a zipper into the catch and zipping (adaptive skill).

_____ At six, he/she exhibits a lack of awareness of simple rules of manners, safety, and socially acceptable behavior (adaptive skills).

What You Can Do Now: Exercises that Stimulate Cognitive Development

When looking at your child's cognitive abilities, make note of how your child learns.

How does your child explore?

What does your child pay attention to?

How well do you feel your child pays attention?

If possible, teach your child a new age-appropriate skill. Maybe this could be drinking from a cup or writing the first letter of his or her name. Watch what happens, as you teach your child for a few short periods of time daily.

Is your child understanding what you want him to do? (Keep showing him.)

Can your child imitate you? If yes, does she remember how to do it minutes later? Or the next day?

You should notice how long it takes to teach the skill.

Were you back to square one each and every day for many days?

If your child learns fast, that's terrific. If your child is having difficulty learning, don't let it upset you, just observe and take note. You are stimulating cognition and affecting change just by working with and engaging your child.

"He doesn't communicate with others"

FOUR

The Development and Disorders of Speech and Language

"My two-year-old son is not talking or using words yet. He seems to understand everything I say to him. I asked my pediatrician, and she said that some kids talk early and some kids talk late, but by five they all usually catch up. I feel like something's wrong, and I want to find out more about this."

You may have already experienced *the comments*. "My child is already using phrases. Aren't you worried because your child isn't saying words yet?" And, "I'm sorry, what did he say? I didn't understand one word."

I remember the questions asked by friends and family about our son's attempts to communicate. He had a lot of difficulty pronouncing words, and he would move his tongue about as if it were simply in the way. The frequent comments made to me about him (and in front of him) left me feeling both uneasy and fiercely protective. The funny part about it was I understood my son perfectly. I knew exactly what he was saying and what he wanted. Some friends and even strangers would carefully inquire as to whether I had noticed (I had) or was doing anything about his speech.

It seemed as if everyone was alert and worried about my child's speech problem—except our pediatrician.

Our pediatrician seemed unconcerned, and after making a remark about how my profession may be making me paranoid, I was told to not rush my son, and to give him some time.

There are times when I do believe it is okay to give a child a little "development time" to carefully watch what may occur during a certain period, but in our son's case, he was becoming frustrated about his inability to make himself be understood, and seeing him struggle was very difficult for my husband and me.

When a child does not appear to be reaching typical speech and language milestones, there seems to be less of an urgency about getting help than with some other areas of development. This should not be. Few really know and understand the vast kinds of developmental skills that speech and language collectively involve. And most parents don't understand the emotional toll prolonged struggling with a speech and language disorder can take on a child.

To help understand how some common communication difficulties can affect a young child, let's take a look at this case study.

A Four-Year-Old at Preschool

Matt's mom is taking him to preschool. He usually does not want to go, and hides or cries in the mornings, but his mom reminded him of the trucks and trains at school, so this morning was not as hard as others. Upon arriving at school, Matt looks around and sees the other kids taking out toys. "Big truck," Matt says to himself. He remembers where the big truck is and skips to get it. "Voom Voom," Matt says while smiling. He begins to hold his legs together and glance around at the children around him. Quietly, Matt hides the truck in the corner next to the Lego table and rushes to the bathroom in a far corner of the room. After flushing and washing his hands, he sees a boy taking his truck. "No!" he screams as he races over and yanks the boy's hands off the truck. The boy cries. Matt hears his name. The teacher tells him to say he is sorry. The boy is still crying, and Matt stares at him. Matt says nothing and is then led to a chair.

Matt turns to look when the teacher says, "snack time." Matt sees the teacher motion for him to go sit at the table. The teacher leans down near him and asks, "Would you like some crackers?" Matt says "crackers." The teacher says, "Say 'yes, please.'" Matt says "yes, please," and the teacher places four crackers on his napkin. After asking for juice with prompting, Matt accidentally spills juice onto the napkin his crackers are on. He looks horrified and looks both at his teacher and the assistant. Neither of them notice. Matt eyes a small pile of napkins near his teacher. He stands up and points over at the napkins, still looking horrified. He begins to walk quickly toward the napkins. The teacher angrily calls his name (the children are not supposed to get up from the table). She takes his hand and leads him back to his seat. Matt looks very upset. For him, it seems snack is ruined. His crackers are all wet.

Matt throws his trash away from the snack and sees the other kids heading to the carpet to sit down. So he heads to the carpet, too. The teacher takes out a book, *Hippo Gets Dressed*. The pictures show a hippo with funny clothes. On one page, Hippo has a spotted hat. Matt raises his hand. The teacher looks at him, and says, "yes?" "Grandpa is funny." Matt laughs. The teacher frowns and returns to reading. Some kids are looking at him now, and Matt puts his head down in his hands. He doesn't look up throughout the rest of the book and lesson.

Communicative Difficulties

Matt is showing some "red flag" behaviors that would warrant investigation by a speech and language pathologist or therapist. Some of Matt's difficulties are very common in children, but sadly, it is also common to mislabel or misjudge difficulties. Some professionals would simply note Matt's aggressive behavior, or that he does not follow directions. Let's see how *you* did in assessing his behavior:

- Matt might cry or hide to protest going to school in the morning. He does not seem able to verbally express his feelings about preschool.

- He seems to have trouble "catching" and processing the verbalizations of his teacher, and his processing may be slow.

- He may only catch the very beginning of what is said, or the very end of what is said.

- Matt did not address a classmate by name (possibly he did not remember the child's name) and became physically aggressive instead of expressing himself verbally. He also had difficulty retrieving the word *napkin* when he needed to use it.

- During a story, Matt's comment seemed tangential and unrelated to what the story was about. It appeared to the teacher that his comment "came out of nowhere."

An observant parent, teacher, or professional would also notice Matt's strengths, and they would use them to help support treatment of his weaknesses:

- Matt used a strategy to help alleviate his own stress: he thought about the trucks and trains at school.

- He was also able to use cognitive skills to plan what to do with his truck before going to the bathroom.

- In the bathroom, he was able to remember the proper sequence of steps to successfully go to the bathroom, and he was able to do his business independently.

- He looks to the teacher and assistant in certain situations, showing he chooses to be communicative.

- He uses visual cues to understand what is going on around him. For instance, he looked to see what the other children were doing and followed suit. He also knew that he should go sit down for snack by seeing the teacher motion to him.

- Matt felt the sensations of needing to use the bathroom, which shows some good sensory awareness.

- Matt could skip, which shows good large-motor coordination and ability.

These strengths show us "ways in" to help Matt feel more comfortable in his environment, while he receives help to develop his weaknesses. This is called using strengths to *compensate*. If the teacher was aware that Matt had speech and language processing issues, she would be able to make some adaptations to help him in the classroom. She could repeat directions twice: "Everyone, please put your crayons away and come sit on the rug. (Pause) Put your crayons away and come sit on the rug." By doing this, the teacher increases the chances that Matt will process the entire direction. She could also walk over to him and quietly say, *"Crayons away, go on the rug."* Here, the teacher has shortened her request, increasing the chances that Matt will process the direction.

In the example, it was also apparent that Matt is visual and will react appropriately to visual cues and motions made by the teacher. The teacher could incorporate more motions, pictures, visual schedules, and visual directions into the day. In addition, by asking some key questions, Matt's teacher could check to see if his seemingly tangential comment was truly unrelated to the book. Possibly, Matt's grandpa once wore a hat like Hippo's.

Without help, atypical patterns of communicative behavior like Matt's can develop into learning and behavioral difficulties. So, it is truly important that each and every concern be investigated. Difficulties in communication may be due to a physical problem—for example, an inability to move the tongue, or a more neurological and developmental problem, such as not being able to process or remember information. If a communication difficulty is detected in your child, no matter if it is mild or severe, your child will need help to overcome it.

Defining a Concern: Speech or Language?

When parents have concerns about a child's speech and language skills, very often they are referring to a child's seeming delay in using verbal language. Yet speech and language problems can entail much more. *Speech* and *language* refer to two separate categories of skills. *Speech* is the production of sound. Producing sound requires cognitive thinking, motor planning, and normal formations of the inner ears, nasal cavities, vocal folds, oral cavity, tongue, and lips. *Language* is the meaningful use of interactive communications. This involves understanding the communications of others and having the ability to make oneself be understood.

Think about your child's difficulty. Does your concern have more to do with your child's speech? For instance, is your child having difficulty forming sounds, or is there an unusual quality to your child's voice? Or does your child appear to have a harder-to-define language difficulty, that relates more to an inability to understand what you are saying, or not being able to communicate wants or needs very well?

Before we discuss speech and language skills and disorders in more detail, it is important to first have a basic understanding of the way these skills typically develop in a young child.

The Development of Speech and Language

The ability to communicate with others is an ability of monumental importance. It is also a basic human need from infancy onward. Very early, an infant will attempt to communicate hunger or discomfort through cries and howls. If responded to, this interaction will serve as the basis for the infant's developing "language." Speech will come later.

The newly developing language of a child is made up of verbal and also nonverbal exchanges. Infants participate in expressing themselves and reacting to others. They are able to recognize familiar voices, including familiar tones, pitches, and rhythms of vocalizations. Many parents are amazed at how their newly born infant seemingly recognizes their voices immediately, and some scientists believe that this familiarity with vocal qualities is established while still in the womb. One of my kids actually stopped his "first cries" in the delivery room when my husband began to talk to him.

While the scientific community acknowledges that speech and language development begins very early, they are divided as to why it occurs. Some experts believe that a baby's language acquisition is actually a form of conditioning that is reinforced by the people in the child's environment, while others believe that a baby is born with some type of "pre-wiring" that makes her extremely sensitive to interactions.

Very early, infants begin to notice the nonverbal qualities of communication, such as facial expressions, gestures, and postures of those who interact with them.

As a baby grows, simply understanding the dynamics of language no longer fulfills the baby's wants and needs. This is when the baby begins to make primitive attempts to imitate and use language. And here, speech comes into play. The ability to produce healthy verbalizations requires the combination of several processes, including healthy cognition, respiration, and motor planning. Also, most areas of the head, neck, mouth, and ears need to be physically well formed.

If these processes and physical factors are present, a typical progression of skills will occur. First, the child will begin to produce single sounds, the smallest building blocks of a spoken language. For example:

A child may use the sound /mmm/ for *Mom*.

Next, these single sounds will later be strung together into a small series of sounds that will form a representative word.

The child may now use the word /mama/ for *Mom*.

With practice, the child will soon be able to form the true word, *Mom*.

As a child becomes more adept at using words to communicate, he will begin to use words together. Through reinforcement and imitation he is able to learn "rules of order" that will allow him to put words together into un-derstandable phrases and sentences. Early on, this is like a verbal puzzle. For example, although a child may begin with "cookie" and then graduate to a phrase like, "want cookie" or "me want cookie," ultimately, the child will learn to say, "I want a cookie," as opposed to, "A cookie I want."

It is also interesting to observe the different word meanings a child as-signs to a word during different stages of his development. A child may, very early, use the representative word *dada* to represent any man he sees. Later, the use of *dada* will have evolved to specifically represent his own father.

This succession of skills may occur early, on time, or late, but they always occur—developmentally—in order. But sometimes something hap-pens along the way and one infant, toddler, or preschooler develops differ-ently from the rest.

Speech and Language Disorders

Let's take a look at some disorders associated with speech and language. Maybe you will see shades of your own child reflected in the stories of the children described here, or maybe you will feel that your child's difficulties are much more subtle and less worrisome than the children described.

Because speech disorders and language disorders are very different in nature, I will present each separately. Speech disorders usually do not affect intellectual acuity, while often, language disorders do.

SPEECH DISORDERS

There are basically three different types of speech disorders:

- **Voice Disorders**—A child with a voice disorder may have unpleas-ant and atypical qualities of the voice.

- **Fluency Disorders**—A child with a fluency disorder may have great difficulty speaking fluidly. The child will usually experience "breaks" in speech and may sometimes struggle to get words out.

- **Phonological Disorders**—A child with a phonological disorder may have difficulty articulating different speech sounds.

A **voice disorder** may be diagnosed if, when assessed, a child exhibits atypical *phonation*, or *resonance* or *prosody* of the voice. Several characteristics determine the *phonation*, which is basically the voice quality. These characteristics include the harshness, loudness, and breathiness of the voice. Pitch breaks and an unusual pitch for the child's age are other signals. (For instance, a seven-year-old boy having a high-pitched, extremely delicate voice.) *Resonance* is the sound resonating from the nasal passages, and clinicians will look for hypernasality, hyponasality and whether there are nasal emissions when forming speech. Hypernasality gives the voice a "nasally" sound, while hyponasality gives the voice a "stuffed nose" sound. Therapists, at times, treat children who speak with dialects that tend to be hypernasal, or hyponasal, though these vocal characteristics are not considered to be abnormal. Atypical prosody refers to unusual speech rhyhms, streses, pauses, and intonations when verbalizing. Children who are found to have voice disorders will learn respiration and vocal techniques that will improve their overall voice qualities.

Note: Because there may actually be some type of physical impairment when voice quality is in question, a medical doctor should always be consulted before asking a speech and language therapist to assess your child's voice difficulty.

Dos and Don'ts
If you believe your child may have a voice disorder,

Do:

- See a doctor, such as an otolaryngologist (an ear, nose, and throat doctor).

- Encourage your child to use a quiet voice when speaking.

- Have your child drink lots of liquids.

Don't:

- Don't call attention to your child's unpleasant voice qualities.

- Don't encourage your child to make sound effects with his voice during play.

Fluent speech is speech that flows and seems quite effortless to produce. When assessing whether a child has a **fluency disorder**, the speech and language pathologist will be counting and noting the dysfluencies, which are hesitations, sound repetitions, word repetitions, prolongations (inappropriate word stretching), and blocks (difficulties in getting sounds out). All of us have dysfluencies at times; for instance, the use of *um* is a dysfluency that many of us use as a "filler" until our speech is back on track. Also, nervousness and tension may at times cause the average person to have an increased amount of dysfluencies. Take a look at the experience of the Briar family:

> The Briars brought their son, Scott, at four years, six months to the evaluation center, expressing concerns about their son's ability to speak. Since his third birthday, Scott seemed to have difficulty getting his words out, and his utterances sounded fragmented with bouts of sound repetitions. Scott's mother had spoken twice to a pediatrician about his speech, but she had been advised that "stuttering-like" behaviors are considered normal until a child's speech is more developed at around the age of five. The Briars felt quite anxious. Although they had seen their son mature, they had not seen any improvement in his speaking. Also upsetting to them was Scott's difficulty during a recent "kindergarten round-up day" at the elementary school he was to attend in the fall. Scott appeared anxious, did not speak to the other children, and whenever called on by the teacher would hold his breath and turn red. His mother believed "he was trying to push and force sounds out." The speech and language pathologist who evaluated Scott immediately noticed his tension in relation to speaking. "I believe that's always a warning sign, when you see so much tension and struggling." The speech and language pathologist believed that Scott was a "true stutterer" and not a "developmental stutterer." This means that what

they were witnessing was not the normally occurring dysfluencies associated with speech development. Scott began to see the therapist twice a week, and the therapist arranged time to discuss implementing a home environmental plan. Scott's parents were advised to be very vigilant and to praise Scott each time he used his speech, and to not comment on, or bring attention to, his dysfluencies. They were advised to give Scott extra amounts of "listening time" and to make sure interruptions were kept to a minimum or eliminated. Also, Scott was not to be pressured to speak, but rewarded and praised for using his speech spontaneously. When Scott entered kindergarten, Scott's mother expressed relief that he seemed more confident, and that after working with the therapist, many sounds were "definitely coming easier for him."

Stuttering is probably the most well-known fluency disorder, and when diagnosing a child as a "stutterer," the speech and language pathologist must be very careful in making sure that the child is a "true stutterer" and not a "developmental stutterer." A "true stutterer" has a fluency disorder, whereas a "developmental stutterer" may be showing stuttering-like behaviors that are known to occur in young children (between the ages of two and five) and are considered completely normal, as they are part of the process of speech development. The way therapists differentiate this is to look for *secondary characteristics*. These secondary characteristics occur in "true stutterers" but not "developmental stutterers," and they are: pronounced eye blinking when verbalizing, excessive tension, holding one's breath, difficulty with respiration, struggling while verbalizing, and straining. When one of these characteristics is present, such as in Scott's case, there is a greater chance of the speech difficulty being a fluency disorder.

Research has shown that stuttering, in many cases, may be genetic in origin. Research has also shown that there is a difference in brain activity during verbalization between typical non-stutterers and stutterers. Typically, language activity occurs in the brain's left hemisphere (based on right-handed people) while verbalizing, but in stutterers, this activity occurs in both hemispheres, simultaneously, when verbalizing.

When working with young children, a speech and language pathologist will usually implement an environmental plan to allow the child to gain confidence and feel more at ease when speaking. If a child is consistently corrected or at times pressured to speak, steps are taken to reduce the focus on the dysfluency. Family members are instructed to focus on what the child is saying, and to not comment on the stuttering. It is not a cure, though the more opportunities the child has to practice verbalizing at ease, the more familiar the motor plans of sounds and phrases will be to the child's brain. And the result will be more fluent speech.

Dos and Don'ts

If you believe your child may have a fluency disorder,

Do:

- Show patience with your child when she is speaking.

- Model relaxed and natural speech when with your child.

- Try to have moments of calm communication even on busy, frenetic days.

Don't:

- Don't correct your child when he is speaking.

- Don't rush your child when she is trying to tell you something.

- Don't tell him to stop "talking like that." (He will need help to overcome this.)

The ability to articulate different sounds typically develops in a predictable pattern. For instance, a child will be expected to form her mouth and move her tongue in various ways to produce certain sounds at different ages, with the more difficult formations occurring at more advanced ages. A child may be diagnosed as having a **phonological disorder** when there is a failure to produce the sounds considered developmentally appropriate for the child's age.

For instance, Lucy was three years and five months when her mother asked to have her evaluated for overall immaturity and limited speech. When observing Lucy at her preschool, I saw her vacillating between shyness and inappropriate aggression, pushing other children and stepping on their toys. She occasionally uttered "uh-huh" for "yes," and "doe no" for "I don't know," and her teacher expressed her unsureness as to whether her refusal to participate in discussions or answer questions was behavioral in nature, or something else that would cause Lucy to be "unable" to participate. Lucy also appeared to have some fine-motor difficulty when having to choose and pick up beads during an art project. During that week, the speech and language pathologist evaluated Lucy, and many articulation errors were found. Something unusual turned up on the speech samples (speech samples are listed, verbatim, utterances by the child, which can be referred to for evaluation). Lucy seemed to form certain sounds at certain times but not at other times, so her articulation was actually very inconsistent. At times she would be able to correctly repeat a word said by the therapist, although if the word were used in a phrase, Lucy would lose her ability to correctly articulate the same word. Lucy was diagnosed with *apraxia*.

Apraxia is a disorder that is motorically and cognitively based. The formation of a sound requires a motor plan, which is a cognitively organized set of steps for the muscles, in this case, the muscles of the mouth, lips, and tongue. The physical apparatus of the mouth uses this plan to form a sound when one verbally communicates. Also involved is cognitive memory, that will store the motor plan for later use. When there is an impairment or weakness in this process, articulation errors will be evident, or at the least, quite inconsistent. Apraxia involves the inability to retrieve the motor plans used to produce sounds, so the sequence of steps used in forming the articulators (the tongue, lips, and mouth area) are unavailable or jumbled. The child with apraxia is very inconsistent in forming sounds, and usually the longer the word or phrase the child is trying to verbalize, the more jumbled and confused the speech becomes.

Some children have malformations of the mouth, lips, tongue, jaw, or face, such as in the deformities, cleft lip or palate. These deformities make articulation very difficult. Also, muscle weakness in a child's head and neck regions can negatively affect articulation.

Dos and Don'ts

If you believe your child may have a phonological disorder,

Do:

- Listen carefully when your child speaks.

- Model appropriate pronunciations of words.

- Play games that will exercise your child's tongue, facial, and jaw muscles. (For instance, move a raisin from side to side in your mouths, lick peanut butter off the tops of your lips, watch each other chew taffy, and laugh about what you both look like.)

- Be vigilant about having ear infections treated promptly.

Don't:

- Don't show frustration with your child when she is speaking.

- Don't try to make your child correct her errors.

Guidelines to the sequence of the development of speech sounds:

- A child will usually master /p/, /m/, /h/, /n/, and /w/ between 1.5 and 3 years.

- /b/ between 1.5 and 4 years.

- /k/, /g/, and /d/ between 2 and 4 years.

- /t/ and /ng/ between 2 and 6 years.

- /f/ and /y/ between 2.5 and 4 years.

- /r/ and /l/ between 3 and 6 years.

- /s/ between 3 and 8 years.

- /ch/ and /sh/ between 3.5 and 7 years.

- /z/ between 3.5 and 8 years.

- /j/ between 4 and 7 years.

- /v/ between 4 and 8 years.

- /th/ (as in thick) between 4.5 and 7 years, and /th/ (as in they) between 5 and 8 years.

- /zh/ (as in pleasure) between 6 and 8.5 years.

Even if a child's sounds develop near the "ceiling age," it is still considered developmentally normal. If a child is lagging behind with sound development, usually a speech and language pathologist will check to see if the sounds are "stimulable." This means there will be an investigation as to whether the child is actually physically able to form the sound in isolation (by itself). A therapist will usually have a child imitate their mouth position in trying to elicit the sound. If a child is able to form the sound in isolation, it is believed with time and practice the child will naturally begin to use the sound. If a child were found to not be stimulable for age-appropriate sounds, further assessment would be needed.

LANGUAGE IMPAIRMENTS

When there are deficits in a child's ability to produce language, understand language, or use language in a functionally appropriate way, his ability to communicate is considered to be impaired, as we can see with Danny's difficulties:

At four years old, Danny did not have a grasp of the basic syntax of English. He verbalized words in unusual word orders, and at times he would completely omit words, and this made him extremely hard to understand. As much as possible he would use two-word utterances, and he preferred to point to common objects rather than say their names. He would rarely initiate conversation with adults or peers and shied away from most social activities. Interviews with Danny's parents revealed that he had had numerous ear infections as an infant and toddler, and he had tubes in his ears the previous year. The speech and language pathologist recommended that Danny's hearing be checked to rule out a hearing impairment. Danny was tested and found to be hearing within the normal range, and the evaluation team met to discuss appropriate services for Danny. The evaluation team felt it appropriate to send Danny to a language-based preschool where he would receive speech therapy as part of a group in class, and also individually in a special therapy room. There, he was exposed to new vocabulary every week, and he participated daily in activities that practiced the use of the new vocabulary. Correct syntax of simple sentences and questions were modeled, and Danny was asked to repeat them. Social interactions were encouraged, and modeling of social phrases gave Danny tools to interact with peers. After several months, Danny began to demonstrate correct word orders in his simple comments and requests. He also expanded his vocabulary and appeared to be more confident about social interactions.

The deficits that Danny had are very common, and his history of ear infections is also common, and a concern. Frequent ear infections can cause temporary (and in some cases, permanent) hearing impairments that affect a child's ability to acquire certain language and sound-discrimination skills during a crucial period of rapid brain development. Even though Danny's hearing tested in the normal range at four years old, it is possible he experienced periods of hearing loss as a result of the numerous infections. This causes a need to "catch up" developmentally, and when caught early, in many cases this can be done. So when there is a suspicion that a child may indeed have some type of language impairment, testing and assessing several processes will create a detailed picture of the child's communication behavior. Most speech and language pathologists will look at a child's:

- expressive language

- receptive language

- word retrieval

- pragmatics

- phonological skills

- syntax

- auditory processing

- listening comprehension

Expressive language is language that is expressed by the child. Words and sentences will be recorded by a speech and language pathologist in a sample that can be analyzed for content, intention, and organization. A young child with expressive language deficits usually has difficulty labeling objects, commenting, asking questions, and answering questions. He may gesture, or point, or not attempt to answer questions at all.

An example of typical expressive language:

The preschool teacher holds up a toothbrush and asks Joey, "What is this?" Correctly, Joey answers, "A toothbrush."

An example of atypical expressive language:

The preschool teacher holds up a cup and asks Ben, "What is this?" Ben answers, "This?"

Ben was unable to label the cup because of an extremely limited vocabulary, and he answered with an echolalic-like response ("Echoing" is a characteristic of echolalia, commonly seen in spectrum disorders such as autism).

Receptive language is language that is received by the child. A child will be checked for an understanding of what is being said or signed, and whether information is being processed and held in memory. It is hard for a young child with a receptive language deficit to answer a question because the child may not process the question to the point of understanding.

An example of typical receptive language:

The preschool teacher asks Leah, "Why do we take baths?" Leah correctly answers, "So we get clean."

An example of atypical receptive language:

The preschool teacher asks Damian, "Why do we brush our teeth?" Damian answers, "Toothpaste."

Damian understood the subject matter of the question by recognizing familiar vocabulary, but he was unable to process the meaning of what was being asked.

Another area looked at is **word retrieval**, which involves accessing one's vocabulary when in the process of communicating. A child with word-retrieval difficulties will have the intention of communicating or responding, but will not be able to locate or iterate known words from his or her vocabulary. This can be very frustrating for the child and listener, and will at times cause the child to not respond at all to a question or inquiry.

An example of typical word retrieval:

The evaluator shows four-year-old Ted a picture of a baseball bat. "What is this?" she asks. Ted correctly responds, "A bat."

An example of atypical word retrieval:

The evaluator shows four-year-old Stewart the picture of the baseball bat. "What is this?" she asks. Stewart answers, "Uh . . . a . . . you hit." He then motions with his arms the swinging of a bat.

Although Stewart understood what was being asked, and knew the answer, he could not access his vocabulary and come forth with the wanted word.

Pragmatics refers to the study of how a child communicates and uses language socially, and whether it is appropriate or inappropriate. It is very important when communicating with another to have good pragmatics. When a child's pragmatic skills are inappropriate, it is frequently off-putting, and other children may shun the child.

An example of typical pragmatics:

Four-year-old Maya was in the front yard with her mother. The seven-year-old girl who lived next store walked over, and said, "Hi, Maya, how are you?" Maya responded, "Hi. Fine."

An example of atypical pragmatics:

Four-year-old Sarah was walking to school with her nanny, and a little girl who was walking with her mother said, "Hi, Sarah." Sarah completely ignored her and did not respond. Sarah's nanny said, "Say hi to her." Sarah asked, "Are you a boy or a girl?"

Sarah did not use her language in what would be considered to be a socially appropriate way, and her poor pragmatic skills negatively affect her ability to relate to others.

Phonological skills are the building blocks for understandable verbal language. Sounds are strung together to form words that will later be strung together to form communicable phrases and sentences. If a child has difficulty cognitively organizing information, frequently this will show in his ability to organize sounds into words, and then words into phrases.

An example of typical phonology:

The therapist holds up a picture of a key and tells three-year-old Jorge, "Say key." Jorge correctly says, "key."

An example of atypical phonology:

The therapist holds up a picture of a key and tells three-year-old Brianna, "Say key." Brianna says, "tee."

Brianna substituted the /t/ sound for the /k/ sound in "key." Sound substitutions are common in children who have phonological difficulties.

When a child begins to use representative words and/or true words, she begins to sequence the words into an understandable order, achieving proper **syntax**. This is very difficult for some children; at times the cognition involved in taking pieces of information and organizing them into a specific order is unavailable or impaired.

An example of typical syntax:

The preschool teacher asks three-year-old Brian to answer her question with a full sentence. "What is the boy eating?" she asks. Brian correctly responds, "He eat a cookie."

An example of atypical syntax:

The preschool teacher asks three-year-old David to answer her question with a full sentence. "What is the boy eating?" she asks. David responds, "Cookie . . . boy."

David was unable to appropriately string words together in a word order characteristic of his native language, English. Also, children with atypical syntax will at times omit word endings such as "ing" and "s."

Auditory processing involves hearing, processing, and understanding meaning from the information one hears. At times it is hard to notice children who have auditory processing difficulties because they have honed and developed excellent visual skills as a compensatory measure. Children with auditory processing deficits will take visual cues from those around them to help them understand what they are expected to do, so it may not be apparent that verbal directions were not processed or understood.

An example of typical auditory processing:

The therapist asks four-year-old Jason, "What do we wear on our feet when it snows?" Jason correctly responds, "Boots."

An example of atypical auditory processing:

The therapist asks four-year-old Raj, "What do we wear on our feet when it snows?" Raj responds after a pause, "Snowman."

Raj may have caught the last word, *snows*, because it occurred last, and it was emphasized with the inflection common in questions. If the therapist held up a visual picture of snow-boots or winter clothing, Raj would have had a visual cue and a better chance of comprehending what was asked.

Listening comprehension involves holding a body of information heard in one's memory, and having the ability to either give facts in response to questions, or infer one's opinion based on what was heard in order to answer questions. For children who have difficulty answering questions, sometimes a picture will be drawn or a scene acted out to demonstrate an understanding of what was heard.

Language impairments can be hugely improved when caught early and serviced through Early Intervention Programs. There are also many special language-based preschools for children who appear to be delayed in their language skills, where children receive specialized therapy and enjoy practicing their skills in a social, school environment with kids their age.

Dos and Don'ts

If you believe your child may have a language disorder,

Do:

- Encourage your child to converse with you and others.

- Speak to your child in phrases and sentences.

- Give your child sentence starters to help him formulate responses. An example would be: "What color crayon do you want? Say I want . . ."

- Feel free to incorporate pictures, and motioning when conversing about different subjects.

- Read to your child.

Don't:

- Don't show your frustration in your face or body. Children with language disorders can often receive visual messages loud and clear.

The information you've just read may have illuminated exactly what was worrying you, or you may still feel a bit puzzled. If you're not sure whether your concern warrants further investigation, use the *Test of Three*.

The Test of Three

Use this technique to help assess your child's speech and language problems, to determine whether your child may need professional intervention or specialized help.

Write down *three* characteristics that concern you. Examples might include:

"She does not use sentences yet and is still not consistently using words."

"She is extremely hard to understand when she speaks."

"Her voice sounds unusually flat."

Decide to intervene with *three* ideas to help your concerns. For example:

- I will speak directly to my child more and will show excitement as well as praise her when I hear her use one of her words.
- I will model how to form certain letter sounds and will show her where I place my tongue to make the sound. I will help her try to imitate what I do.
- I will model expression in my voice and will try to get her to imitate my voice inflections.

Work on your interventions daily for *three* weeks, or if you are unable to do this, work on them intermittently for *three* months. Either way, write down specific characteristics that you see. If you can, include verbatim utterances from your child. Do not be afraid to critically watch your child's development over a three-month period. Some children develop in uneven spurts, so you might observe big leaps in skills, or you might continue to see a lag in skills, which would warrant further assessment.

At the end of the chosen time period write down what you observe. Write down how your child performs in the specific areas of concern. Compare your notes with the notes you took in the beginning. Are there any differences? Has there been progress? If you have chosen to work on your interventions daily, you should see some progress in three weeks. If the additional and focused stimulation is only scratching the surface of the difficulties, and your child has not shown obvious progress, it may be time to look into getting further help. After three months, your child has had time to grow, develop, and interact in many different types of situations. How is she doing? Did she have a developmental growth spurt? Or is reaching milestones still a struggle, slow and incremental? If it is the latter, she may need help.

Important Considerations Before Diagnosis

Before a final diagnosis of a speech and language disorder is given, several considerations should be taken into account. For example, is the child not able to perform a certain skill due to a lack of exposure or practice? There is a big difference between not having learned a skill or not having been exposed to a skill (yet having the ability to perform it once exposed) and having a true developmental roadblock or deficit that prevents the child from learning like their same-age peers. All children have different talents and are unique, so a child's learning style should also be looked at.

Factors including the nature of the environment and home life of a child lend information about whether the child has had communication-building experiences. This can be of great importance when a child is adopted after infancy, or has lived in an abusive or otherwise deficient environment (for instance, if a child is malnourished).

Another factor looked at is English as a Second Language. ESL children tend to have unfamiliar syntax, word-retrieval difficulties, and many speech errors, which may appear similar to common speech and language impairments. A therapist will find out from the ESL child's parents whether she developed her first language without apparent difficulties.

A Word on Nonverbal/Alternative Communication

When a child is unable to verbalize due to his or her specific deficit or syndrome, or when a baby or young child is not vocalizing at all, an augmentative and/or alternative communication (AAC) system may be put in place. Sign Language is used in many cases to help facilitate communication, as is specialized communication software and AAC devices (sometimes called "assistive technology"). Some of these devices "talk out loud" as the child chooses pictures or words with a keyboard, mouse, or special attachment. Usually, a communication specialist (a speech and language pathologist who facilitates communication with nonverbal children) will choose a device that is right for the child's specific needs and lifestyle. Many parents would like their children to have devices that are portable, lightweight, and easy to carry. One popular system that parents and teachers use is PECS (Picture Exchange Communication System). PECS allows for a parent, teacher, or specialist to choose from numerous square pictures representing words and actions, to make individualized communication boards or wallets that a child can exchange for access to the object that is pictured. For instance, a child may exchange a picture of a glass of juice to receive juice. One young boy I had the pleasure of working with recently used a PECS communication wallet. We would clip the wallet to his pants so that he would not drop it accidentally, or have to hold onto it when not wearing pants with pockets. Inside the wallet were pictures depicting "bathroom," "help," "juice," "eat," "book," "music," and "hug." This boy was completely nonverbal and severely impaired due to a genetic syndrome. Although he was cognitively impaired and had no functional language, he was able to communicate some basic needs by using the PECS system as an augmentative alternative communication device.

Red Flags of Atypical Development in Speech and Language

Red flags can act as warning signals that development may not be progressing as it should. Below, you will find a list of characteristics that commonly accompany speech and language difficulties. Don't panic if you check one or more; there is no way to "score" your child here. Simply use the list as a tool that will assist you in defining and gauging your child's vulnerabilities, so that you can find her the help she may need.

Birth to Three Months

_____ Baby is extremely quiet.

_____ Baby consistently has difficulty latching on and/or feeding.

_____ Baby cries excessively for no known reason.

Four to Six Months

_____ Baby avoids eye contact.

_____ At four months, baby is not imitating sounds.

_____ At six months, baby is not laughing or squealing.

Eight to Ten Months

_____ Baby does not use vocalizations to get your attention.

_____ At nine months, baby does not babble.

_____ At ten months, baby does not respond to his/her name.

Twelve to Eighteen Months

_____ At twelve months, there is no gesturing, such as waving "bye bye."

_____ At twelve months, he/she does not communicate "hurt" or the need for help.

_____ At fifteen months, he/she does not have a couple beginning words, such as "mama" or "dada."

_____ At eighteen months, he/she does not have at least six beginning words.

Twenty to Twenty-two Months

_____ At twenty months, he/she does not point out objects of fascination.

_____ At twenty-one months, he/she does not follow simple one-step directions.

_____ At twenty-two months, he/she is unable to point to very familiar people, pictures, or objects when named.

Twenty-four to Thirty-six Months

_____ He/she seems uninterested in playing with other children.

_____ He/she shows interest in interacting with adults only.

_____ At twenty-four months, he/she does not string two words together.

_____ At thirty months, he/she is unable to point to common body parts upon request.

_____ At thirty months, he/she does not imitate the words and/or actions of those in her environment.

_____ At thirty months, his/her verbalizations cannot be understood by immediate family members.

_____ At thirty-three months, he/she is unable to identify an object by usage ("Show me what we brush your teeth with").

_____ He/she seems to have a vocabulary of gestures.

_____ He/she seems to have lost words he/she previously used.

_____ He/she verbalizes with confusing word orders.

_____ He/she seems to have difficulty getting sounds and/or words out of the mouth.

_____ At thirty-four months, he/she is unable to respond to "where" questions.

_____ At thirty-six months, he/she is unable to make simple sentences.

_____ At thirty-six months, he/she is unintelligible to strangers.

_____ At thirty-six months, he/she is unable to answer "why" questions.

_____ At thirty-six months, he/she does not ask questions.

Three to Four Years Old

_____ He/she has a peculiar voice quality.

_____ He/she does not respond appropriately to yes/no questions.

_____ He/she does not speak in simple phrases.

_____ He/she is unable to answer "who" questions.

_____ At three and a half, he/she is unable to follow two-step directions.

_____ At three and a half, he/she consistently does not say the ending sounds of words.

_____ Near four, he/she does not respond appropriately to "which" questions.

_____ Near four, he/she does not respond appropriately to "why do we" questions.

_____ He/she has not begun to use adjectives in his verbalizations.

Four to Five Years Old

_____ At four, he/she is continuing to exhibit stuttering-like behaviors.

_____ At four, he/she is still frequently unintelligible.

_____ He/she is not stringing at least four words together.

_____ He/she is unable to follow three-step directions.

_____ He/she does not seem to understand statements with negations.

_____ He/she is unable to initiate an interaction or conversation appropriately.

_____ He/she is unable to sustain a conversation for several conversational turns.

What You Can Do Now:
Exercises that Stimulate Speech and Language Development

You can help encourage appropriate speech and language skills. One way to do this is to set up situations that will present your child with the need to communicate.

- Get your child to *request*.

  By placing favorite objects or favorite foods out of reach, you will put your child in a position where he/she will have to communicate in some way a request for a wanted item.

- Get your child to *negate*.

  By offering your child food or activities he/she dislikes, you can get your child to communicate negations.

- Get your child to *comment*.

  By handing your child something other than what was requested, or by purposely setting up "silly oddity" situations, such as putting your clothes (or your child's clothes) on backwards, you can get your child to comment.

- Expose your child to as many appropriate social situations as possible. These may be family functions, activities, or schools for young children, or simply a playground where other children will be playing.

- Show your child the way your mouth looks, including where your tongue is, when making different sounds. See if your child can imitate you.

- Introduce new vocabulary to your child by labeling objects, and showing your child many different things. Reading books to your child is a good way to expand his/her vocabulary.

- Encourage conversational "turn-taking" even if you have to completely model what should be said next. For instance, you might say, "Say, 'may I play with you?'"

To successfully grasp speech and language skills, your child must be exposed to and be actively involved with the use of language every day. The more your child practices his language skills, the more successful he will be when communicating with others.

*"She's very aggressive
toward other children"*

FIVE

The Development and Disorders of Social and Emotional Behavior

"Our daycare center asked us to withdraw our daughter for the safety of the other children. I am at the end of my rope! She disregards rules, throws, bites, kicks, will not mind me, will not mind the teachers, and I just don't know what to do anymore! We tried everything—time-out, rewards . . . what are we supposed to do now?"

Before our children are even born, we daydream about what their personalities may be like. "Will he be quiet and serious like his father?" "Will she be a free spirit and a rebel like I was?" We find ourselves looking forward to seeing our children's unique talents and individualities unfold, and we feel excited about the opportunities to guide them through life's ups and downs. It will be blissful and meaningful, we think, to share with our children the things we find amazing and joyous about life, loving, and family. We envision wonderful children, intimate close relationships with them, and happiness even in hard times.

We usually don't imagine our little sweeties hitting pets or small babies, or screaming, "I hate you!" in front of all the neighbors. We don't imagine getting a phone call from the preschool director to pick up our child because he is just completely out of control.

In reality, we find ourselves discussing our children's "temperament" with doctors and friends. We begin to notice sensitivities in them, and whether they are energetic or sedentary. We begin to notice traits that really are a little bit like Mom and Dad. We begin to realize we need to let our children know what proper behavior is or looks like, in many different locations, and we start to set limits and discipline our children so that they will learn how to conduct themselves properly. We try to help them socially interact in positive ways with others.

Sometimes a child is unable to conduct him or herself in what is considered to be a socially appropriate manner. Sometimes, a child does not see or experience joy in life's pleasures, or behaves in a truly unpredictable or erratic way. Some of our children will have social or emotional difficulties or disorders, and when this is the case, a child's entire family can suffer the effects.

Social and emotional difficulties tend to have a stigma attached to them because of common beliefs and fears about problems that may come under the categories of "psychological" or "psychiatric." As you learn more about the ways social and emotional skills develop in children and the corresponding problems many of our children may deal with, I hope you will drop any biases or stigmas you may hold and approach this fascinating area of development with understanding. The development of a healthy "psyche" and social and emotional skills is truly important to the overall well-being of a child.

Many professionals who treat children with social and emotional problems still assume that more discipline, or "not giving in" to a child will lead to positive change. Of course, these approaches will work in some cases, but research has shown many behavioral difficulties to be linked to our biological makeups. Each child, even in the same family, is biologically individual from one another. Often, an emotionally difficult child will have siblings who do not exhibit the same negative, explosive, or impulsive behaviors.

To help understand how some common social and emotional difficulties can affect a young child, let's take a look at Bayley, a five-year-old boy, at home.

Bayley Won't Behave

Bayley is playing with his favorite race car in the kitchen. He notices the time on the wall clock. "It's time for Spongebob," he says. "Spongee!" he yells as he runs in a beeline for the family room TV, right past his seven-year-old older brother, Kyle, who is already watching a program. Bayley presses the channel button rapidly over and over, and jumps up and down when he spots the cartoon character. Kyle protests, "No! I was watching something, Bayley!" Kyle reaches for the remote, and almost instantly Bayley hurls himself toward the remote and bites Kyle's hand. Kyle runs off screaming for their mother while Bayley calmly sits down again on the floor in front of the TV watching Spongebob and the other cartoon characters on the show. A few seconds later, Bayley notices his brother Kyle coming back into the room, and his mom is walking into the room, too. She walks up in front of him and turns the TV off. "Nooo!" Bayley shouts. His mom gets close to him and says, "Bayley, you can't just walk up to the TV and change the channel." Bayley immediately stands and forcefully shouts, "You always take his side! I hate you! You stink!" Bayley's mom, looking furious, yells, "You don't talk to me like that, you apologize now!" Bayley turns and bounds up the stairs, right into Kyle's bedroom. He grabs a model airplane and slams it against the wall. Bayley then sees his father walking into the bedroom toward him. "Get off! Get off! I can't breathe!" Bayley screams as he's scooped up, kicking as hard as he can. "Get off! Get off of me! I can't breathe!" His father tells Bayley to calm down and he'll let go. Bayley screams, "Shut up! Shut up!" Bayley is now on his own bed in his own room. Bayley looks at his father with rage. "I hate you! You want to make me die!" Bayley grabs a toy truck from his bed and raises his arm, ready to hurl it right at his dad, but his dad is quick and grabs the truck. Bayley, shaking with anger, glances toward the doorway and sees his mother standing in it. "I bet you'd be glad if Dad makes me die!" Bayley screams.

Social and Emotional Difficulties

Bayley is showing some "red flag" behaviors that would warrant investigation by a psychologist, a psychiatrist, or a behavioral specialist. You probably noticed some of Bayley's emotionally reactive behaviors and inability to stop and think before acting. You may have also noticed his inability to calm himself once wound up, and the negative self-talk he engaged in. Some professionals may reason that Bayley's inability to control himself or respond in an age-appropriate manner may be due to Bayley's learned behavior, meaning that Bayley has learned that if he screams or has tantrums long enough, he will get his way. Many child professionals would see Bayley's symptoms as a sign of an overall "family problem." Let's see how *you* did. Here are some of the behaviors of concern:

- Bayley appears to act impulsively. He runs into the family room to watch a favorite show without stopping and thinking first. Bayley showed a lack of awareness for his brother's presence, and a lack of awareness or caring about what was happening in the room already when he entered.

- He did not show any want or need for social interaction, discussion, or problem solving.

- He interprets his brother Kyle's actions, for instance when Kyle made moves to reclaim his show, as a personal attack.

- Bayley became physically reactive and aggressive when he bit Kyle. He also did not seem to show remorse or a conscious "knowing" that this act was inappropriate.

- He viewed his brother and his mother (and later, his father, too) as people "who are against him."

- He displayed a clear lack of self-control as he became verbally and physically explosive.

- He destroyed his brother's property purposefully and without remorse.

- Bayley made a connection between his situation and death.

An observant parent, teacher, or professional would also notice Bayley's strengths and would use them to help support his weaknesses. Here are some of the positive behaviors and skills that Bayley displayed:

- Early on, Bayley showed that his play and entertainment interests were age-appropriate. He would have many interests in common with peers.

- He displayed some good memory and conceptual skills when he was able to tell what time it was by using the clock (without knowing how to tell time). He remembered when one of his favorite shows came on.

- When confronted by his mother, he chose to escape (flight instead of fight) when he felt uncontrollable anger. This was a good choice at that moment, and probably kept him from aggressively fighting his mother or acting in a more verbally or physically violent way toward her.

These strengths are very important because the teachers and professionals who might help Bayley can use these strengths to develop strategies that can help Bayley learn new skills that can help him feel more positive and interact with others better.

Doctors and child professionals can speak with Bayley's parents and encourage them to help Bayley express his needs and problem solve before situations get heated. Child professionals could help Bayley's parents learn to recognize points of stress and common situations that Bayley may find difficult to handle. With this knowledge, Bayley's parents might be able to "run interference" and guide a situation so that Bayley's need to aggressively act could be diminished. Also, with this knowledge, Bayley's parents could position themselves as Bayley's "partners," "helpers," and even "translators" in his daily life activities, as opposed to people who, in his eyes, are against him. His brother, Kyle, could be involved in this process as well.

Doctors and child professionals could observe Bayley and learn about Bayley's developmental history, to investigate what may be the roots of his misbehavior. Bayley's moods, language skills, sensory integration, and attention could be investigated as well as any additional symptoms that may point to certain disorders or conditions. It would be important to know whether there is any history of developmental or psychiatric disorders in Bayley's family.

Bayley's teachers and parents could help Bayley use his age-appropriate interests to form friendships and enjoy activities with peers. Both Bayley's teachers and parents could help to set up social learning situations that purposefully involve Bayley's interests. For instance, they could use the characters of *Spongebob Squarepants* to help teach important social lessons. Also, in school and at home, Bayley could be given "social scripts." These are scripted sentences that have already been written out or memorized and can be used to help children problem solve and have appropriate phrases at hand, when they themselves are unable to think of what to say.

Without help, atypical patterns of social and emotional behaviors can develop into a cycle of nonacceptance by peers, and a resulting self-worthlessness that can lead to feelings of hopelessness and risky behavior. Untreated serious social and emotional difficulties can lead to aggression or self-medicating behaviors such as drinking or drug habits. It is truly imperative that parents be observant and vigilant when it comes to their children's social and emotional development. All children, in their development, experience some social and emotional challenges, but whether your child simply could use a little more practice with social skills, or whether you are suspecting an actual condition, it is important to be proactive about any concern as early as possible or when symptoms become apparent. Early detection of social and emotional difficulties and their underlying causes can allow for early help to make a child's daily experiences with family, friends, and school, more normalized, happy, and successful.

Defining a Concern: Emotional Disorder or Condition? Social Maladjustment? Or Interfering Condition?

The social and emotional development of children refers to a wide range of skills that reflect children's mood, behaviors, and personal and interpersonal relations. Severe emotional disorders and conditions only make up a fraction of the different types of social and emotional difficulties children face daily.

Usually, a child's social or emotional difficulties will fall into one of three different categories. These categories are: *emotional disorders and conditions*, *social maladjustments*, and *interfering conditions*. Difficulties in any of these categories, whether mild or severe, can impede a child's ability to interact and relate successfully.

The disorders that affect a child's emotional health can be hard to differentiate and diagnose. To help in the understanding of the vast and very different types of social and emotional difficulties children have, we will look at examples in each of the three categories separately.

But before we discuss each of these social and emotional difficulties in more detail, let's first take a look at how social skills and emotion develop in our children.

The Typical Patterns of Social and Emotional Development

When your bundle of joy arrives and is placed in your arms, you can be sure that she has arrived pre-wired with her own unique temperament and newborn emotions. You will probably hear your baby wail with the taking of her first breath, and then witness her become more comfortable when wrapped tightly and securely in her receiving blanket.

Your baby's temperament, mixed with her daily experiences and interactions, from this point on, will make up her "personality." So, though a child is born with the genetic wiring that can give her a predisposed temperament, her actual personality and how she reacts and socially behaves is a combination of the pre-wiring of her brain, and her environmental experiences, relationships, and interactions with others. As with our cognition and language, emotion stems from the brain, mainly in its right hemisphere.

Experts believe that although newborns do have social and emotional experiences, they do not experience emotion in the way older babies or children do. Newborns are also not able to exert control over their emotions. It is not until a baby reaches about six months old that he begins to knowingly experience emotion and show some control over his emotional reactions.

Although a baby of six months shows social and emotional ability that a newborn does not, your child's social and emotional life really do begin as soon as she is born. Barely minutes old, a newborn is able to imitate the facial expressions of others. Newborns will also cry or wail to seek comfort through being held, fed, or changed. When a baby receives food or comfort as a result of her early beckoning, she will learn to continue to interact in ways that will get her needs met, and this will result in the baby beginning to feel secure. If a baby is unable to anticipate comfort in these ways, for instance, if care is not consistent or comforting, the baby will not develop the needed, basic feeling of security that will support her in developing healthy emotions.

In a baby's second month of life, he begins to smile, and with this new ability, he attracts prolonged interactions with his caregivers. And as baby grows, he becomes even more socially imitative and interactive, as he begins to coo and babble as if he is conversing with you. I remember my own children cooing, smiling, and looking directly at me, as they would "talk" a blue streak from their infant seats while I did laundry or cooked a meal. These little "conversations" definitely brought them positive social responses and interactions, which encouraged them to continue these early social behaviors.

And at about six months of age, a baby will truly begin to have some control over her emotions. As opposed to infancy when facial expressions of impending doom might have corresponded to the natural and physical act of having a bowel movement, now, facial expressions and emotional reactions stem from actual "feelings." Babies at this time pay close attention to their environments and begin to cognitively attach meaning to actions and events. Babies are also becoming more and more aware and familiar with the people in their lives and can anticipate emotionally how it may "feel" to be with each person.

At about eight months of age, an emotionally healthy baby will become attached to the parent or caregiver that is her closest, most focused and comforting relationship. Babies will try their best to keep the person of attachment close at hand, and they will frequently fuss when separated from this desired person. This first connected relationship helps babies learn about the emotional feelings of others, as well as more about their own emotions and feelings.

Yet with this new, wonderful ability to emotionally attach to another, comes some different and more difficult emotions and reactions that can appear when a child is near someone that is unfamiliar to him, or when he is to be separated from his person of attachment. Child experts call these emotions "stranger anxiety" and "separation anxiety" and they are common in emotionally healthy babies. Your baby may fearfully stare and reach out for you when a well-meaning unfamiliar person approaches him, or he may wail in desperation when handed to a baby-sitter or caregiver.

In your presence though, or in the presence of a familiar and trusted caregiver, your little one will begin to explore and venture away from you for short periods, yet return to you frequently to "check in." Some experts believe this is a type of emotional "refueling" before venturing out once more. And as your child explores, she will be demonstrating a style of exploration that many studies show to be highly correlated with her genetically given temperament. Experts look at a child's "degree of approach and withdrawal" and label their styles of exploration and comfort in novel situations as "inhibited" or "uninhibited." Inhibited children are very cautious and will not readily explore or respond in novel situations. Uninhibited children will freely and fearlessly check out novel toys, people, or places.

For most children, these characteristics of inhibition remain a part of their temperaments and can be repeatedly witnessed as they grow older and confront new situations. Though there may be the tendency to think that being "inhibited" will not be good for a child, in actuality inhibited children often become good students who are able to conform to rules. Involved and vigilant parents frequently expose their inhibited children to many different types of novel experiences, giving them a comfort level for new experiences that they did not have before.

As a child grows, it is not only through their early intimate relationships and exploring that a child develops her social and emotional skills, but also through *play*. Most researchers and child experts consider play to be essential in the development of social skills and adaptive skills. It is through play that children experiment with their own ideas, bodies, and surroundings, which helps them to understand more about their environments and their own abilities. Through play, many children practice work skills that they have witnessed adults perform.

Play is also important for the development of social skills. Typical children who have play experiences seem to develop a desire to relate to and "do" with others as they grow. Many experts have documented a pattern to the growth of social skills through play. For instance, a child less than two years old will usually engage only in "solitary play," when among other children. This means that the child's play would be self-centered and unrelated to the actions of other children. A child who is two years old will frequently engage in "parallel play," meaning that the child will enjoy playing among other children and seek out places that children are playing, but will still remain self-centered in her actual play activity and will appear to be playing "next to" other children. At three years old, many children begin to engage in "cooperative play." In this stage, children actually seek out other kids' company and will cooperate as one of a group in simple and imaginative games and activities. When children are four, they are frequently observed to have "highly cooperative play" skills. In this developmentally advanced phase of play, children partake in highly organized games and activities. They are seen to brainstorm, make rules, negotiate, and take turns.

The Disorders that Affect Social and Emotional Well-being

Let's take a closer look at some of the disorders associated with atypical socialization and emotions. Maybe you will see shades of your own child reflected in the stories of the children described here, or maybe you will feel that your child's difficulties are much more subtle and less worrisome than the children described.

EMOTIONAL DISORDERS AND CONDITIONS

The puzzle of what is or what is not normal emotion can be complex and elusive. Experts do know that many emotional disorders and conditions "run in families." Experts also know that early childhood neglect and abuse can cause lifelong social and emotional disorders, as well as damaging biological changes in the developing brains of children. But experts know that emotional disorders and conditions occur in children who have good parents, too. Parents can be quick to blame themselves or feel blamed when they or others suspect an emotional disorder or condition in their child. In school systems, there is a diagnosis of "emotionally disturbed" that is frequently and purposely avoided. I have seen not only parents, but also child professionals use any diagnosis they can to avoid labeling a child as "emotionally disturbed." There is often fear and a mysteriousness attached to the concept of an unhealthy "psyche" and there are, of course, stigmas of being "crazy" or "mentally ill." Because of these fears and stereotypes, families often avoid seeking help for their children, when early intervention is truly the key to regaining emotional health and social well-being.

Emotional disorders and conditions are considered to be long-term or lifelong conditions. They are frequently workings of the brain's biology, and many sufferers show a genetic family history or predisposition. Many emotional disorders and conditions are listed medically as "psychiatric disorders," and this wording can be scary for parents initially. Really, the term "psychiatric" refers to the relationship of the brain's chemistry to a person's inner thoughts and outward behavior. When properly diagnosed and treated, children with emotional difficulties can show great progress and interact more typically with family and peers. Proper early treatment of emotional disorders and conditions help children to be more available for learning and relating, and these children enjoy greater success with their relationships as well as their academic schoolwork. Some examples of emotional disorders are bipolar disorder, schizophrenia, Obsessive-Compulsive Disorder (OCD), oppositional-defiant disorder, and depression. ADHD (Attention Deficit Hyperactivity Disorder) is also considered to be an emotional disorder because the origin of ADHD is also in the chemistry of the brain and probably in the genetic makeup of the affected child.

Over the years, child experts have defined various types of emotional disorders and their symptoms, several of which I will highlight here. Most of these disorders do leave clues to their presence, such as in Evan's case:

Evan's parents wondered what to do with their five-year-old son's un-usual fearless behavior and seemingly hyperactive motor-driven peri-ods. Evan's parents told us that sometimes Evan wouldn't sleep for more than a couple hours for days at a time. A recent dangerous event where Evan ran into traffic believing he was Superman and could stop cars with his bare hands, convinced Evan's parents that they needed help. Though earlier in Evan's life, they had laughed about their son's "imagination" and energy level, they were now con-cerned, scared, and convinced that this was no laughing matter. As Evan's parents described him more thoroughly, it also became appar-ent that Evan would sometimes have crying jags, and periods where he didn't want to leave the house. He at times would want to be left alone and wouldn't eat. We immediately referred Evan's parents to a psychiatrist who is knowledgeable about child psychiatric disorders and symptoms. Three months later, after careful observation and eval-uation, Evan was diagnosed with **bipolar disorder**.

Bipolar disorder is a condition marked by extreme mood swings. Chil-dren who have bipolar disorder go through periods of extreme elation followed by intervals of deep depression. Bipolar disorder is different from the typical mood swings that children and most people go through from time to time. The "high" periods have a manic quality to them, where a child may hardly need to sleep at all, may talk excessively jumping from thought to thought, and where a child may have unrealistic thoughts and beliefs that can lead to extremely dangerous and daring behaviors. Elements of the "manic phase" of bipolar disorder can look similar to hy-peractivity in some children, and this is why it is important for knowl-edgeable child professionals and medical professionals to observe both "phases" of this disorder before a diagnosis is made. The "low phase" of bipolar disorder is marked by a period of diminished energy, irritability, feeling worthless, and even thoughts of death or suicide. Bipolar disorder is a lifelong but treatable condition, and the earlier symptoms are recog-nized and treated, the better the developmental outlook for the affected child.

Justin's symptoms were recognized when he was four:

Justin's parents had received numerous phone calls from his pre-school teacher about his odd behavior. The teacher had even used the word "creepy" to describe Justin's behavior. Apparently Justin would tell other children that he "sees fire behind them," and that his god told him "to set anyone who doesn't do what I say on fire." Justin was not physically aggressive, and he was even relatively quiet. He would walk around the room, pace, and quietly murmur and talk to himself for a large part of the time. Justin's teacher described her "dis-trust" of Justin and what he "may" do. "I really found myself uneasy and afraid to be around this little boy," she relayed. "The things he would say . . . and the flat monotone voice he would use . . . he was just in his own scary world." Justin's parents did agree that his "seeing things" had become more prevalent, and they would see him talking to himself frequently at home. After a little coaxing, the Pratts brought their son to a major university's child development center and had Justin evaluated. After careful consideration, experts concluded that Justin should begin treatment for symptoms of childhood **schizo-phrenia.**

A diagnosis of **schizophrenia** is very unusual in a young child. Most cases of schizophrenia are diagnosed in the teenage years or in young adulthood. Children who are suspected of having symptoms may demonstrate unusual moods, a disinterest in socializing, expressionless speech, hallucinations, and delusions. Early on, the general "affect" of children who may be de-veloping schizophrenia may look like other disorders, such as Asperger Syndrome, because children with Asperger Syndrome also frequently have a flat, expressionless way of interacting. With schizophrenia, though, the presence of recurring hallucinations, where the child "knows what was seen as real," is a serious departure from typical fears of children that can be logically relieved by turning on a light or discovering the cause of a shadow. Children with schizophrenia are actually seeing or hearing things (or both), and they will react to or become active participants in these ex-periences. Children who have healthy imaginations can usually differenti-ate between what is real and pretend, and they will say, when confronted, that "they were just playing." Children with schizophrenia may be driven by their own beliefs, from the voices they hear, or from the delusions of missions they feel they must accomplish. They are typically disorganized, illogical, and at times paranoid.

Schizophrenia can be successfully treated in most cases, the most common form of treatment being medication and therapy. Medications can help control or stop the hallucinations and delusions, while therapy can help children and their families adjust to and learn more about the disorder. Once treated, children relate much more appropriately and find it much easier to concentrate on learning social and academic skills. Left untreated, schizophrenia and other emotional disturbances make focusing in a learning environment very difficult.

A seven-year-old little girl named Gerri also found it difficult to focus at school.

Gerri's first-grade teacher asked the school psychologist for help with a situation that was affecting her whole classroom. Apparently Gerri, who had been previously asking for baby wipes to wipe down her chair upon entering the classroom, was now demanding that no one touch her chair or desk. If another child even brushed by her chair or desk, she would be on the verge of tears and refuse to sit at her desk until she could wipe it down with baby wipes again. Gerri's teacher also described a certain way she had to hand papers to Gerri, and that Gerri had a specific way of holding her fingers to receive papers from her. If a paper or pencil of Gerri's dropped on the floor, she wouldn't pick it up or even touch it. The school psychologist met with Gerri (Gerri had to baby wipe the chair she was going to sit in first), and Gerri told the psychologist that she didn't want to get strep germs or bring strep germs home to her baby brother. "Strep can lead to worse things. It's dangerous." The psychologist asked if she knew that nowadays there are many antibiotics that can kill strep germs, and Gerri replied that she knew, but that she also knew "some germs and strep germs are now resistant to antibiotics." The psychologist met with Gerri's parents, who both described a worsening of Gerri's preoccupation with catching germs. Gerri's parents called their pediatrician and got a referral to a psychiatrist. After meeting with Gerri and her family, the psychiatrist developed a plan to help Gerri with her symptoms of **Obsessive-Compulsive Disorder**.

Like Gerri, a child with **Obsessive-Compulsive Disorder** will be obsessive or unusually worried and distressed over a specific issue. Children affected by this disorder are frequently aware that their obsessions and compulsions may not be logical, and this can cause an even greater sense of embarrassment and shame. Obsessive-compulsive children may have certain rituals and self-inflicted rules that they abide by to help them avoid their individual fear, and if they are forced to miss or interrupt one of these rituals, the children can truly experience anguish. A common symptom of this disorder is the anxiousness children feel when they experience obsessive thoughts. The children themselves experience their own obsessions as unwanted thoughts. Many children express an inability to make the obsessive thoughts go away or stop the rituals that help them cope. Behavior therapy has been very successful in treating Obsessive-Compulsive Disorder, and some children have found relief with medication. Obsessive-Compulsive Disorder's onset may be slow or sudden, but the condition is treatable, and children can find relief and successfully progress under the care of knowledgeable child professionals. Gerri's progress helped not only Gerri, but also helped her parents feel hope.

Hopelessness was a feeling Andrew's parents knew well.

Andrew's parents described the past twelve months with their six-year-old son as "simply awful." "Andrew has been irritable and negative just about every moment of every day. He will argue with me about everything. Even silly little things." They relayed that Andrew was also having a difficult time at school. His teacher reported that he was extremely argumentative and would challenge her constantly. He would not follow the rules of the classroom and would sometimes have a tantrum or shout at his teacher. The school psychologist (who described Andrew as a "loose cannon") had been called in midyear to help Andrew's teacher "handle" him, but the second half of the year was no better, especially after finding out that Andrew had been lying to his parents and teacher about events at school or home, and blaming classmates, the teacher, or his parents, for his frequent out-bursts. Feeling like they were ready to try anything that may help An-drew and their family as a whole, Andrew's parents accepted a referral to a psychiatrist and were thrilled with the planning of team meetings that would include the school professionals, outside profes-sionals, and themselves, to devise a behavioral plan that would help Andrew in the classroom and at home. The psychiatrist treating An-drew joined the meetings and participated in fine-tuning a behavioral plan that helped Andrew cope with his anger and lack of self-control. The psychiatrist felt Andrew was displaying symptoms of opposi-tional-defiant disorder.

Children with **oppositional-defiant disorder** are notoriously frustrating, even to the calmest and most patient of parents and teachers. Children with this disorder do not accept guidance or instruction and will argue and challenge rules. They also frequently lie. These children are often irrita-ble, "on edge," and show a lack of awareness for authority figures. For in-stance, a child with oppositional-defiant disorder may challenge and argue with an adult in the same way he would with a peer. Most children are nat-urally aware of a difference between dealing with a teacher, parent, or same-age "friend" and adjust their behavior accordingly.

Many children with oppositional-defiant disorder find themselves in trouble at school and at home. They are labeled as "trouble makers" who have "behavioral problems." But psychiatrists who treat these kids have ar-gued that many of them are not in control of their moods and irritability. Some experts believe that children with oppositional-defiant disorder are developmentally behind in fundamental abilities such as flexibility and tol-erance. Experts have found that oppositional-defiant children improve with behavioral therapy and guided interactions.

Child professionals can demonstrate to parents and teachers ways they can diffuse an "argument" with an oppositional-defiant child before it truly gets started. This can be done by giving the child choices and as much con-trol as appropriately possible over his day. Acting as if you are a "partner in success" who is willing to listen can also be helpful. Keeping a calm de-meanor, so as not to escalate a situation, is also important and helpful.

Many parents and teachers find that distracting or using humor with their oppositional child helps to avoid conflict. Also, involving oppositional-defiant children in activities that they love can help to encourage more positive demeanors.

Sometimes a child's negativity can be so profound that help is needed.

At six years old, Didi felt she was ugly and didn't want to go to school anymore. She would cry in the morning and seem extremely irritable in the evening. Her parents thought that something may be happening at school; perhaps she was being bothered by another student. Didi's mother noticed that she was bringing home a good portion of her school lunch uneaten, and that her appetite at home was not what it used to be. Didi was also not completing her schoolwork, and she had always been a very responsible student. Didi's mother also noticed a similarity to the down and hopeless feelings she had seen her own sister (Didi's aunt) display when they were growing up. Her sister had been diagnosed with **depression**. "But Didi is only six. How can she be depressed?" her mother wondered. After about three months of trying different things to get Didi to "snap out" of her down mood, Didi's parents took her to see their pediatrician and learned that their daughter indeed may be showing symptoms of depression. The family was referred to a child psychiatrist, who through a combination of therapy and later on, medication, helped Didi to make an enormous turnaround. "She is back to herself again. She is happier. We are all happier," her mother reports.

Most of us know that **depression** is common in the general population. We usually picture adult women struggling with this disorder. Most of us are unaware that many children struggle with depression, too. Children with depression are not experiencing the typical "sadness" most children feel now and then. Depression causes an ongoing sadness, irritableness, and fatigue that may appear with no apparent reason. Sometimes children will become depressed in reaction to a situation or event. When a child is sad, with time and adult guidance, the child usually "recovers" and resumes her typical mood and activities. When a child is depressed, the mood of sadness may last for days and even weeks, wreaking havoc on the child's ability to concentrate, sleep, eat, and relate to others. Children with depression may be anxious, nervous, and may act out or tantrum. Most children show a decline in their ability to perform at school. And sadly, though it is rare, children as young as six can even have thoughts of suicide.

When experts suspect depression in children, they look for an episode of "sadness" that lasts for two weeks or more. This helps them to differentiate between what may be a typical and passing event or mood, and what may truly be depression. They also review the child's symptoms and behaviors, the child's school performance, and even the child's feelings, if she is able to share them. True depression is not a condition that a child can mentally or physically control, so it is very important that a child professional, preferably a psychiatrist, be contacted if it appears your child may be experiencing symptoms of depression. Depression is a treatable condition, and with proper treatment, a child can speedily get back on track. Getting on track, and giving their difficulties an actual name, helps many children cope, for when they realize that they are not expected to handle the difficulties by themselves, and that the difficulties are not their fault, they often feel a sense of relief and are treated more gently by those around them.

Six-year-old Stewart felt a sense of relief when he was diagnosed with ADHD. He felt he was actually not, after all, a "bad kid."

"We got a note from Stewart's kindergarten teacher saying that he needed to learn to follow directions, listen better, and keep his hands to himself. We kept hearing about inappropriateness, but at that time, it was hard for us to believe, because we weren't seeing anything wrong at home. Stewart was such an early reader and ahead academically, so we thought he was probably bored." Mrs. Ladd went on to say that when Stewart began first grade, he was put on a behavior plan, and she called a meeting with his teacher in disbelief that they were talking about Stewart as if he were a behavioral problem. "When I went in for the meeting, I purposefully walked down the hall to where Stewart's classroom was and looked in the doorway window. I was shocked at what I saw, to say the least. Stewart kept getting out of his seat, talking when he shouldn't have been talking, and just seemed really wound up, like he couldn't settle down. I did not like the way the teacher spoke to him, but I had to admit, I, myself, was getting annoyed at him as I watched. After that, I started noticing many things I hadn't noticed before. I noticed how he would quietly run back and forth across his room when it was time for bed, how he was disorganized, and he just could not really settle down, even when he tried hard to do it." Stewart was taken to see a pediatrician in the family's pediatric group, who specialized in diagnosing **Attention Deficit Hyperactivity Disorder (ADHD)**. Stewart's parents and teachers filled out checklists to decipher whether Stewart might have ADHD. After observations at school and at home, Stewart was diagnosed as having a form of ADHD. Mrs. Ladd reported, "With this diagnosis, we are relieved. Stewart is receiving help, his school is more understanding, and he doesn't feel like a bad person anymore. Right now, things are going very well for him."

Attention Deficit Hyperactivity Disorder has become a well-known condition in recent years, with large numbers of children being diagnosed with the disorder. There are a few different forms of this condition. Children with one form of ADHD show symptoms of inattention without the hyperactivity. Children with another form have hyperactivity and impulsivity, but are able to attend. Some children have yet a different form of ADHD and show symptoms of both the inattention *and* hyperactivity. The distractibility and impulsivity that is typical of children with ADHD can cause all kinds of problems in a school or academic setting, and can be very socially off-putting to peers. Children with ADHD are also frequently reprimanded by adults for their undesirable "behaviors," resulting in poor self-esteem in many cases. When child professionals consider an ADHD diagnosis, they are usually looking for the symptoms to have begun before the child reached seven years of age. If the symptoms appeared at age seven or later, other possible explanations would be considered. Child professionals also look for the symptoms to have been present for six months or more. Symptoms of an attention deficit might include being easily distracted, being forgetful, being disorganized, and having difficulty staying focused on the task at hand. Symptoms of hyperactivity might include running about as if propelled by a motor, talking excessively, fidgeting, and possessing an inability to sit still.

Impulsivity is also a common symptom of ADHD. Children will act or blurt out answers before considering the consequences of their actions or words. Some of you may recognize these symptoms in many of the children you know, but ADHD truly causes difficulties at home and at school. Children find it much harder than their peers to sustain friendships, complete schoolwork, and maintain a healthy self-esteem. The symptoms of ADHD are present most of the child's waking hours, so periodic "bouts" of these symptoms, when a child has more typical behavior the majority of the time, would not be considered to be ADHD.

ADHD can be successfully treated once identified. Treatments usually include a combination of therapy, medication, school interventions, behavior modifications and classroom adaptations. Some children with ADHD find success with therapy and school interventions alone.

Therapy and school interventions can help children who struggle with anxiety. Anxiety is common to us all, but thankfully, for most of us, the disturbing feelings pass with the passing of the anxiety-provoking events we encounter. We usually resume our lives and activities until once again we are "thrown for a loop." It is hard to imagine feeling anxiety or nervous and anxious almost *all* the time. For children, it can be overwhelming. Children who have a *generalized anxiety disorder* feel anxious and threatened by the numerous possibilities of events and outcomes that typical children simply accept. Though children may experience anxiety when attempting new skills, or may even have a specific fear, children with an anxiety disorder frequently refuse to participate in typical childhood activities, and they may react inappropriately and disproportionately to these activities as if they were being faced with life or death situations. When child professionals suspect a child's overly concerned and nervous behavior to be an anxiety disorder, they usually see a pattern of behavior that has occurred for six months or more. Typical children may have periods of anxiety that can last a few weeks, usually resulting from a specific event. But children who truly have an anxiety disorder are not able to control their anxious thoughts, even when they make great efforts to try and make them stop. Children with a generalized anxiety disorder find their worries getting in the way of making friends and participating in social activities, interfering with their concentration and ability to perform at school, and enjoying time at home with their families.

Anxiety disorders are also very treatable, and children respond well to psychotherapy, behavioral therapy, and in some cases, medications. Some children learn relaxation techniques that are simple and that they are able to do whenever needed.

Autism Spectrum Disorders

You may hear child professionals and parents talking about emotional disorders and conditions that are "on the spectrum." Usually, they are referring to disorders that have autistic-like qualities that may range from very mild to severe. I will introduce you to the two most commonly known spectrum disorders, autism and Asperger Syndrome. Let's start by taking a look at Luke's story:

"When Luke was a newborn baby, I was thrilled because he slept through the night from the start! Little did we know then that that was probably the first sign of his autism. He seemed to develop well during his first year. He wasn't a cuddly baby and would not really make good eye contact with us, but we would catch his eye sometimes before he would look away. Sometimes we would make a game out of trying to catch his eye. I feel a little foolish about that now. Luke did begin to talk and use words . . . not well, but he used them. I think it was about the time Luke was a year and a half when we starting seeing him regress into an irritable child who had no interest in us, really at all. He stopped using words he had previously used, and stopped playing with his toys. He wanted to do things that most little ones wouldn't want to do like pull threads from the carpet for hours. Luke was diagnosed with autism when he was about three, and he started to attend a special preschool where he got therapy, too. He is seven now, and he's doing well. He does talk; we are very lucky.

Some of his classmates don't talk. We do have struggles daily, but we have a very bright boy, and he is very lovable in his own way."

Autism is a disorder that can have a mysterious and sometimes terrifying onset. Children do sometimes show symptoms from birth, but often children seem to develop normally, and then simply begin to regress into their own worlds. Communicating and interacting become challenges, and many parents experience a feeling of desperation when they fight to keep the child they know and love from "slipping away." Experts believe that autism possibly results from abnormal development or growth of the brain, but there are many theories and hypotheses to still be researched, and still much more to be learned about this puzzling disorder. Children with autism have great difficulty with, and frequently show a lack of interest in, communicating and socializing. They tend to want to remain alone and may become agitated or even have a tantrum when disturbed. Children with autism may have difficulties understanding or using language, and some have unusual responses to language such as echoing what was said or repeating phrases from overheard conversations or TV shows. Many children with autism have odd habits and use their bodies in unusual ways. Some of these children will open and close cabinets, or turn on and off lights for hours. Many children rock their bodies, flutter their fingers, or flap their arms. Sometimes, children with autism have special talents and abilities that may be considered to be extraordinary.

Children with autism may share symptoms, but they are also quite individual from one another. Plans for treatment are also individualized and are influenced by the knowledge and influence of the doctors, parents, and teachers in the child's life. Some doctors prescribe medications for certain symptoms associated with autism and see great improvements in their patients. Some parents swear by a learning technique called Applied Behavioral Analysis (ABA). Many autistic children receive special help at school and therapies to help them learn better communication, socializations, and adaptive skills (everyday skills, such as dressing, toileting oneself). Sometimes children with autism will be treated with many approaches at once. With help, children with autism can and will improve. It is important to begin help as soon as symptoms are apparent.

Asperger Syndrome has similarities to autism, although the symptoms are much less severe. Children with Asperger Syndrome are usually able to function among peers in typical classrooms and keep up academically with schoolwork, but to those on the outside, there is an "oddity" about the child, or a "strangeness" that can lead to social isolation. Many children who have Asperger Syndrome avoid social interaction, or they may even see it as an unwelcome annoyance. They also may avoid eye contact, and although most children with Asperger Syndrome communicate at an age-appropriate level, their speech and language frequently has an unusual, formal quality to it. Also, the child may have difficulty communicating or understanding things that are not blatantly literal. Children with Asperger Syndrome like to have a routine that they follow, and changes in routine can cause them stress. Many have obsessive interests and hobbies.

Asperger Syndrome is also treated with special learning techniques, such as social skills programs and, at times, medications. Adaptations and extra attention from teachers and therapists at school can also help a child with Asperger Syndrome to progress.

Dos and Don'ts

If you believe your child may have an emotional disorder or condition,

Do:

- Seek help from qualified professionals as soon as you are aware of seemingly atypical social behaviors or emotions.

- Begin to take notes about situations that are very difficult for your child, and the moods your child experiences daily. Also take note of the environments and circumstances in which your child is most comfortable.

- Help to create opportunities for your child to socially interact with peers. Continue to encourage your child in this regard.

- Set a good example for your child by handling situations or unexpected circumstances in a calm way, and without a heightened reaction. Try to model problem solving for your child.

- Try to have a basic routine to your day, and discuss with your child any changes that may affect the routine.

- Compliment and notice your child's good qualities and moments.

- Remember that it can be exhausting at times to live with or work with children with emotional disorders and conditions. Take time for yourself to refuel, so that you can be at your best.

Don't:

- Don't isolate yourself, your child, or your family. Go out, leaving your child with a family member or a sitter, if needed. Or, take along a "helper" to focus on your child if your child finds certain environments to be uncomfortable. (For example, a helper could take an ADHD child for a walk while waiting for food at a restaurant.)

- Don't simply accept the diagnosis and advice of a psychologist or educational evaluator if your child's symptoms are severe. Severe symptoms that affect behavior and emotion need medical attention because certain medical conditions may be the cause. Also, psychologists and educational evaluators cannot diagnose certain psychiatric conditions because they are not qualified to do so.

- Don't expect your child to be able to control or stop behaviors or emotions that may be due to an emotional disorder or condition.

- Don't let your child lose his positive interests and strengths as a consequence of his inappropriate behavior, and notice and reward appropriate behaviors. Discuss behavioral modification plans with child professionals and what consequences might work for your child. Activities that encourage socialization and gross motor activities, such as sport activities, can be very beneficial. Losing computer games, TV privileges, or time outs may be appropriate as consequences for problem behavior.

- Don't forget that your child needs your love and caring, even if he doesn't show it.

Social Maladjustments

Social maladjustments are considered to be temporary social and emotional difficulties. Though a child may need treatment for a social maladjustment, they are not considered to be long-term or lifelong disorders of the child's "psyche." A child is considered to have control over the maladjusted behavior, so in a way, social maladjustment is a form of "acting out" or withdrawing. The term "social maladjustment" usually refers to a behavior or behaviors that directly result from a situation or experience. Some examples of the situations that may cause social maladjustment behaviors in children are: a death in the family, certain situations involving sexual abuse, being bullied, or having a difficult reaction to divorce.

There is some disagreement among child professionals as to what social maladjustments really are. Some experts believe that social maladjustments refer to disorders such as oppositional-defiant disorder, and conduct disorders, which include behaviors that are clearly violent. This way of thinking led many to try to judge true emotion from social acting out, for children with true emotional disorders would receive interventions and services in schools, but children with social acting out behaviors would not receive these special services. This caused some very needy, difficult children to be without help, and in some cases be suspended or expelled due to poor behavior. Cases have been disputed in court to somehow come to terms with the questions, What is truly an emotional disorder? and, When is behavior a social maladjustment?

Current thinking allows us to see that social maladjustments are caused by various traumas in children's lives, and not by permanent or long-term brain deficiencies, or developmental abnormalities characteristic of emotional disorders and conditions. Experts consider social maladjustments, even those that require treatment, to have short-term durations, and this difference in affliction "length" also differentiates social maladjustments from emotional disorders and conditions. The different types of traumas that cause most social maladjustments fall into a few distinct categories. These are *grief, interpersonal trauma, transitional trauma,* and *physical trauma*.

Grief can be a very difficult emotion for children to handle. Children may withdraw, become fearful, or depressed, or they may act out in behaviorally inappropriate ways. Many times we hear that children are just "not themselves" anymore, and this can be heartbreaking to those who love them and want what's best for them. A death of a cherished person, or the death of a favorite pet, or the loss of "the personality of a person the child knew" due to illness, an accident, or drug addiction (the person still being alive), can all weigh heavily on a child's emotional stamina, and cause social maladjustments.

Interpersonal traumas result from socially traumatic relations and interactions with others. Children who show social maladjustments as a result of interpersonal trauma may be struggling with social situations such as being bullied by another student, being physically or sexually victimized by adults or youths (where frequently children are threatened to "not tell" or horrible things will be done to them or their families). Explosive or unhealthy parent/child relationships can at times cause social maladjustments in children, as can the loss of friendship from a peer in socially less-resilient children.

Some children experience transitional traumas that result in social maladjustments. These children find big changes in their lives very difficult to deal with. The inability to adjust to new surroundings, such as in a move to a new house or city can cause a problematic period of discomfort and loneliness that can lead to depression or aggressive acting-out behaviors. A child diagnosed with a serious illness or whose family member is diagnosed with a serious illness may experience a social maladjustment due to the "change of life" that may largely be unwanted and unexpected by the child.

Social maladjustments in children may also be caused by physical trauma. A traumatic accident may cause negative changes in personality and attitude, and a child may seem to completely lose interest in, or even fear, formerly loved activities or people. Another example of physical trauma that may cause a social maladjustment in children would be the child who is having difficulty dealing with ongoing pain and may feel unable to "take it" for another hour or week or month.

Children with social maladjustments can be helped and encouraged. Caring child professionals and parents can help children to grow and learn new ways to cope with their difficult situations. When addressed early (when symptoms become apparent), with help, many children can get past the temporary hardships that change them socially and emotionally.

Dos and Dont's

If you believe your child may have a social maladjustment,

Do:

- Seek help from qualified child professionals if you see "acting out" or withdrawing behaviors that are uncharacteristic of your child and that don't appear to be going away.

- Seek help if your child's personality has suddenly "changed" for no apparent reason.

- Seek professional advice if you see your child engaging in acts or showing knowledge that you do not consider to be age-appropriate.

- Try to have your child spend time in environments and with people he considers to be safe.

- Communicate with your child's school professionals about your concerns and ask for support if needed.

Don't:

- Don't assume that all children are resilient. Some are not.

- Don't try to force your child to "snap out of it" with the threat of consequences or punishment.

- Don't underestimate the danger of your child's feelings of hopelessness, even if the origin is simply a transition or negative peer interaction.

- Don't stop reaching out and being proactive until you get your child the help he needs.

Interfering Conditions

Interfering conditions are varied developmental conditions and disorders that can interfere with the ability to successfully interact with others. They may include speech and language difficulties, physical abnormalities, or learning disabilities. Frequently, a child's struggle with any type of developmental problem or disability will make socializing somewhat challenging. Sadly, for some children, the feeling of being different or ostracized can be emotionally devastating. When children are born with or are found to have any type of developmental difficulty, there is usually an emphasis on improving that particular area of development. In some cases, time needed for play and socializing will be left behind in the quest to remediate the developmental weakness. This may leave some kids unprepared for the peer interactions they are destined to encounter. Parents need to be extra vigilant, for any developmental condition or disorder has the potential to be an interfering condition, socially or emotionally. An example of an interfering condition would be **Nonverbal Learning Disorder**.

Antonio, who was diagnosed with **Nonverbal Learning Disorder** this year, won't play with any of his first-grade classmates because he says they are all "too dumb." I asked him how he knew his classmates were dumb, and he said that they say he wears baby pants. Antonio went on to tell me that his pants were obviously a size six or seven, a size for big kids. He also said that there is a rule that you have to keep your hands to yourself, and his classmates always touch each other, and it drives him crazy. Antonio has recently seen the school psychologist and will be a member of a special peer "social group" so that he can learn some new social skills, as well as how to be a friend.

A child with Nonverbal Learning Disorder (NLD) will frequently understand what is said literally, but will not "catch" the underlying meanings embedded in spoken words or facial expressions. The reactions of peers and adults can be very confusing and frustrating to an NLD child, causing unexpected emotional reactions and social difficulties.

Sensory Processing Disorder is another example of an interfering condition:

> Harry hates kindergarten and will tell you so, if you ask him how he likes school. He says he hates the noise, and that everyone is always yelling. If you observe his class, though, the noise level does not seem any different from any typical kindergarten class at work. Harry, when at his table, will frequently cover his ears and growl, "Stop it!" over and over. Harry also doesn't like to get paint or glue on his fingers because he can't stand how it feels to have "stuff" on his fingers or hands. When a classmate accidentally spilled her juice on Harry, getting a sleeve of his shirt wet, Harry completely lost control and began kicking the little girl and crying uncontrollably. Harry is not a well-liked boy in his class right now, although with help from an outside occupational therapist to address his sensory sensitivities, and with additional help from the school social worker, who will teach him some better social skills, things should be looking up for Harry soon.

Children with *Sensory Processing Disorder* and sensory integration difficulties may favor solitude, away from noise and the frenetic feeling of chaos they may feel in the presence of other children. They will try to avoid at all costs activities and situations that make them uncomfortable. This avoidance, and their efforts at trying to "hold it together" can be exhausting for these kids, and the inability to "get away" from the sources of discomfort can cause extreme irritability, distractibility, and even rage. When children have to deal with sensory discomforts, it is very difficult for them to focus on socializing or relating to other children in a friendly and pleasant way. Occupational therapists can be very helpful in reducing sensory sensitivities to a degree, and special educators can help to reduce the sensory discomforts the affected children experience in the classroom.

Dos and Don'ts

If you believe your child may have an interfering condition,

Do:

- Make social and emotional well-being a priority for your child.

- Prepare your child for social situations by discussing beforehand what your child might expect, and prepare for or practice different situations your child may encounter.

- Try to "touch base" with your child daily and encourage him or her to discuss or express both the ups and downs of his or her day.

- Seek the help of child professionals if your child has any ongoing social or emotional difficulty.

Don't:

- Don't assume that hopelessness or ongoing sadness is just part of your child's atypical development or disability.

- Don't feel timid about asking your child's school or teacher for information and support.

- Don't wait and see if problematic social situations or behaviors will go away. Get help for your child.

The Test of Three

Use the test of three with your child's social and emotional concerns to help assess whether your child may need professional intervention or specialized help.

Write down *three* characteristics that concern you. Examples include:

"She doesn't make eye contact."

"She doesn't interact with children when around them."

"She is extremely anxious about going to school."

Decide to "intervene" with *three* ideas to help your concerns, for example:

• I will touch her shoulder and ask her to look at me.

• I will guide her over to children at the park, and model how to initiate play.

• I will talk with my child and try to establish a bedtime and morning routine.

Work on your interventions daily for *three* weeks, or if you are unable to do this, work on them intermittently for *three* months. Either way, write down specific characteristics that you see. If you can, keep notes on your child's moods and reactions. Do not be afraid to critically watch your child's development over a three-month period. Some children develop in uneven spurts, so you might observe big leaps in skills, or you might continue to see a lag in skills, which would warrant further assessment.

At the end of the chosen time period write down what you observe. Write down how your child performs in the specific areas of concern. Compare your notes with the notes you took in the beginning. Are there any differences? Has there been progress? If you have chosen to work on your interventions daily, you should see some progress in three weeks. If the additional and focused stimulation is only scratching the surface of the difficulties, and your child has not shown obvious progress, it may be time to look into getting further help. After three months, your child has had time to grow, develop, and interact in many different types of situations. How is he doing? Did he have a developmental growth spurt? Or is reaching milestones still a struggle, slow and incremental? If it is the latter, he may need help.

Important Considerations Before Diagnosis

A child who is experiencing social and emotional difficulties needs to be observed very carefully so that the true problem at hand can be properly pinpointed. Symptoms of disorders can usually be observed over time, and the suspicious behaviors are expected to be present more than not present. Another key to proper diagnosis and helping a child to improve is to become aware of "what just happened" right before the child's inappropriate behavior or reaction. For instance, what just caused the child to bite? Was it in reaction to another child grabbing away a toy? Did the child bite to protest something? Do you think the child bit because he likes the way it feels? Professionals call this "before the behavior moment or occurrence" the *antecedent* to a behavior. It is important to know what the antecedents are to your child's behaviors, because behaviors may be in reaction to many different causes, yet the resulting behaviors look very much alike. Some children may be reacting in purely socially inappropriate ways and would be in need of some help learning social skills. Some children may be having difficulty integrating sensory stimuli from the environment (for instance, she *just can't stand* the noise anymore and wants to get out!) and this can leave a child in an extremely agitated state. A child such as this would find a "sensory diet" helpful and would possibly benefit from occupational therapy. Some children behave inappropriately due to an inability to express themselves verbally. A speech and language therapist may be helpful in situations like this to help establish appropriate ways to communicate. As you see, it is very important to carefully ascertain what a child's inappropriate behavior is in reaction to, or what its "use is," by noticing what is happening right before.

It is also important to recognize what happened right after the behavior. For instance, what was the child's *consequence*? What was your reaction to her behavior? What was said to the child in direct response to her behavior? What was done? Did the child get hugs or kisses? Did the child get a wanted object after all? Was she carried to her room after her inappropriate behavior?

Making note of your child's behaviors of concern, the antecedents to the behaviors, as well as the resulting consequences, will help child professionals to properly make a diagnosis and form a plan of action to help reduce inappropriate behaviors and encourage more appropriate behaviors in their place.

A Word on Medicating Children

Nothing ignites debate among parents and professionals like the subject of medicating children. I often hear a common belief that when doctors prescribe medications to treat various disorders, they are "drugging" our children, and that this mode of treatment needs to stop. This thinking is not helpful and can influence parents to rule out a treatment that may really be beneficial for their child. The idea that a child is being "drugged" lends one to believe that a child is being sedated or "warped" into a state where they are not able to partake in the undesirable behaviors the adults don't like. In truth, medications that treat many of these disorders (such as ADHD or bipolar disorder and autism) help to replace a faulty amount of brain chemical in the brain. Many medications actually "normalize" chemical amounts in the brain, resulting in more normalized behavior. I have seen medication help children to succeed and feel better about themselves. When medication works well for children, their families often enjoy a better home life, too.

On the other hand, I must admit that I do see a "rush" to medicate by some professionals before true effort is put forth to find the true nature and causes of disorderlike symptoms. Symptoms resulting from different origins can look alike, and care needs to be taken before medications are prescribed. Also, medications do have side effects, and these side effects can sometimes result in new unforeseen problems for the child and his family. Some children stop eating and do not feel hungry while the medication is in their systems. Some children develop insomnia and are unable to sleep at night.

When deciding whether to try medication for your child, speak frankly with your physician about your concerns, and try not to let pressure from your child's educational environment sway your thoughts. Information from teachers is helpful and valuable to both you and your child's doctor, but different teachers have different levels of tolerance. You must, with the advice of a physician, make the best decision for your child. Medicating as a treatment should by no means be taken lightly. And the possibility to help children through medication should not be ignored or criticized.

Red Flags of Atypical Social and Emotional Development

Red flags can act as warning signals that development may not be progressing as it should. Below, you will find a list of characteristics that commonly accompany social and emotional difficulties. Don't panic if you check one or more; there is no way to "score" your child here. Simply use the list as a tool that will assist you in defining and gauging your child's vulnerabilities, so that you can find her the help she may need.

Birth to Three Months

_____ Your baby is not making distinct eye contact with you.

_____ Your baby is not waking herself to feed.

_____ Your baby is consistently inconsolable.

_____ Your baby is consistently and unusually quiet most of the time.

Three to Twelve Months

_____ He/she at six months is not laughing or smiling.

_____ He/she at nine months is not showing clear signs of attachment to a favored adult or primary caregiver.

_____ He/she at ten months is not responding to his/her name.

Twelve to Twenty-four Months

_____ He/she at eighteen months does not demonstrate interest or curiosity by pointing to objects or people.

_____ You struggle to get his/her attention (or to get him/her to acknowledge you).

_____ He/she at eighteen months does not imitate or pretend to perform simple actions: many children at this age will pretend to talk on the telephone or feed a doll with a cup or spoon.

Twenty-four to Thirty-six Months

_____ He/she spends time engaged in unusual activities such as rocking or flicking switches repeatedly.

_____ He/she at thirty months shows no interest or reaction when another child is hurt or cries in his/her presence.

_____ He/she at thirty-five months is unaware of whether he is a boy or a girl.

_____ He/she at two and a half to three years old remains unaware of common dangers, such as crossing streets or walking off from a primary caregiver.

Three to Four Years Old

_____ He/she at three and a half is unable to pay attention to a simple, short story.

_____ He/she shows no interest in participating in activities with family or peers.

_____ He/she shows no interest in attempting to converse with same-age peers.

_____ He/she is not interested in or is consistently confused by others' emotions.

_____ He/she consistently uses violent means, such as biting, hitting, or kicking when angry or annoyed.

Four to Five Years Old

_____ He/she has extreme difficulty separating from a parent or primary caregiver in familiar surroundings.

_____ He/she does not interact or converse during times of "togetherness" (such as breakfast or dinnertime) with family or familiar persons.

_____ He/she is extremely explosive or has tantrums several times a day.

_____ His/her speech and expressions seem flat and odd.

Five to Six Years Old

_____ He/she is repeatedly unsuccessful at forming a friendship.

_____ He/she seems sad or withdrawn most of the time.

_____ He/she does not seem to need more than a few hours sleep for days at a time.

_____ He/she talks excessively or runs about excessively most of the time.

_____ He/she has rituals (such as washing his/her hands a certain number of times) that, if interrupted, cause anguish and anxiety.

_____ He/she frequently harms property, or has harmed a pet or other animal.

What You Can Do Now: Exercises That Stimulate Social and Emotional Development

You can help encourage healthy social and emotional skills in your child. One way to do this is to set up a safe, supportive environment, as well as an environment that is open to communication. Also, the following exercises will be helpful.

Choose to involve your child in activities and family events that will give her chances to socialize. Help her prepare by doing the following:

- Tell your child what she will need to know about the situation, for instance, what will be involved, and what she may expect to see and experience.

- Teach your child the rules of the games that may be played, and the phrases used during the games before the social event.

- Make your expectations about proper behavior clear, and relay them as simply and briefly as possible before you arrive at the activity or event.

- Practice through role-play what your child may expect at the event, and how she may handle different social situations.

- Privately give your child social pointers, if needed, without reprimanding or embarrassing your child. Some children notice "social cues and rules" better than others. Think of yourself as a supportive coach.

Begin to help your child learn to communicate his feelings by doing the following:

- Make yourself available to talk with your child and try to keep interruptions at a minimum. You need to help him feel like his feelings and what he says are important and worth hearing.

- Help your child to learn the names of different emotions and talk openly about what different emotions may look like and feel like. This will help your child to identify his own emotions and the emotions of others, and will allow him to speak more comfortably and freely about "feelings."

- Try to model patience and support in difficult situations. Ask your child what you might be able to do to help.

Begin to confront any social or emotional difficulties you may be experiencing as a parent, teacher, or therapist by doing the following:

- Find some support from community parent groups or from colleagues at work.

- Discuss difficulties with your doctor or get a referral for a counselor or therapist.

- Form a "getaway plan" for the moments you feel you are not handling your child well. Enlist the help of family or friends. They may enjoy the same opportunity to get away at times, with your help.

- Practice acting calm and understanding, even if you may not be feeling calm or understanding. You may find that with enough practice, you may actually begin to feel calmer and better able to "keep your cool" and handle trying situations.

It will also be helpful to note the situations that your child finds enjoyable, and those he finds stressful. And don't forget to let your child have some unstructured time in a safe environment to just be himself.

"He isn't walking yet"

SIX

The Development and Disorders of Motor Systems

"My son is seventeen months old, and he doesn't even pull himself up to a standing position! I read that it's normal to not walk until eighteen months, but I don't want to wait any longer. My baby's pediatrician said that he'll probably pull up in a couple weeks, but his legs are not strong at all, so I don't think so. How do I get him to start doing this?"

They are hard to miss at the playground and at playgroups: those parents and grandparents that just cannot hide their smiles and joy over the fact that their little ones are sitting up or walking early. "He has always been very advanced for his age," they may say. Some of us may remember a feeling of envy as we wondered when our own children would take their first steps. "She likes to sit and take it all in," some of us would say. But really, a baby is not able to "take it all in" unless she is exploring her environment and the objects and people in it. Luckily for most of our on-time and "a little slow" sitters and walkers, research has shown that early motor development does not predict a higher IQ, nor does development on the slow side predict low intelligence. The window of development that is considered to be normal is relatively expansive when it comes to motor skills, so for now, take heart and breathe a sigh of relief.

At the playground and at playgroups, there are also kids who choose to stay on the sidelines instead of joining in with physical games or sport activities. Some kids noticeably prefer to socialize and sit with the adults on the playground benches. Many of these children have motor difficulties and would be considered to be "uncoordinated" or "non-athletic."

And there are certain kids at school who capture the attention of teachers and peers because they are clumsy or have difficulty holding a pencil. Some of these kids are teased because they find themselves unable to button their pants after using the bathroom, unable to open their potato-chip bag at lunch, and unable to complete a writing assignment, at least without the teacher commenting on the messy handwriting. Children who experience situations like these may be having motor difficulties, too, though some of these children, unfortunately, may be labeled as having a learning disability.

Motor development, though not a predictor of intelligence in infancy, is believed important enough to affect other areas of development over time, such as cognitive development and social and emotional development. Motor skills are more predictable and observable than most other areas of development because skills are acquired in a predictable pattern, even when a child is not acquiring the skills "on time."

To gain an understanding of what some common motor difficulties may look like in a young child, let's take a look at five-year-old Orlando at day care:

Orlando Looks Lazy

Orlando's face looks sad on the way to day care. In the car, he repeatedly says, "I don't want to go! I want to watch TV!" Upon arrival, Orlando's mom hugs him while trying to lift him up a little. "Careful, you feel like you're going to slip down, Orlando," his mom says. "Pull your socks up more," she calls out as she waves and leaves out the main door. Orlando looks down at his socks, leans his side against the wall, and tries to bend down to pull up his socks. Unsuccessful, he then slowly lowers himself to the floor. Orlando gives his socks a couple pulls and leans back against the wall to look at his socks and shoes. "Orlando!" the teacher calls out, "get off the floor and come into the room! Remember to sign in." Orlando twists over onto his hands and knees and tries to get up as quickly as he can. "I'm up," he says breathlessly as he walks into the room. Orlando walks over to the sign-in sheet and picks up the pencil. He leans down a little sideways and pushes his fist against the paper. The letters of his name go into Danielle's space some. He walks to his table, pulls out his chair, and awkwardly sits down. The teacher announces that they will be reading a "Miss Spider" story. Then they will be playing spider catch, a game where each child has a partner, and together they look like a spider. Orlando appears happy about that. The teacher calls the children to a carpet in the corner of the room for the story. Orlando pulls himself up from his chair, tries to push his chair in with one hand, and then uses both of his hands to push it in. He walks to the carpet, takes a deep breath, and lowers himself.

The teacher begins to read, and Orlando, enjoying the story, lies back against the comfortable carpet. "Get up, Orlando!" some of the children begin to murmur. "Get yourself up right now, Orlando!" the teacher angrily says, "What a lazy bones!" Orlando quickly starts moving his arms and legs to try to get up. "Ouch! Don't kick me!" a couple kids yell. Finally, the teacher tells the class to line up at the door for spider catch on the blacktop. The students are told to pick a partner. The students pair off, but no one picks Orlando. His teacher tells a girl to be his partner. She reluctantly walks over. Orlando watches some of the other pairs catch the ball like a spider, and then it is his and his partner's turn. Orlando stands behind his partner and puts his arms through her arms, and together (using all of their arms) they will have to try to catch the ball. Orlando looks at the ball thrower and is ready. The ball is thrown . . . he moves forward and tries to catch it with his partner, but suddenly he feels himself lose his balance and fall forward. He lands on his partner on the ground. The girl begins to cry. "I'm sorry. Are you okay?" Orlando says again and again. The teacher and kids help the girl. No one asks Orlando if he is okay, too.

Motor Difficulties

Orlando is showing some red flag behaviors that would warrant investigation by a pediatrician, physical therapist, and/or occupational therapist. The suspicious behaviors in Orlando's case are relatively subtle, but they are common occurrences in children with certain types of motor difficulties. So if you were able to detect just a couple, you are ahead of the game. Sadly, children with Orlando's difficulties may be considered to be social outcasts, lazy, or even worse, behavioral "problems." Some professionals would even wonder if Orlando's awkwardness and seemingly "odd" behaviors were signs of a learning or emotional disorder. Here are some of the behaviors and elements of concern:

- Orlando's body felt like it was going to "slip down" from his mother's grasp when she lifted him.

- He needed to use the wall as a support surface when trying to pull up his socks.

- Getting up from the floor was strenuous for Orlando.

- He found writing his name to be awkward, and he was unable to keep his letters in his designated space.

- Manipulating the classroom chair was also a challenge for Orlando while sitting down, getting up, and while trying to push it in.

- He had trouble maintaining a sitting position and lay back onto the carpet.

- He had great difficulty getting up from the carpet, from a lying down position.

- Orlando had difficulty maintaining his balance and fell forward during spider catch.

An observant parent, teacher, or professional would also notice Orlando's strengths, and would use them to help support his weaknesses. Here are some of the positive behaviors and skills that Orlando displayed:

- Orlando separates from his mother and transitions into his day quite well.

- He willingly follows directions without any opposition.

- Orlando problem solves; for instance, he was able to find a way to pull up his socks when his first attempt to do it was unsuccessful.

- Orlando has a good social sense and showed empathy, for he immediately apologized to his partner after falling on her and was concerned about her.

These strengths are very important because the teachers and therapists who might help Orlando can use these strengths to help Orlando thrive despite his motor difficulties. Here are a few ways Orlando's teacher, parents, and other child professionals may help:

- If Orlando's teacher were aware that he might be experiencing some motor difficulties, she could help plan ahead of time for possible problems. The teacher could suggest to Orlando that he sit against a wall, or a large pillow could be placed on the carpet for Orlando to lean against. Lessons that she would typically teach at the carpet could be taught while the children sit in their chairs at their tables.

- Orlando's teacher could ask Orlando directly what things or activities he finds difficult or strenuous, and together they could form a plan where they might have a special sign if Orlando needs extra help or a break.

- Orlando's teacher could meet with Orlando's parents and form a plan for work completion or possibly reducing the amount of work that requires motor skills. Together they might think of creative ways that Orlando may be able to do some of his work. For instance, he could tell a story or describe an event into a tape recorder and play his "homework" in class the next day.

- Both Orlando's teacher and parents could seek the advice of staff therapists and inquire as to whether Orlando needs to be evaluated so that he may receive special help for his motor difficulties.

- Assignments that require neat and legible writing could be graded according to effort. This would bring Orlando a much greater amount of praise and positive reinforcement in class.

Without help, motor difficulties can affect a child's self-worth, and his ability to socialize among peers. They can also keep a child from experiencing his environment and may limit the child's play and opportunities. Sometimes, motor difficulties can affect a child's health (circulation, respiration, sleep, joint and muscle health). Be vigilant for the possible signs of motor difficulties in your child, because early detection will allow for children to receive help and interventions before motor compensations or bad habits have solidified. When detected early, many motor difficulties improve with therapeutic help and help at home. Children can progress rapidly in many cases, and these children will have a better start at school, and a better start forming friendships and sharing with peers.

Defining a Concern: Gross Motor or Fine Motor?

Motor skills are commonly broken down into two separate categories that are evaluated and treated separately. Developmental skills that involve the use of the large muscles of the arms, legs, and torso are called gross motor skills, while developmental skills that involve the use of the small muscles of the arms and hands are called fine motor skills. Gross motor skills allow a child to crawl, walk, run, and jump. Fine motor skills allow a child to pinch, grasp, grip, and perform activities that require dexterity of the fingers. Some children have difficulty using muscles in their mouths and oral cavities. These oral motor difficulties affect a child's ability to successfully feed or form speech sounds.

Gross motor issues are usually addressed by a physical therapist. The child will learn exercises and participate in activities to help improve her large muscle issues. Fine motor issues are commonly addressed by an occupational therapist. This type of therapist will help a child work to improve the use of his hands, wrists, arms and fingers. Visual-motor skills, eye-hand coordination, and sensory issues are also addressed by an occupational therapist. Both therapists may work on posture and stability. A speech and language pathologist will help a child with his oral motor difficulties.

Think for a moment about your own child's difficulties. Is your child having a hard time balancing on his legs? Is she unable to lift her head or remain upright while sitting? These would be *gross motor difficulties*. Maybe your child is unable to grasp with her fingers or hold a crayon in her hand to draw, when her peers are already doing these things with ease. These may be *fine motor difficulties*. Is your child having difficulty feeding, and refusing different food textures? Maybe your child is drooling excessively. These would be *oral motor difficulties*.

We will discuss these motor difficulties in greater detail, but first it is important to have a basic understanding of the ways motor skills develop in children.

The Typical Patterns of Gross and Fine Motor Development

Motor development is like a complex mathematical puzzle. The neural development needed for motor skills matures down in the spine first, and then travels up through the frontal regions of the brain. Though these mechanisms mature from the bottom up, we witness this maturation process and ability to perform motor skills from the top down. As we watch our babies, we witness new motor skills in their faces and necks first. Then we see their arms and trunks strengthen. Next, we see our babies use their legs as they begin to explore their environments. Movements go from uncontrolled to controlled. Controlled movement develops in a pattern, too, from side to midline, to across the midline of the body, as the brain perfects itself for movement.

A baby shows movement while still in his mother's uterus. From early in a pregnancy, this movement can be seen with ultrasound technology. I remember being amazed at the sight of my own children twisting and kicking on the ultrasound screen when I was nineteen weeks pregnant. Little arms would be flailing, and little feet would be kicking outward in short, quick kicks. I also have distinct memories of later in pregnancy, feeling the twists and kicks quite strongly. Many an expectant parent joyfully speculates that their little fetus is going to be a slugger, a gymnastics star, or a pro soccer player. The flipping and kicking movements help your baby develop and prepare for the motor skills he will need in the outside world.

When your baby is born, she has several preprogrammed reflexes. One commonly known reflex in newborns is the rooting reflex: when your newborn baby is touched on the cheek, she will turn her head to that side, and open her mouth to feed. This reflex and corresponding motor movements are considered to be involuntary movements because your baby is not in control of them. The baby is not purposely moving her head, limbs, fingers or toes. She is simply performing one of the innate reactions that infant babies throughout the world perform no matter their race or culture.

The pattern of motor development in your baby is considered to be predictable. Experts believe that by watching this pattern, especially in the first year, information is gained about a child's neurological growth and health. Parents worldwide witness their babies gaining motor control of their heads and necks, rolling over, reaching, and then sitting. Babies then begin to creep and crawl, and then stand up on their legs while holding on. And about the time of their first birthday, they reach the important and highly anticipated milestone of walking independently.

How is it that babies can learn all of that in one year? The answer is, through healthy growth and practice. Remember, babies have actually been practicing certain motor movements from their days in the womb. Later, with every reach and every kick, they are forming distinctions and strengthening muscles. And to help encourage this, doctors and therapists are also now stressing the importance of "tummy time" for babies. These are short periods of time where babies are placed on their stomachs for play and exploration. Tummy time helps babies to strengthen important muscles needed for motor stability and growth. Exploration and experimentation in safe environments are very important for babies, for it is by trial and error that they are able to learn new motor skills and use their muscles in new ways.

At about one month of age, a baby can lift his head, and possibly turn his head to the other side. He might get his hands to his mouth and suck on his fingers, which strengthens the muscles of his face, jaw, and mouth. At about three months, a baby might bring both of his hands together and hold them like that often. He will grasp objects in a tight hold, but he will not be able to release his grasp or let go. He will learn to "let go" later, around the time of his first birthday.

Researchers note a baby's reaching, which occurs between two and seven months of age, as an important milestone, because it is the beginning of a baby's attempt to manipulate objects in his environment. Good vision is needed for this motor milestone, for "seeing" a desirable object stimulates a baby to reach for it.

In the second half of the first year, a baby will begin to use her fingers in more precise movements. She will begin to master a pincer grasp, which will allow her to pinch small objects between her thumb and forefinger. She may pinch and lift pieces of food to feed herself, or lift objects for a closer look. Being able to use her fingers in this new way will help her begin to use tools, such as utensils, and will help her strengthen muscles in her fingers, hands, and wrists.

At about eight months of age, a baby may be pushing himself up to a sitting position, and playing from a new vantage point. Sitting up allows a baby to concentrate on using his hands to manipulate toys. The baby's creeping, pivoting, and rocking on his hands and knees to this point have strengthened his trunk and shoulders, so that he is able to balance himself well while using his hands and fingers.

Crawling and walking are also milestones of note, because both motor abilities allow a baby to make independent choices about where to go, what to play with, and who to be around. Both skills involve complex motor plans that coordinate both sides of the body. Good balance is needed to perform these skills, as well as lots of practice. Babies typically begin to crawl and pull to a stand at nine months, and often walk at about twelve months old.

In the second year, all of that motor practice can make for active, on-the-go toddlers, and nervous, tired parents. A little one, with his newfound muscle strength in his hands, and nimbleness in his fingers, just may pick up that red crayon and decorate the living room wall with large scribbles.

And if he's in the second half of the second year, he may run from you if you try to take that crayon. Many parents, though, also express how much fun their kids are at this time, as they learn to throw balls, build with blocks, and enjoy artistic activities such as finger painting.

Preschoolers truly begin to refine skills that we consider important for preparing for school. Children draw with intention and use voluntary movements of their hands to work scissors and squeeze glue. They begin to use their fingers and manipulate their bodies to dress and undress, and begin to use their muscles to "hold" their bodily eliminations until they are safely at a toilet. On the playground, three- and four-year-old children run with ease, climb stairs, and jump off steps. As children near their fifth birthday, balance and acute body awareness is clearly evident. Children of this age descend stairs step over step, balance on one foot for several seconds, and begin to coordinate their movements into voluntary actions used in sport activities and physical games. Children are also able to hold a pencil or crayon in a relatively correct grasp at this age, and they can continue the grasp for a period of time with their increased muscular stamina. With continued physical practice, five-year-olds learn to skip, which requires considerable coordination. Also, it is not uncommon to see a five-year-old confidently attempt to jump off a high surface, to the dismay of their parents and teachers.

But sometimes a child's motor skills don't seem to develop as they should, and one infant, toddler, or preschooler is unable to physically keep up with, or function like her peers.

Gross and Fine Motor Disorders

Now we'll take a look at some disorders associated with atypical motor development. Maybe you will see shades of your own child reflected in the stories that will be described here, or maybe you will feel that your child's difficulties are much more subtle and less worrisome than the children described.

There are several common types of motor disorders. The first type is an obvious impairment or diagnosed neuromuscular condition. An example of this would be a child who is unable to use an arm and leg on one side of her body, such as in cerebral palsy. Children who have neuromuscular conditions may be born with these conditions or they may begin to show symptoms in early childhood. Some children develop neuromuscular conditions from injuries sustained during accidents.

Another type of motor disorder causes kids to have a significant lag in the acquisition of the predictable pattern of motor skills. An example would be a child who is "late" but does learn to crawl, pull up to a stand, and walk. This child may be considered to have a developmental delay. Children with developmental motor delays may demonstrate ongoing struggles with coordination or problems with strength and tone. Some children have difficulty with the muscles in their mouths and oral cavities, making feeding and sound/speech formation hard. Children who are born prematurely also frequently exhibit atypical patterns of motor development and display a set of motor behaviors distinctly tied to their "too early" births.

Environmental factors can also negatively affect a child's gross and fine motor skills. Improper or negligent care of an infant or child can result in less than optimal motor development.

Neuromuscular Disorders

Neuromuscular disorders may be detected in the womb, or later on with the onset of motor difficulties. We will discuss three common disorders whose symptoms may range from mild to severe. They are *muscular dystrophy*, *spina bifida*, and *cerebral palsy*. Let's first take a look at Bobby's experience:

Bobby was five and a half and a kindergartener when he began to sit out of recess and walk out of gym class to sit. Several teachers in his school were noticing that Bobby was having trouble getting in and out of his seat, and that he had an unusual and constant "fatigue." Bobby's parents were called in for meetings with his teachers and with the school nurse. At first, many believed that Bobby had a type of virus or a strep infection that can settle in the hips. Others wondered if he was "low tone." But since Bobby did not have a previous history of being low tone, Bobby's parents decided to make an appointment with their pediatrician. After examination, the pediatrician felt that one serious possibility needed to be checked out. The pediatrician inquired as to whether any members of the family on the mother's side had muscular dystrophy, and he found that an uncle did have the disorder. After a blood test and an electromyogram (a test used to measure electrical activity of the muscles), Bobby's doctor made a preliminary diagnosis of muscular dystrophy.

The doctor and Bobby's parents decided to have Bobby go through genetic testing to be sure, and one month later, Bobby was officially diagnosed with Duchenne muscular dystrophy. Bobby, almost immediately after his diagnosis, began physical and occupational therapy to help keep his muscles strong and to maintain the range of movement in his joints. He learned new ways to approach activities that had become difficult and seemed to improve a little with the extra help. Bobby currently still walks, though his gait appears to be uncoordinated. Bobby is now in the third grade and continues to be a well-liked, good student.

Muscular dystrophy is the result of several genetic disorders that cause muscles to degenerate over time. They are inherited through the mother, but although a woman or girl may carry a gene that causes muscular dystrophy, only boys will be affected. This is because the gene that causes muscular dystrophy is on the X chromosome, and boys don't have an extra X chromosome to "take over" the work, as girls do. The defective gene affects different elements needed for proper muscle cell growth. Duchenne muscular dystrophy is one of the more common forms, and can begin to affect little boys in their preschool or early elementary school years. Affected boys will usually begin to experience weakness in their hips, and then their shoulders. Physical activities, as well as walking, may become awkward and strenuous. Many boys who have Duchenne muscular dystrophy need ambulatory assistance, such as a wheelchair, in their pre-teen years.

Spina bifida is another neuromuscular disorder that may leave children in need of ambulatory help, like Esther:

When Esther was born, she needed surgery. An open area in her back left her spinal cord exposed, and nerves around her spine appeared to be damaged. Surgery would close this open area, prevent infection, and prevent further damage to her spine and surrounding nerves. Esther also had fluid on the brain and needed a shunt implanted to drain it. This required an additional surgery. Initially, it was very difficult for Esther's parents to accept that their baby daughter had spina bifida. They knew nothing about the deformity and what it would mean for their daughter's future. Esther began to receive early intervention services when she was about eighteen months. Up until that point, a lot of time was spent in and out of the hospital. Esther received physical and occupational therapy, and really progressed quickly. She is an outgoing girl of normal intelligence, and is currently in second grade. Esther uses a walker to get around and has given a presentation on her disability to her class. Her teacher has recently asked Esther if she might do a presentation for the school's parents at a PTA meeting.

While still in the uterus, an embryo may experience a malformation known as *spina bifida*, which causes a portion of the spinal cord to be defectively left open and unenclosed. Spina bifida is probably the most commonly occurring birth defect that causes permanent paralysis in children. Though babies with spina bifida can undergo surgery to close the open lesions, the motor control of their lower bodies will be compromised or nonexistent. The motor difficulties and paralysis resulting from the lesions along the spinal cord will be different depending upon where the lesions are. Some children with spina bifida walk, while others will not be ambulatory and need to use a wheelchair. Spina bifida frequently causes children to have elimination difficulties, and these children will need medical care for issues with their bladder and bowels. Many children with spina bifida have average to superior intelligence, though some experience learning problems. Experts believe that environmental exposure to heat in the earliest weeks of pregnancy, such as hot tubs or fevers, may cause spina bifida in some cases. Experts also encourage women to take a proper dosage of folic acid during their childbearing years as a preventive measure.

Cerebral palsy is the most well-known neuromuscular disorder. Here is Cynthia's experience:

> Cynthia was born in what would be considered to be a typical vaginal delivery to a mother who experienced high blood pressure in the later months of pregnancy. To this day, Cynthia's mother wonders whether her high blood pressure contributed to her daughter's disability. When Cynthia was only seconds old, it was apparent to the doctor and nurses that her legs were stiff, almost "like they were frozen." Cynthia's mother reports, "I could tell that something was not right with her. The looks on the faces of those in the room told me the whole story." Cynthia was examined and diagnosed with cerebral palsy while still in the hospital. "Specialists needed to come and show me how to feed her. I was so scared. I felt like I wouldn't be able to do it." Cynthia, now seven, attends her neighborhood elementary school and uses a walker to get around. Cynthia is able to walk, although her leg movements are extremely wobbly and unsteady, and her arms and hands are a little weak. Her speech is also hard to understand at times. Cynthia says, "Some people will point at me and tease me, but my friends tell them to leave me alone, and tell them I am way smarter than them." Cynthia receives physical and occupational therapy for her motor difficulties, and speech therapy for her articulation difficulties. Says Cynthia's mother, "They told me she would be in a wheelchair. They told me she would be mentally retarded. Look at her! She's beautiful, she's smart . . . we are blessed."

Cerebral palsy is one of the most common physical disabilities in children. About one child out of every five hundred will have some form of cerebral palsy. The word *cerebral* means "of the brain," and the word *palsy* can mean "muscle weakness" or "an inability to control one's muscles." Hence, this disorder causes a child to have great difficulty with her movements, and an inability to make her muscles do what she wants them to do. Cerebral palsy can be mild or severe, and it can result from an event that causes bleeding in the brain or a lack of oxygen to the brain during pregnancy or during the birth process. Many times, the causes remain unknown. Some known causes are a mother's contraction of rubella during pregnancy, and a new-born infant's contracting of a serious illness or infection in the first weeks of life. Accidents can cause cerebral palsy, such as motor vehicle accidents or near drownings. Cerebral palsy is not a genetic, inherited condition.

There are different types of cerebral palsy that are defined by the different characteristic tones of the muscles and the portions of the body that are affected. Sometimes a child's muscles will be very tight and spastic, while another child, upon trying to move a certain way, may experience uncontrolled, random movements. Other children experience muscle tremors.

Cerebral palsy may affect some children on only one side of their bodies, while others may be affected in mostly their legs. Still other children with cerebral palsy are affected throughout their bodies, including their legs, arms, trunk, neck, and face. Some children find that they are able to get around without any special tools and are able to learn to perform most typical daily tasks. Other children with cerebral palsy need special tools and devices to help support their bodies during movement and activities. Some children need therapeutic support in eating, chewing, and swallowing.

Many children with cerebral palsy have average to superior intelligence, while some children with cerebral palsy are intellectually disabled.

Dos and Don'ts

If you believe your child may have a neuromuscular disorder,

Do:

- See your doctor promptly if you suspect your child is displaying symptoms of a neuromuscular disorder.

- Ask your doctor and school system about early intervention services for your child.

- Involve your child in school, social, and recreation activities with same-age peers. Your child can participate in a modified way if needed.

- Encourage open and communicative relationships with your child's therapists.

- Remember that your child has feelings, goals, and dreams. Help to prepare your child for life situations, successes, and disappointments.

Don't:

- Don't remain with a therapist that makes your child or you feel uncomfortable or inadequate.

- Don't forget to celebrate even little successes and milestones.

- Don't forget your needs as your child's parent or caregiver. Research parent groups that can support you or get support that will help you address your concerns for your child, your marriage, or your family life.

- Don't overschedule your child daily with strength building and motor activities. Allow your child to have some downtime, and leisure activities of his/her choice.

- Don't forget to approach tasks or frustrating situations with a sense of humor. Your modeling patience and humor will help your child learn to approach daily situations and/or setbacks in a calm, confident, and humorous way.

Gross and Fine Motor Developmental Delays

As we move about and perform our daily tasks, many of us never stop to appreciate how very complex each of our motor movements really are. We don't realize that we must first have a thought-out intention of which direction or in what way we want to move. We use our knowledge from our previous motor experiences to aim or direct our movements in the fashion needed to perform a certain task. With each step or swing of a tennis racket, we are aligning information, intention, and directed muscular instruction to complete a movement. And at the end of each movement, we release or "let go" of the movement and ready ourselves for the next intended act. Any subtle interruption, in any one of several different types of information pathways needed for fluid motor performance, can visibly make a motor skill uncoordinated and unsuccessful.

Recently, a diagnosis called Developmental Coordination Disorder (DCD) has gained some popularity, even though the phrase has been around for many years. This diagnosis will at times be given to children who experience more difficulty with their coordination (either gross or fine motor) than their same-age peers. Children with DCD are considered to have coordination and motor difficulties, but no neurological disorders. Because the diagnosis is nonspecific and may involve any one or more of many different types of motor difficulties, many doctors and experts, when observing motor difficulties, choose to use more specific labels and the term "developmentally delayed." Children diagnosed with DCD may be unique from one another and display very different symptoms, from visual perceptual difficulties, to low tone, to sensory processing difficulties. A child diagnosed with DCD may need an additional child expert to help more specifically define the weaknesses and delays that need to be addressed, and to plan appropriate interventions.

GROSS MOTOR DIFFICULTIES

School-age children with gross motor difficulties are frequently victims of teasing by peers. The lack of ability to perform large motor skills is very visible to others, and children may be repeatedly chosen last for playground games and sports teams. The humiliation of being unable to move and perform in the way your mind wants you to can be frustrating and discouraging. This experience of nonacceptance due to poor motor performance can negatively affect the self-esteem of even the most intellectual and logical child. It is important to catch gross motor difficulties early so that a child can receive help for gross motor delays or deficit areas. Here are some of the stumbling blocks that can cause gross motor delays and deficits in children:

Weak Muscle Tone

When a child has weak muscle tone or is considered to be "low tone," simple daily movements and activities can feel exhausting and strenuous. Weak tone or low tone is not the result of being lazy or sedentary. When a child has weak tone or low tone, her muscles do not have the right amount of tension at their natural relaxed state. This will require her to work even harder than the typical child to use her muscles for motor tasks, such as walking, running, and getting to a standing position from a sitting position on the floor. Children with weak or low tone can appear floppy, lazy, and fatigued. They tend to dislike sport activities. These kids do need to be included and encouraged to participate in large motor activities. Any strengthening of their muscles is helpful and may make symptoms less noticeable.

An Inability to "Motor Plan"

Some children are unable to interpret information from the environment and from their bodies. They are unable to put information to use when trying to perform a large motor skill. The successful execution of any complex large motor skill requires a sequence of intended movements that make up a motor plan. Children with motor-planning difficulties find themselves kicking out before reaching the ball, tripping when trying to leap over a rock or puddle, and spilling or knocking over items when trying to strategically reach across a table.

A Lack of Motor Evaluation

Some children have good muscle tone and initiate their movements with a focused intention, but somehow lose track of their movements as they are being performed. These children experience a breakdown in the split-second monitoring and adjusting of large motor movements. Most of us don't realize that we make minute adjustments in our large motor movements, and that we are constantly evaluating our movement so that we get the desired result. Children who experience motor-evaluation difficulties find complex large motor skills extremely frustrating. Though they may be able to understand and visualize a motor plan, the inability to monitor and maneuver while performing a skill makes successful completion of complex large motor skills rare.

A Lack of Coordination

Unlike children who have difficulty monitoring their movements, some children experience great difficulty in instructing their muscles to perform large motor tasks. These children have great difficulty using their muscles together in a synchronized fashion and often are poor at motor planning. Children with these difficulties are commonly called uncoordinated, and may appear to be clumsy.

A Weak "Memory" for Movement

Most children demonstrate a strong "motor memory" for repeated or practiced movements. Though first attempts at motor movements require concentration and focus, later attempts seem to come more naturally. A child does not have to relearn a movement every time he wants to perform it. A child who learns how to throw a ball can then throw balls, as well as other items without having to relearn the motor movement. Children who have a weak motor memory for previously learned large motor movements find themselves unable to remember how they used their bodies. The motor plans and motor knowledge from previous experience doesn't stick. This can be very frustrating for children.

An Inability to Translate a Direction into Movement

Children who can perform large motor skills and motor plan sometimes find it very difficult to take instruction and translate verbal instructions into movement. These children are usually accused of "thinking too much" and advised to "just go for it." Children who experience this kind of motor difficulty can become embarrassed and confused at their failure to be able to carry through or follow verbal-physical directions. Many of these children become hesitant to join sport activities or try new skills in front of peers.

Weak Use of Visual Cues

Children who have poor visual perception and visual skills often have difficulty predicting and judging distances during large motor activities. They also neglect to use important visual cues when motor planning and maneuvering. Children need to use their vision when catching or aiming to throw a ball. They need to use vision to readjust their movement according to what they see happening. Children who demonstrate weak visual skills and a weak use of visual cues have great difficulty with many kinds of large motor tasks and activities.

Weak Sensing of the Body's Position

Some kids are unable to perceive where their bodies are in space. They are weak in sensing their body's position, even when sitting or standing still. These kids may make large exaggerated movements, may jump up and down excessively, or use objects or people in the environment to gain information about where their own body is in relation to others. For instance, a child may walk with his class in line down the hallway of his school while running his hand along the wall. This gives the weak-sensing child information about where his body is in space. Many times, a child will use his visual skills to look and see where his body is while trying to imitate a physical task. Many children with weak sensing of their body position are considered to have sensory processing difficulties, which we will discuss in depth in Chapter 7.

FINE MOTOR DIFFICULTIES

Sometimes, a baby has difficulty manipulating her arms. She may later experience difficulties controlling her wrists, hands, and fingers. Her early attempts at reaching and grasping for objects or pieces of food may be strenuous or unsuccessful. The inability to successfully manipulate objects in the environment can cause a baby to stop trying. Many times, a baby's caregiver will step in and simply hand her the toy she is reaching for. And this lack of independently manipulating objects, coupled with the readily accessible help, can cause an even greater decrease in strength and motivation, and a greater delay in the fine motor skills she will need for her future.

Fine motor skills are needed for academic success. This is why parents and professionals look for difficulties with fine motor tasks when a child enters preschool or kindergarten. Many of the activities in early schooling involve beginning writing, drawing, cutting, gluing, and tracing. Children also begin to independently perform daily living skills, such as using utensils, using tools, and tying shoes. Children with fine motor difficulties may display difficulties with their grasp, hand strength, or finger dexterity (using their fingers separately from one another). Some children may have difficulty using their wrists, or have bad habits with arm, wrist, hand, or finger positioning that may cause them fatigue. Children with fine motor difficulties often try to avoid tasks that require them to use the fine motor skills that cause them discomfort. Some kids become oppositional or will have tantrums when encouraged to participate in fine motor activities. Older children who have fine motor difficulties tend to try to avoid writing assignments.

Graphomotor dysfunction is a name given for the inability to produce writing or written work. Many professionals describe children with graphomotor dysfunction as children who have wonderful ideas and who can orally tell stories as well as complete hands-on or verbal assignments. But if asked to write their answers or stories on paper, these same children will produce written work that is frequently illegible and sparse in content (if they participate at all). When comparing these children's oral performances to their written performances, there are major discrepancies. It is unclear whether graphomotor dysfunction is truly a disability or whether a name is simply being given for poor writing performance in an academic environment. It is also unclear whether the difficulties resulting in the poor written work are fully due to fine motor difficulties. Some children labeled as having graphomotor dysfunction have poor

visual skills in combination with poor motor skills, and some have difficulties with independent organization and memory. We do know that
there truly are kids who experience a breakdown of sorts when engaging
in writing. A child may forget how to form letters. He may be unable to
picture the letter in his mind, or he may, when picturing a letter, forget
how to move his hand and hold his grip to form the letter. Some children lose track of where their hand is, or while in the process of forming a letter, forget where they are in the movement. It is frustrating for
the children who experience this. Many of these children are successful,
even gifted, in other academic areas. Children with fine motor and graphomotor difficulties may also be highly successful with gross motor activities, and sports.

ORAL MOTOR DIFFICULTIES

A child needs to use muscles in her mouth and oral cavity to suck,
chew, feed, and move her lips and tongue to form sounds for speech. As
your baby grows, her tongue begins to move independently from her jaw,
and with practice, a baby can gum, chew, swallow many different textures
of food, and make numerous sounds by moving her tongue and lips.

Sometimes, though, a baby does not develop her oral motor strength
as most typical babies do. This baby may resist food textures, and she may
be unable to close her lips over a spoon or make sounds that require movement of the tongue and mouth.

Children with oral motor difficulties are often sensitive to the feeling
of having something in their mouths, and many children with oral motor
difficulties are slow to speak and require the help of a speech therapist to
improve their articulation and oral motor strength.

When a child's oral motor strength affects his ability to produce
speech, the child may be diagnosed with a condition called *dyspraxia*.
Children with dyspraxia have great difficulty pronouncing different speech
sounds, as well as combining the movements needed for different speech
sounds, into a fluid motion, to make words. Children frequently work very
closely with speech pathologists to strengthen their facial and oral cavity

muscles, and to practice oral "motor plans" for each difficult sound. Dyspraxia is at times also referred to as "developmental apraxia of speech."

How Premature Birth Affects Motor Development

Premature birth is a risk factor for motor delays. Simply being born before the thirty-seventh week of pregnancy can have an effect on a child's motor development.

In the last several weeks of pregnancy, the womb is quite cramped, and the baby must assume a curled-up or "flexed" position, also known as flexion. This position has great importance for motor growth. Some consider it as the basis or "beginning position" of normal motor development. A baby will maintain flexion after birth, and it is through flexion that a baby develops the right muscle tone, visual cues, and neuromuscular foundation for the growth of weight-shifting skills and movement.

Premature infants, never having had to assume a curled-up position in the womb, don't experience flexion, and usually lay flat after birth. With limbs outstretched from their bodies, these infants begin to tighten and use muscles that do not promote a healthy pattern of motor growth or muscle use. Premature infants frequently experience difficulties such as stiffness, low muscle tone, and muscles that are too tight and too tense. Surgery and other medical interventions can also leave a baby immobile.

Some hospitals and programs provide early intervention services for premature newborns so that therapists can help position babies to promote healthier motor development. Therapists may try to position babies in a flexed position, which not only helps babies' motor development, but can also help babies to feel more secure. The rewards of this early intervening can be seen later, when many children who were born prematurely display typical postures, strength, and skills.

Environmental Factors that Affect Motor Growth

To develop his motor skills, a baby needs lots of practice. This requires time and freedom to move about and use his muscles. Being motivated to move is also very important, whether it be motivators such as moving toward a friend, sibling, or caregiver for social interaction, or the attraction of a bright and interesting toy, a baby with a reason to reach or crawl will practice his skills much more readily than a child who remains confined with little to interest or stimulate him.

Dos and Don'ts

If you believe your child may have a gross or fine motor delay,

Do:

- Speak with your doctor if you believe your child is having difficulty acquiring motor milestones.

- Call your school system and ask for your child to be evaluated, or call a local hospital for names of physical and occupational therapists in your area.

- Speak with your child's teachers and physical education teachers about your concerns, and your wish to help create positive motor experiences, and opportunities to increase your child's self-esteem.

- Ask your child's daytime caregiver or teacher to watch your child's motor performance and give you updates on your child's progress.

- Offer to support your child's therapist (and your child) by working with and practicing with your child at home. Ask your child's therapist if he/she can show you what to do.

The Test of Three

Use the test of three with your child's gross or fine motor concerns to help assess whether your child may need professional intervention or specialized help. Write down *three* characteristics that concern you. Examples would be:

"She doesn't reach for toys."

"She isn't crawling and all the babies in her playgroup have been crawling for quite some time."

"He isn't walking yet."

Decide to "intervene" with *three* ideas to help your concerns:

• I will place her on her tummy and put attractive toys just out of her reach. (If your baby is not reaching for toys, also have your baby's vision checked.)

• I will play with my baby on the floor and by using games and toys, I will encourage her to try to chase or move after me.

• I will reduce the time my baby is in his exersaucer (or walker), and try to set up an environment where my baby can easily pull to a stand in several locations. I will try to give him more freedom of movement and freedom to explore in a safe environment. (Also let your doctor know of your concern.)

Work on your interventions daily for *three* weeks, or if you are unable to do this, work on them intermittently for *three* months. Either way, write down specific characteristics that you see. If you can, keep notes on your child's progress and on whether you see your child favoring an arm or leg. Try to carefully watch the way your child is moving his/her body, and even videotape his/her motor movements when you begin. This will help you to see any progress that is made. Do not be afraid to critically watch your child's development over a three-month period. Some children develop in uneven spurts, so you might observe big leaps in skills, or you might continue to see a lag in skills, which would warrant further assessment.

At the end of the chosen time period write down what you observe. Write down how your child performs in the specific areas of concern. Compare your notes with the notes you took in the beginning. Are there any differences? Has there been progress? If you have chosen to work on your interventions daily, you should see some progress in three weeks. If the additional and focused stimulation is only scratching the surface of the difficulties, and your child has not shown obvious progress, it may be time to look into getting further help. After three months, your child has had time to grow, develop, and interact in many different types of situations. How is he/she doing? Did he/she have a developmental growth spurt? Or is reaching milestones still a struggle, slow and incremental? If it is the latter, she may need help.

Don't:

- Don't wait and see if you feel your child's motor skills are lacking.

- Don't criticize your child for clumsiness or accidental mishaps (even when you are fatigued or frustrated).

- Don't allow therapy sessions to eliminate your child's involvement in school, social, or favorite recreational activities.

- Don't force your child to participate in activities that may bring about feelings of humiliation. Discuss situations beforehand, and possibly encourage your child once the uncomfortable possibilities are known.

- Don't forget to celebrate your child's many strengths.

Important Considerations Before Diagnosis

Doctors can diagnose neuromuscular disorders accurately, but subtle muscular and motor developmental problems can be more difficult to label as normal or atypical. To help with this, many experts and therapists try to emphasize the difference between motor skills being "on target" or "tenuous." If your child is reaching motor development milestones on the later side, but the skills she does have are performed well, she may be developing fine, but at her own rate. Many experts stress that a situation like this is much better than a scenario where a child acquires skills on time, but his movements are shaky and tenuous. Children who acquire skills but perform them with little control or an inability to regulate their balance may have motor issues that would require intervention. It is better to be "on target" a little late than on time but "tenuous."

Another consideration to be taken into account is that to be able to perform fine motor skills well, a child must have gross motor strength. Some children who are experiencing fine motor difficulties have underlying gross motor weaknesses. A child needs good stability in her shoulders, arm mobility, and solid postural tone to be able to successfully perform fine motor tasks. Wrist stability is also important. When fine motor difficulties are assessed in your child, inquire as to whether there are any signs of gross motor weaknesses as well.

A Word on Hand Dominance

Will your child be left-handed or right-handed? Many parents wait with anticipation for clear signs of their child's hand preference. If you're a betting person, you should place your money on right-handed. About eighty-five to ninety percent of children end up right-handed. Left-handers frequently have left-handers in the family, supporting the idea that handedness is passed down genetically. Researchers, though, have not yet figured out exactly how this hand preference and "one sided" comfort zone develops. Some experts believe that a fetus's position in the womb favors the right side, by allowing for more movement, while others believe that newborns favor turning their heads to their right side. This turning of the head allows a baby to observe his right hand and its movement, stimulating early visual-motor experiences. Also, experts reason that most newborn infants are held in their caregivers' left arms, encouraging the preference for turning to the right. Some experts think that right-handedness is the norm, and left-handedness is either a genetic difference or the result of some type of subtle neural injury.

You may see a preference for one hand or the other in your child quite early. Many children begin to have a preference before they even reach two years old. Be alert, though, if your child shows a distinct hand preference before the age of eighteen months. Clearly preferring one side this early may be a sign of muscle weakness on the non-preferred side. In this case, a doctor should be called. Generally, most doctors and child experts wait until a child is four or five before declaring a definitive hand preference. Some children develop a hand preference later, at age six or seven.

Another interesting fact about handedness is that it can be switched. Several cultures do not look kindly upon going left, and many children are forced to practice using and preferring their right hands. Early in a child's life, when the brain is still rapidly growing and "plastic," this can be done successfully. Most, however, see no need for extreme measures when they observe their child's preferred hand. Most view their child's handedness as simply a characteristic or quality, and a unique milestone to witness as our children grow.

Red Flags of Atypical Motor Development

Red flags can act as warning signals that development may not be progressing as it should. Below, you will find a list of characteristics that commonly accompany motor difficulties. Don't panic if you check one or more; there is no way to "score" your child here, and checking one or more red flags does not necessarily mean your child has a developmental delay or disability. It does mean you should become vigilant, watchful, and check with your pediatrician. Use the list as a tool that will assist you in defining and gauging your child's vulnerabilities, so that you can find him the help he may need.

Birth to Three Months

_____ Baby appears to have very tight muscles, seems stiff, or appears to be exceptionally strong.

_____ Baby at three months is unable to hold up her head when picked up, or her head rolls from side to side when you lift or hold her.

_____ Baby at three months does not adjust his head to an upright position when turned toward the side or turned sideways.

_____ Baby is consistently having difficulty latching on or feeding.

Three to Twelve Months

_____ At three months, baby is not holding his head up.

_____ At three months, baby's hands are tightly fisted.

_____ At four months, baby is unable to bring toys to her mouth.

_____ At four months, baby is not yet reaching, or appears as if she is unable to extend her arms.

_____ Baby repeatedly reaches with the same arm.

_____ At six months, baby does not transfer toys or objects from one of his hands to the other.

_____ Baby appears to have "hand dominance" and favors using one hand clearly more than the other.

_____ At six months, baby feels like she may slip from your grasp when you lift her.

_____ At six months, your baby still has his newborn reflexes such as his/her "startle reflex" or your baby still turns his/her head and "roots" when you touch his/her cheek.

_____ At eight months, your baby doesn't try to use the whole outside portion of his hand, from pinky finger to wrist, to rake up and grasp small objects.

_____ At eight to nine months, baby is unable to sit independently.

_____ At ten months, baby appears to drag limbs when crawling, or has an unusual or "lopsided" way of crawling.

Twelve to Twenty-four Months

_____ He/she appears to resist bearing weight on his/her feet.

_____ He/she consistently walks on his/her tiptoes.

_____ He/she is unable to pick up small objects or cereal O's with his/her thumb and index finger.

_____ At eighteen to nineteen months, he/she is not walking.

_____ At one-and-a-half, he/she is unable to rip paper.

_____ He/she "W sits" often, where his/her knees are forward, and legs flat and backward.

_____ He/she refuses many food textures and will only accept a couple of different textures.

Twenty-four to Thirty-six Months

_____ He/she is not chewing solid foods, or refuses solid foods.

_____ He/she repeatedly chokes on solid foods.

_____ He/she fears typical playground equipment and will not grab onto, walk across, or swing on various playground pieces.

_____ He/she is having difficulty sitting on the floor for a period of time without support.

Three to Four Years Old

_____ At any time between three and four, he/she begins to experience weakness in his/her pelvis.

_____ He/she consistently gives up writing and drawing activities soon after beginning them, or gives up on trying to manipulate small toys.

_____ He/she finds climbing stairs difficult, and uses his/her arm strength in conjunction with the stairway rail.

_____ He/she drools excessively.

Four to Five Years Old

_____ He/she consistently holds a crayon or pencil in a fist grasp.

_____ He/she avoids physical games that may require gross motor skills such as skipping or hopping.

_____ He/she has not established hand dominance by five years old.

_____ You have noticed his/her motor skills have regressed.

_____ He/she begins to experience weakness in his/her pelvis.

Five to Six Years Old

_____ When writing or drawing, he/she consistently uses his/her entire arm and shoulder.

_____ He/she begins to adopt avoidance techniques when asked to participate in fine motor or gross motor activities.

_____ He/she is unable to copy movements or remember movements in supervised recreation or sports activities.

What You Can Do Now: Exercises that Stimulate Gross and Fine Development

There are many things you can do at home to help stimulate motor development in your baby or child. Wrap your newborn baby in her flexed, curled-up position in a receiving blanket, and allow her to feel the feeling of security she gets from being in this position. Unwrap your baby, and for short periods of time, while supervised, place her on her stomach with interesting toys nearby to look at. If you can, get down on the floor with her and call her name or massage her a little; in doing so, you will be helping to stimulate many areas of your baby's development at once.

As your baby gets older, he will not want to be wrapped up. Place him on his stomach for short periods, and place toys just out of his reach. Sit nearby and call his name, or make a toy dance or light up. You are trying to ignite a motivation in your baby to move toward or reach for the toy.

Sing songs to your baby and make up hand movements to go with the song. Maybe you will gently take your baby's hands or feet and try to do the movements together. Later, see if your baby will imitate you as you sing and model the movements. You may hear your baby sing along in her own way.

Try to have at least one truly babyproofed room where your baby will be able to creep, crawl, and explore safely. Make sure there are toys and attractive things to explore at a level baby can reach. Get down on your hands and knees and take a look for yourself to see if the environment is stimulating from your baby's point of view.

Shop for toys that are age-appropriate for your baby. Try to include toys that encourage crawling, walking, or spinning, as well as toys that engage a baby's hands.

Take your toddler to age-appropriate playgrounds. Get in on the fun and model for your child how the equipment is used. Model how much fun climbing, running, and sliding can be.

Have safe crayons, markers, paints, and dough on hand, for fine motor practice, and rainy-day activities. Drawing, painting, and shaping dough help to strengthen your child's wrists, hands, and fingers, and will help your child prepare her hands for school.

Try to make sure your child has at least one gross motor activity and one fine motor activity every day. These activities can be incorporated into a busy daily schedule. For instance, have your child assist you in the kitchen by opening the fridge, unscrewing caps from bottles or opening plastic bags. Maybe your child can use a spreading knife to spread butter on bread, or she can fold napkins. Have your child take out small bags of garbage, rake leaves in the yard, or pull clothes out of the dryer.

To strengthen oral motor skills, children should be encouraged to suck and chew. Have a supply of toys that are safe for your baby to mouth and chew on. Some of these "chewy" toys will have different weights and textures and can help a baby to strengthen her oral motor muscles.

Give your older child chewy granola bars, taffy, and fruit chews, which can all help to strengthen the muscles needed for oral motor skills. Some healthy choices are bagels, carrots, and pieces of meat that require a good amount of chewing. Children that need to increase their oral motor strength can also suck liquids through straws. Milkshakes, fruit shakes, and other blended drinks, which require some hard sucking to move the liquid up through the straw, can all help to increase oral motor strength.

SEVEN

Sensory Integration and Sensory Processing Disorders

"Our son's preschool teacher says our son is inattentive and inappropriate. He refuses to participate in art projects, and he's pushy with the other kids. He also covers his ears when the teacher tries to speak with him. He is a different child at home. I would say he's calm, even quiet. He is an excellent reader at four. Why is he acting this way at school?"

"Do you believe in that sensory processing stuff?" This question was posed to me with quite a bit of skepticism at the end of a recent meeting. I answered with a simple "Yes, I do," but the idea in some circles that sensory processing difficulties may just be a fad saddens me. Sensory registration, modulation, and integration are neurological processes of perceiving, sorting, and organizing an ever-constant bombardment of environmental information. Together, they make up our sensory processing. I didn't tell this woman that she was processing sensory information that very moment. I didn't tell her that her sensory systems were supporting her as she turned her head in my direction and as her eyes followed me as I proceeded to walk from the room. Earlier, she had transitioned from a seated position to a standing position smoothly, and I didn't remember her being distracted by the "wind tunnel" sound of the air-conditioning during our meeting.

Sensory processing is serious business. It is critical for proper development. When child professionals look at and work with a child's ability to register, modulate, and integrate sensory information, they may be taking an even deeper, and more probing look at the root of the child's motor, cognitive, emotional, or attention difficulties, especially when the causes are unknown.

Those of us with healthy sensory processing are constantly perceiving and interpreting environmental and orienting information. And although most of us grew up thinking that there are only five senses, I have news for you. There are more.

When teachers or therapists express concern about a child's sensory processing, they are usually referring to concerns about a child's use of his tactile sense, or the lesser-known vestibular or proprioceptive senses. The *tactile sense* perceives touch sensations. Our skin acts as our tactile sensor, while our sensory integration affects whether we perceive temperature, pain, or pressure when touched. The *vestibular sense* tells us whether we are upright or where our bodies are in relation to gravity. There are vestibular sensors in the inner ear that affect our balance, and bodily orientation. The *proprioceptive sense* tells us how our body is positioned at any given moment, without our having to look at each one of our limbs. It also helps us to judge how much force we need to exert in our movements. There are proprioceptive sensors in our skin, muscles, ligaments, and tendons.

These three senses are fundamental information systems that can translate and send our brains information that's needed to keep us upright and in control of our faculties. These senses also serve as a basis for growth and learning.

Most of us experience occasional moments of compromised sensory processing. Have you ever had an ear infection or illness that caused you to feel dizzy upon standing up? Have you ever felt carsick or seasick, where your vestibular and visual senses send your brain incompatible information and therefore don't integrate? Have you ever attended a dance or exercise class that did not have a mirror, and you found yourself having difficulty knowing if you were copying the instructor's movements properly? In this case, your proprioception was compromised without the ability to integrate additional visual cues from a mirror. You may have found yourself having to look at your arms or legs to see if you were properly mimicking the instructor.

Children with sensory processing difficulties experience symptoms like these daily. The constant bombardment of environmental stimuli can leave these children frustrated and irritable. It is estimated that seventy percent of children who have a developmental delay or disorder, have underlying sensory processing difficulties. Many child professionals have found that sensory difficulties can be handled by manipulating the environment, using sensory diets, and administering sensory "fixes." Sensory diets can give children the sensory input they need, or desensitize children from the sensory experiences they find hard to tolerate. Sensory "fixes" are short breaks with a calming sensory component, to help a child reorganize in a stressful setting. Also, the act of increasing or decreasing a child's sensory input can, at times, hugely affect a child's sense of well-being and ability to focus.

When all systems are functioning well, children are aware of their movements and are able to self-regulate their reactions. They are able to selectively focus and selectively ignore environmental stimulus. For children with sensory sensitivities, the tag on the inside neckline of their shirt, or touching the inside of a pumpkin may be just too much to bear.

Sensory processing difficulties often correlate with many different types of developmental disabilities and disorders. It is estimated that over two-thirds of children with disabilities have inefficient sensory modulation and self-regulation. *Sensory modulation* is the combining of information from the senses to give a child "the big picture" of himself within his environment. *Self-regulation* is the desired result of perceiving and processing sensory messages. Children with the ability to self-regulate can selectively focus on or ignore stimuli in their environments. They are able to appropriately "read" environmental cues and bodily cues, and react accordingly.

Too much sensory information may cause "sensory overload," resulting in inattention, hyperactivity, irritability, hostility, or an overall "shutting down." It is quite common to see children experience sensory overload in preschool and elementary school. Frequently, classroom walls are colorful and stimulating, and children must process this visual stimulation along with peer noise and movement around them. In addition, children must weed out and focus on the words and movements of the teachers (and not attend to the beautiful wall decorations, or their own itchy tights), while retaining in their memory a host of instructions, previous learned knowledge, and motor plans for classroom tasks. This sensory multitasking is essential for success in many daily settings, so sensory hypersensitivities and hyposensitivities can truly be sources of frustration and distraction. Even simple daily activities such as eating and sleeping can be negatively affected by sensory processing difficulties.

For a better understanding of what sensory processing difficulties can look like in a young child, let's take a look at five-year-old Yoshio in his kindergarten class:

Yoshio Stresses Out

"I want to go home. I hate school," Yoshio says to his dad as he gets in his kindergarten line outside of his school. More of his classmates begin to line up, so Yoshio moves off to the side. Yoshio looks to see if his dad is gone and proceeds to take off his jacket and backpack, even though it is chilly. The teacher comes out and begins to lead the class inside. Yoshio waits and lets all of his classmates go first. He then follows his class in, leaving a distance between himself and the very last person in line. Inside, Yoshio takes out his take-home folder and puts his things away in his cubby. He walks quietly to his table and places his pencil in front of him. Morning work is on his table, so Yoshio takes his pencil and begins his work. Kids at his table are talking and laughing. Yoshio looks anxious and covers his ears. After a moment, he picks up his pencil again with a very unusual grip and (while grimacing) completes his work. Though his markings are hardly readable, he does the work correctly. The teacher calls the children to the rug for morning circle and a morning lesson. Yoshio waits for all of the children to sit on the rug, and then he sits down a good distance behind the other students. "We will be going to art, so please after our lesson, get your smocks on," the teacher says. Yoshio looks nervous and does not pay attention to the lesson. When the kids get up to get smocks, Yoshio walks to the classroom water fountain. "Let's go, my friend, get your smock," the teacher says as she looks directly at him. Yoshio looks at the line of kids with their smocks and suddenly makes a beeline run into the classroom bathroom, locking the door. Everyone can hear Yoshio stamping his feet on the bathroom floor, over and over. "Your behavior is unacceptable, Yoshio!" the teacher says as she calls the principal.

Sensory Processing Difficulties

Yoshio is showing some red flag behaviors that would warrant investigation by child professionals and therapists. Sensory processing difficulties can be a potent underlying cause for many types of childhood struggles, yet they too often go unrecognized or misdiagnosed. So a child like Yoshio needs to be observed very carefully so that child professionals can intervene and give help where it's truly needed.

If you were able to note even a few red flag behaviors and their possible causes, you are truly on the right track. Here are some of the behaviors and elements of concern:

- Yoshio expresses dislike about going to school. Children who are Yoshio's age usually love to attend kindergarten, and enjoy participating in the variety of activities kindergarten offers. Although some children initially have difficulty separating from their parent or caregiver, an ongoing dislike of a school environment should be a cause for concern.

- Yoshio tends to move off to the side of or the end of the line, instead of standing "in line." He seems to want to keep a distance between himself and the other children. He also took his jacket and backpack off, which may have been discomforting him, even though it was chilly.

- Yoshio struggles with his pencil. He may have difficulty sensing where his hand is as he tries to form letters.

- He covers his ears in reaction to others talking and laughing, which may show a sound sensitivity or inability to handle auditory stimulation.

- He did not want to get his smock and tried to use avoidance techniques, as when he got a drink and locked himself in the classroom bathroom to help escape a situation he may deem as too stressful to deal with. Possibly he does not like the feeling of having the smock on, or possibly he does not like the feeling of touching art supplies, such as glue or paint.

An observant parent, teacher, or professional would also notice Yoshio's strengths and would use them to help support his weaknesses. Here are some of the positive behaviors and skills that Yoshio displayed:

- Yoshio separates from his parent without a problem.

- He is able to remember and perform a sequence of daily activities successfully. For instance, upon entering the classroom, Yoshio was able to independently take out his take-home folder while putting his other things away, find his seat, and sit down to work.

- Yoshio did his morning work correctly, even though his handwriting may not be up to par. He may be quite bright.

- Yoshio did not show aggression toward children or adults, even when anxious.

- Though Yoshio didn't know it (and Yoshio's teacher may not have known it), he showed a sensory coping strategy when he began to repeatedly kick the floor. The repeated vestibular information from the forces and pressure in his legs each time he kicked the floor had a calming and organizing affect on Yoshio's brain. (You will learn more about this later in this chapter.)

These strengths are very important because the teachers and therapists who might help Yoshio can use these strengths to help him thrive despite his sensory difficulties. Here are a few ways that Yoshio's parents, teachers, and therapists can help him:

- Yoshio's teachers and parents could help Yoshio prepare in advance for different environments, settings, and activities. They could warn Yoshio about how loud or chaotic different settings would be or what certain tasks would entail. This way, Yoshio could participate in forming a coping plan, so that there would be no surprises, and expectations would be clear. For example, if a task would require Yoshio to do something he finds uncomfortable, the teacher and Yoshio could make a deal. His teacher might suggest, "Yoshio, if you finger paint for five minutes, then you can immediately wash your hands and use the computer until the end of the activity." This would help Yoshio feel much more secure. His "escape" would be approved by his teacher.

- Yoshio could be taught to recognize the early signs of feeling irritated or anxious. He could have a place to go, or a "help person" to turn to, who would help him.

- An occupational therapist could recommend a *sensory diet* for Yoshio. The sensory diet could help him tolerate sensory input better, and sensory fixes could be welcome breaks that might calm and organize him for the next task at hand.

- Yoshio's teacher could set up a "quiet corner" in the room. Yoshio could possibly put on earphones and listen to soft, calming music. Yoshio might even be interested in working on a computer while wearing headphones.

Without help, sensory processing difficulties can affect a child's ability to function at his best. The constant focus on or defending oneself against confusing sensory messages, or the constant drive to *seek out* sensory experiences, can frustrate and fatigue a child to a point of despair. Without early vigilance and early help, children with sensory processing difficulties are frequently misdiagnosed and labeled with many different types of disorders, from learning, to emotional, to motor disorders. And yet they continue on with the discomforts of poor sensory processing. Early intervention can help children become more "available" for learning and interacting with others.

Defining a Concern:
Tactile? Vestibular? Or Proprioceptive Dysfunction?

Think for a moment about your own child's difficulties. Is your child having a hard time tolerating clothing against her skin? Does she avoid hugs and other simple affectionate touches? These may be tactile difficulties. Maybe your child panics when he is held up in the air, held upside down, or spun. Possibly she refuses to play on or try out playground equipment. These may be vestibular difficulties. If you feel your child is having difficulty gauging her movements—for instance, using so much pressure when drawing that the crayons break—she may be exhibiting proprioceptive difficulties.

We will discuss these sensory difficulties in greater detail, but first it is important to have a basic understanding of the ways the tactile, vestibular, and proprioceptive senses develop in children.

The Development of the Tactile Sense,
the Vestibular Sense, and Proprioception

When our babies are born, we hold them close, gaze into their tiny faces, and speak to our new members of the family with joy and anticipation. Can she hear me? Can she see me? Does he recognize my voice? Most of us know that healthy newborns can peer back at us from a close distance and listen to our voices, sometimes with knowing recognition.

But few of us stop to marvel at our babies' ability to sense if they are upright, or their innate ability to orient themselves outside of the womb.

We don't really think about the millions of receptors in our baby's skin, muscles, joints, and inner ears that are constantly in action, translating information from the environment into electrical messages that travel to the brain. We wonder if our babies are able to feel touch, temperature, pressure, and pain. Actually, our babies' tactile sense is the most established sense at birth. Many a parent has shed a tear as their little newborn undergoes the typical poking and prodding from tests and vaccinations. Newborn babies do feel pain, although they will not remember these early and unpleasant tactile experiences.

At just several weeks old, an embryo reacts to touch in sensitive facial areas, and at the beginning of the second trimester, a fetus reacts to touch over most of his body. As a fetus grows and develops, his perceptual awareness of touch begins to emerge. And at birth, a newborn's detection of touch is unorganized but highly informative.

Tactile sensation, like motor control, develops from the head and face down through the baby's toes. A baby's tactile receptors are all over his skin, but early on, his mouth and cheek area is one of the most sensitive areas. Young babies use their mouths and tongues to explore, and this helps them to adjust and feed successfully. Very young babies even have a specialized tactile reflex that causes them to turn their heads to feed in response to a touch on the cheek.

Tactile stimulation of the skin helps a baby to develop proprioception, which will help a baby begin to gain an awareness of, and "keep track" of, his limbs and body position. As a baby grows, he will be able to integrate tactile stimulation and proprioceptive information, and "tell" where a touch has occurred on his body.

Positive tactile stimulation and touch experiences are critically important for a baby in her first months of life. Research has shown that a lack of positive tactile or touch experiences can negatively affect the development of typical tactile sensitivity, and research with animals shows a resulting atypical development of the brain's cerebral cortex. There is no doubt that early tactile stimulation can encourage healthy brain development.

A baby's vestibular sense is also well developed at birth. With proper formation of the inner ear, this sense will help a baby seek to stay upright and lift himself against gravity. Without even knowing it, all of that bouncing, rocking, and strolling that we do with our babies is helping to provide vestibular information that will stimulate brain development, as well as stimulate further integrating of the senses. A baby's ability to integrate vestibular information will help her adjust her eyes to look at mom, even if she does not yet have the strength to turn or lift her head. It will help her try to "right" her head when turned sideways, and will help her begin to use her balance in conjunction with motor skills. Using her vestibular sense, she will be able to sense directional motion, such as movement forward or movement backward. Like tactile experience, vestibular experience has been shown to be critical to a child's overall development. Weak sensing of vestibular information is common in children with learning disabilities, motor delays, social and emotional difficulties, and even autism.

As children grow and process sensory information more readily, vestibular information from activities like spinning, bouncing, and jumping continue to have an "organizing" and at times calming effect on the child's brain. These activities, which exercise a child's balance and orientation, have been shown to positively affect cognitive aptitude for a period of time after the vestibular stimulation. So recess is important.

With healthy proprioception, a child is able to successfully direct his motor movements, and this gives a child a "movement confidence" that allows him to direct his attention to the cognitive, or social aspects of a task or activity. When a child has weak proprioception, he will not have this confidence with his movements, and his attention will be "split" between having to visually grade every movement and having to focus on tasks. Healthy proprioception gives a child an innate knowledge or map of where his arms or legs are, even if his eyes are closed.

Most preschool and kindergarten children love tactile activities and will willingly finger paint, squeeze dough, and get their hands dirty with cooking activities. Most children also love the feeling of playing in a swimming pool, a bath, and being hugged. These different tactile experiences will continue, as they grow, to give children sensory experiences that they will integrate when making cognitive decisions, social decisions, motor judgements, and efforts to interact.

Sensory Processing Disorders

Now we'll take a look at the different types of difficulties children with sensory processing disorders experience. Maybe you will see shades of your own child reflected in what will be described here, or maybe you will feel that your child's difficulties are much more subtle and less worrisome.

Children with sensory processing disorders tend to have a disorganized way about them and tend to *overregister* or *underregister* sensory information from the environment. If a child is overregistering, she may have a heightened sensory awareness and be overreactive, extremely defensive, and overly sensitive to stimulus (sound, action, color, touch) in the environment. This is called *hypersensitivity*. A child who is underregistering sensory information has a muted sensory awareness, and may not feel sensations such as hunger, fullness, or the need to use the toilet. These children may need to make much larger movements to get the same sensations that other children would receive more readily, and they may constantly be trying to seek out sensory experiences that will give them information about their bodies. This is called *hyposensitivity*.

To gain a better understanding of the types of difficulties associated with sensory processing disorders, let's take a closer look at children with tactile and vestibular hypersensitivities and hyposensitivities, as well as children with proprioception problems.

TACTILE DYSFUNCTION

Tara's parents were very concerned. They could not understand their four-year-old's "violent tantrums" at bath time, and in the mornings and evenings when Tara would have to get dressed for school or bed. Tara's parents expressed that though they were embarrassed to admit it, they frequently punished Tara when she would run and hide to avoid brushing her teeth. Tara's mom said, "I would think to myself, 'What just happened to my nice little girl?' At one point, I actually wondered whether my daughter was schizophrenic! And I would just get so angry at her."

Tara's teachers were seeing some of the same patterns of behavior. Tara refused to finger paint or participate in activities where she would have to put her hands in shaving cream, sand, beans, or dough. She would also panic and cry if she or a peer spilled liquid near her. One of Tara's teachers said, "The year we had Tara, we were slowly changing our program a little bit, to a more multisensory program, because multisensory approaches are supposed to be good for all children. But for Tara, the more multisensory activities we did, the less she wanted to be with us."

Tara's parents, on the advice of their pediatrician, sought help from an occupational therapist, who observed Tara at her preschool. Tara now sees the occupational therapist on a regular basis to help with her tactile hypersensitivities. Tara and her parents now speak openly about how textures feel to her. Tara and her mother shop for clothing together, and Tara tries on and/or decides whether she will wear an item or not. She will also now feel the textures of different toothbrushes briefly to decide which one she will use. At school, Tara and her teachers "make deals" about participating in tactile activities. Sometimes sitting alongside a peer is enough, and at other times Tara is required to participate for a couple minutes. Tara is currently a very successful kindergartener.

Tara has sensory processing difficulties. Her sensitivities and reactions to tactile input are heightened and extreme. Tara is not "deciding" to be oppositional when faced with a tactile activity. She actually feels and experiences true discomfort, possibly even pain, through the tactile receptors in her skin. Tactile hypersensitivity can be overwhelming, because children with this type of dysfunction go about their days in an almost constant state of defensiveness. The sensations they receive through their skin are distracting and uncomfortable, and this makes attending to learning or socializing difficult.

Occupational therapy can be very helpful for children with tactile hypersensitivity. By participating in tactile exercises and activities, children develop a better tolerance for tactile stimuli, making them less tactile defensive. For some children, progress can be slow and incremental, while others develop a tolerance for tactile stimuli quite quickly. With a new familiarity for tactile textures, children frequently let go of their anxiousness and defensiveness when they experience or anticipate tactile sensations.

Tactile hyposensitivity can also be difficult for children. One little kindergartener I know, named Griffin, was not well liked in kindergarten, and classmates would readily tell many reasons why, such as, "He lays down in the sandbox. He always tries to hug and kiss everyone. He gets food all over his face, and goes in his pants and doesn't even care." Griffin's teacher suspected his constant need to touch everything and everyone wasn't normal. To help him, a school-based occupational therapist recommended a sensory diet to help with his tactile hyposensitivity. Griffin's parents and teachers met together to decide how this could best be done both at school and at home. Griffin was given several tactile experiences upon entering school, and this decreased his inappropriate seeking of tactile stimuli. Griffin was also allowed to chew fruit chews while he worked. In addition, while at home and at school, Griffin would engage in conversational lessons about appropriate ways to touch and "be around" his peers. And Griffin was taught to catch bodily "clues" that could possibly be telling him that he may have to use the toilet. He was required to visit the bathroom frequently and was taught to use a napkin to wipe his mouth after every three bites.

Tactile hyposensitivity may cause affected children to seek out tactile sensory input frequently and at times inappropriately. Children with hyposensitive skin may touch or shove others, rub against objects and people, or may constantly try to handle whatever catches their visual attention. All of this seeking of tactile information helps these children get sensory information from their environments, information that most typical children understand and synthesize more readily. But children who are hyposensitive to touch sensations do not register the more subtle tactile sensations that most kids do. Typical children will readily integrate and use tactile sensations to act, react, or to make adjustments if they feel tactile discomfort. For instance, a child may take off his sweater if he feels too hot. Another child may adjust the water running from the bathroom sink to a comfortable temperature for hand washing. Children with tactile hyposensitivity do not clearly receive the tactile messages that might help them make these simple actions and adjustments. The sensations involved in scraping a knee, or feeling temperature, do not evoke a reaction that is typical.

Oral Defensiveness

Oral defensiveness refers to a tactile hypersensitivity inside the mouth. Foods that same-age peers enjoy may cause an oral-defensive child to gag. Children who are oral defensive may have tantrums if pressured to eat certain foods or forced to participate in activities (such as brushing teeth) that cause them oral discomfort.

VESTIBULAR DYSFUNCTION

Javier, at six years old, says that he hates recess, gym class, and boys at his school, and he also vows that he will never again play soccer. Javier says that he always forgets which way he's supposed to run with and kick the ball. Over the past couple years, Javier's mother and father both had had concerns about what they believed at first to be a nervous stomach. They thought Javier was overly nervous about trying out swings and amusement rides, for they believed his consistent vomiting in these situations was probably due to anxiety. They would try to force Javier to try rides and activities, but Javier began to adamantly refuse and at times, have a violent tantrum. He would even lock himself in his bedroom to avoid having to participate in activities with motion and movement. A turning point came when Javier's uncle (whom Javier adored) visited the family. "Javi was so excited and all smiles," his mother said, "and then I see my brother toss Javi up and give him a kiss. When he put Javi down, I saw him stumble like he's dizzy, like he's a drunk man. I saw Javi was still smiling, but I also saw him hold his stomach for a moment like he does when it feels bad. I ask, 'Javi, are you dizzy?' And he says, 'Yes, Mommy.' I called his doctor the next day." Javier's doctor recommended that Javier be screened by an occupational therapist. Javier currently receives occupational therapy for his vestibular hypersensitivity. He is showing a great deal of improvement with tolerating motion sensations.

Javier also has sensory processing difficulties. But the difficulties Javier experiences are different in nature from children who have difficulty synthesizing tactile sensations. The vestibular receptors in Javier's middle ear give Javier's brain information about his head position and body position in relation to gravity. These receptors in Javier's middle ear also give Javier information about motion and direction, including whether he is moving forward, backward, up, or down. Javier shows hypersensitivity to motion and directional confusion. This makes everyday activities difficult and active activities unfavorable.

Children who are hypersensitive to vestibular sensations feel dizzy or disoriented in reaction to very subtle movements. Many movements that cause these children discomfort would not faze most typical children. Most typical children enjoy "rush," speed, and spinning sensations, beckon for more, and incorporate movements that create strong vestibular sensations as part of their play. Hypersensitive children try to avoid these activities. Hypersensitive children experience changes in position and movements that require adjustments in balance as threatening. Some children become physically sick in reaction to vestibular stimuli.

Rusty has difficulty with his vestibular processing, too:

> Rusty, at four, is well known at his preschool as the "little bull in the china shop." His teachers felt that he had no sense of his body, for he would constantly (and his teachers believed purposefully) bump into or push kids and adults. He would also hurl himself onto the carpet or against the wall when excited, and impulsively and dangerously jump from high corners of the playground equipment. At times, Rusty would clearly bruise or injure himself, though he would not stop for help and would sometimes even laugh hysterically at his "accident." A visiting occupational therapist (for another child in the class) called

Rusty's parents, feeling that he should be screened. Rusty does now receive occupational therapy for his hyposensitive vestibular system. Rusty's therapist expressed that in the beginning, he could spin and spin and not get dizzy, but that now he definitely feels pain when he scrapes himself or falls outside.

Rusty shows symptoms of another distinct kind of sensory processing difficulty. His vestibular system is hyposensitive, making Rusty less sensitive to body position, speed, or motion. Rusty needed heavy-handed, large motor movements to register the vestibular sensations that would give him pertinent information about where his body was in space. When Rusty began occupational therapy, his vestibular reactions and eye movements were atypical after a number of activities that involved spinning, flipping, and jumping. Rusty began to work weekly with the occupational therapist and daily at home to further develop his vestibular awareness.

Many children like Rusty find themselves seeking out vestibular sensations in inappropriate ways. To the children, the "rush" they get from extreme movement is pleasurable and exciting. To adults and peers who are with these children daily, the constant seeking of large motor and balance thrills can be frustrating and off-putting. Many classmates of children with vestibular hyposensitivity talk of being accidentally shoved, bumped, and/or pressured by the affected child to try or participate in a dangerous game or action.

Gravitational Insecurity

Gravitational insecurity is a common symptom of vestibular dysfunction. Children who have gravitational insecurity experience a sensation of imbalance and disorientation when lifted off the ground, or when bodily senses give the brain information that puts them at an "uncomfortable" height. Even when holding the hand of a parent, a child with gravitational insecurity may, when walking out onto a balcony of a theater or high-rise apartment, feel a sensation that tells them they will lose their balance or fall at any moment. Some children feel that they are tipping sideways and will lose their balance. A tendency of children with gravitational insecurity is to get closer to the floor, or to get down to the lowest they can be. At times, touching the floor with both feet and hands helps a child to "right" himself and feel reorganized and balanced again. "Crouching down like a frog" can be very helpful, even for just a moment, to help a child get through the anxiety and fear provoking sensations of gravitational insecurity.

Bilateral Integration Difficulties

Another symptom of vestibular dysfunction is bilateral integration difficulties. Children with bilateral integration difficulties find it extremely hard to get both sides of their bodies to work together. Bilateral integration begins very early, when babies learn to cross their bodies' midlines with their arms and hands, a result of their right brain and left brain learning to talk with and communicate with each other about position and movement. Purposeful motor movement requires bilateral integration, and children with bilateral integration difficulties are frequently unable to participate in age-appropriate motor activities or academic activities without difficulty.

For instance, an art project may need one hand to steady a piece of paper, while the other hand draws, writes, or glues. Both sides of the child's brain must together remain aware, anticipate, and communicate the movements that will eventually complete the art project. Walking up and down a flight of steps also requires bilateral integration. Each side of the brain works one side of the body, so both the right brain and left brain must communicate to make fluid ascending or descending movements. Beginning reading and math skills often require bilateral integration of the eyes. A child's eyes must move across text in a left, across midline, to right pattern, and then the eyes must quickly and fluidly return to "way left" to begin this pattern again. This reading pattern must be practiced over and over again with many children whose bilateral integration is weak.

Coordinating both sides of the body is, for most children, simple and natural. Children with bilateral integration difficulties can become frustrated with seemingly simple tasks, and they can appear highly uncoordinated or motor delayed. Practicing simple bilateral integration skills daily, and then slowly progressing to more difficult bilateral skills can be very beneficial to children with this particular type of vestibular dysfunction.

PROPRIOCEPTIVE DYSFUNCTION

Abby didn't want to go to kindergarten, and her mother made an appointment with Abby's teacher. Abby's teacher had invited the music teacher to attend the meeting as well. There, Abby's mother learned why her daughter didn't want to attend school. Apparently, practice for a Thanksgiving show was taking up a good deal of both the morning and afternoon time. Abby was finding it difficult to pick up all of the movements to the songs, and others were teasing her about it. Her teacher assured Abby's mother that teasing was not tolerated, but Abby herself was starting to rudely scream, "I *am* doing it!" when the teachers would try to remind her of the proper movements. The teachers also believed that Abby was now trying to misbehave on purpose so that she would have time-out during rehearsal. "I heard what they were saying," Abby's mother said, "but part of me wanted to defend my daughter, because their frustration with her was really visible. They kept saying, 'We keep trying to work with her, but she can't get the movements.' I thought they wanted me to say something like, 'Oh, don't worry, she doesn't have to be in, or mess up the show.' " At the end of the meeting, Abby's kindergarten teacher mentioned that Abby also appeared to be uncoordinated in physical education. "My daughter was always a bit uncoordinated, but this mention of physical education kind of made me put two and two together. At home, I was seeing Abby have a hard time getting dressed and undressed. It was even hard for her to put on and take off her jacket, that is, unless she was standing in front of my mirror. She always said she dresses better in front of my mirror." Abby was evaluated by a physical therapist and occupational therapist, and she was initially going to be evaluated for cognitive problems as well, but this was later dropped after observing her in class. Abby now receives occupational therapy and a physical therapy consultation, where she practices using her visual cues in conjunction with her motor skills. After motor skills and motor plans are repeatedly practiced using multisensory cues,

Abby attempts the skills without the additional sensory information (for instance, without looking in a mirror). Her mother currently reports that her therapy has made "a world of difference."

Abby's sensory processing difficulties make it difficult for her to synthesize and integrate proprioceptive information received through her muscles, joints, and ligaments. Healthy proprioception is important for a child's ability to effectively carry out gross and fine motor movements. It is also an important factor in a child's ability to grade her movements, that is, be effective in using different amounts of pressure or pull when handling objects. A child's proprioception receptors help to form a mental "map" of the body. A visual or verbal instruction for movement can cause a child to call forth this integrated map. This map will help a child to perform a movement with an inner knowledge of whether the movement is "right on," "almost there," or "not it at all." A child with weak proprioception will not be aware of their resulting movement. A child with weak proprioception may have to purposefully look with her eyes to see if her arm is up like it is supposed to be, or whether she put the right foot out and forward.

Unclear proprioceptive information also causes children to have a "muddled memory" for motor plans. Proprioceptive information is important when we carry out motor activities, and we remember the proprioceptive (as well as the vestibular) sensations, and repeat movements easily and fluidly using our previously learned sensory experience and knowledge. Children with weak proprioception find it difficult to integrate the proprioceptive information, so the information is not "held on to" for future use.

Dos and Don'ts

If you believe your child may be having sensory processing difficulties,

Do:

- Watch your child's behaviors across different environments. If you notice your child is stressed, try to reduce the amount of sensory stimuli, or leave the environment.

- Discuss your sensory concerns with your pediatrician or an occupational therapist that is knowledgeable in sensory issues.

- If your child is old enough, talk with your child about how he/she feels in certain situations. Your child, even at three years old, may be able to tell you what he/she finds hard "to deal with."

- Try to make your child's bedroom (or a section of your home) "a comfort zone" for your child, where your child can let down his/her defenses or play, bump, and fall without injury.

- Talk to other parents who, through personal experience, know about sensory integration and have "been there."

Don't:

- Don't force your child into activities your child appears to loathe or fear. Try to find out what makes your child refuse, act defensive, or act fearful.

- Don't force feed your child.

- Don't try to desensitize your child to certain sensory stimuli, by yourself or without expert advice.

- Don't forget that with early help, sensory integration can improve.

Important Considerations Before Diagnosis— Premature Birth and Adoption

Premature birth and adoption can both present some special sensory processing issues. Babies born prematurely are frequently unable to handle the immense amount of sensory stimulation in the environment outside the womb. Their premature brains and sensory systems are not fully developed, and "sensory overload" is a frequent result of this inability to handle sensory information. Too much sensory input causes premature infants

The Test of Three

Use this technique to help assess your child's sensory processing concerns, to determine whether your child may need professional intervention or specialized help.

Write down *three* characteristics that concern you. Examples include:

> "He cries or hides when it is time to get dressed."

> "He refuses to go on the playground equipment."

> "He gets extremely angry and irritable in busy places."

Decide to "intervene" with *three* ideas to help your concerns, for example:

- I will ask my child to help pick his clothes for the day. I will also ask my child if he can tell me or show me what makes dressing so upsetting for him.
- I will encourage my child to try the playground apparatus by playing side by side with my child, and by demonstrating what to do, as well as how much fun a playground can be.
- I will take time to tell my child what he might expect in different busy locations, and have a plan or sign we both have knowledge of, that will help my child to tell me that he is beginning to "lose his cool."

Work on your interventions daily for *three* weeks, or if you are unable to do this, work on them intermittently for *three* months. Either way, write down specific characteristics that you see. If you can, keep notes on your child's behaviors and reactions. Do not be afraid to critically watch your child's development over a three-month period. Some children develop in uneven spurts, so you might observe big improvements, or you might continue to see the questionable behavior, which would warrant further assessment.

At the end of the chosen time period write down what you observe. Write down how your child performs in the specific areas of concern. Compare your notes with the notes you took in the beginning. Are there any differences? Has there been progress? If you have chosen to work on your interventions daily, you should see some progress in three weeks. If the additional and focused stimulation is only scratching the surface of the difficulties, and your child has not shown obvious progress, it may be time to look into getting further help. After three months, your child has had time to grow, develop, and interact in many different types of situations. How is he/she doing? Do his/her difficulties continue to persist? If so, he may need help.

stress, and this stress manifests itself in many physical and behavioral ways. A baby's heart rate and oxygen level may drop, and his blood pressure may increase due to sensory overload. Parents and hospital staff may see their babies avert their eyes, cry more, and eat less. Some babies will gag or stiffen their bodies in reaction to too much sensory stimulation. Often, the bright lights and noises of the neonatal intensive care units, as well as the tactile input from medical procedures, can cause some premature infants to experience an almost constant degree of stress.

Though many neonatal intensive care units used to discourage touch as a way to avoid overstimulating infants, recently, with the help of research, experience, and experimentation, many NICUs are now encouraging a calming touch, infant massage, and skin-to-skin contact between infants and their parents. Making the environment more peaceful for infants is also a goal of many NICUs. This helps premature babies remain in a more relaxed state for feeding, and it reduces the startling (reflex) in reaction to sudden movements or sound. Some parents like to play their babies soft music or record and play a tape of a parent singing softly or speaking softly.

Parents are advised to look at their environment and try to reduce some of the sensory stimuli in it if they feel their baby is stressed. Maybe a parent can turn down the volume of the TV or turn off the bright light nearby. Possibly a parent will need to speak in a softer voice, or stop rocking or bouncing their baby.

Helping your premature baby avoid sensory overload can at first feel a little daunting. Remember, as your baby grows, little by little, he will be able to handle and organize more and more of the typical daily sensory experiences his full-term peers experience.

The adoption of older babies and children has also led parents to have to confront numerous forms of sensory processing difficulties. Many families adopt (locally and from overseas) children with histories of early deprivation or neglect. Some children arrive at their new homes with only the experience of life in an institution. The lack of stimulation and sensory input early on leave many of these kids at a developmental disadvantage. Many of these kids are unable to synthesize or integrate their new overstimulating environment, resulting in atypical behaviors, from withdrawal, to hyperactivity, to self-stimulation. Parents find that early intervention and therapy are key in helping their adopted babies and children improve and tolerate new sensory experiences. Early intervention and therapy has also been found to help (formerly) disadvantaged kids to develop calming and self-regulating behaviors.

A Word on Distortions and Synaesthesia

Children with sensory processing difficulties may also experience uncomfortable and confusing sensations that are known as *distortions*. They may also experience a more rare sensation (or "sensory experience") called *synaesthesia*.

Distortions cause an object to be perceived as moving when it is not. For school-age children, sensory distortions may cause the lines of text in their books to appear as if they are moving forward, backward, or diagonally. Distortions may cause a child to see halos around objects or people, or may cause a child to see stripes moving across the shirts and pants of peers.

Synaesthesia can cause a child to see colors when subjected to certain sounds, or may at times cause a child to become dizzy after standing in a dimly lit room. Children with synaesthesia may even become fearful of, or overly "hungry for," these sensations.

Red Flags of Atypical Sensory Processing

Red flags can act as warning signals that development may not be progressing as it should. Below, you will find a list of characteristics that commonly accompany sensory processing difficulties. Don't panic if you check one or more; there is no way to "score" your child here. Simply use the list as a tool that will assist you in defining and gauging your child's vulnerabilities, so that you can find her the help she may need.

Red Flags of Sensory Processing Difficulties in the First Year

_____ Baby cries excessively or consistently shuts down and sleeps in public or noisy environments.

_____ Baby has great difficulty learning to roll over.

_____ Baby appears to want to "skip" creeping and crawling, and may opt for an atypical scooting in a seated position.

_____ Baby is extremely fussy during diaper changes, clothes changes, or bath time.

_____ Baby is not mouthing toys.

_____ Baby becomes extremely upset the moment he/she is tipped backward on a changing table or lowered into a crib.

_____ Baby gets upset at the jolting or bumping of the stroller or carriage.

_____ Baby displays discomfort and frustration when held.

_____ Baby does not appear to be reaching motor milestones.

_____ Baby is consistently having a difficult time feeding and may resist the introduction of solid foods or cereals.

Red Flags of Tactile Dysfunction

_____ He/she partially or completely disrobes whenever possible.

_____ He/she avoids activities or tasks that involve getting his/her hands wet, sticky, or messy.

_____ He/she has tantrums at bath time or when it is time to brush teeth.

_____ He/she loathes certain pieces of his/her clothing.

_____ He/she consistently makes inappropriate choices of clothing for the season, either dressing clearly too light or too warmly.

_____ He/she does not seem to notice newly inflicted scrapes or bruises.

_____ He/she shows a lack of awareness for food on his/her face, chin, and neck during or after eating.

_____ He/she expresses irritability or discomfort when hugged or kissed.

_____ He/she dislikes being barefoot.

_____ He/she loathes wearing shoes on his/her feet.

_____ He/she inappropriately wants to hug or physically be against family members or friends.

_____ He/she seems to have a need to touch and handle all that is around him/her.

_____ He/she reacts negatively and excessively to unexpected touch or contact.

Red Flags of Vestibular Dysfunction

_____ He/she (at or nearly after age two) does not show a hand preference.

_____ He/she becomes upset when you or family members lift him/her high in the air.

_____ He/she avoids being turned upside down or activities that involve being turned upside down, like rolling, flipping, hanging, or somersaulting.

_____ He/she becomes nauseated or physically ill from riding in a car, bus, train, or plane, or from movement activities.

_____ He/she appears to be very clumsy and frequently collides with objects, or falls from his/her chair.

_____ You see him/her crouching down to the ground to keep from falling in seemingly nonthreatening situations.

_____ He/she seems to reach out with his/her hands from furniture piece to furniture piece for stabilization, or he/she walks the hallways of his/her school running a finger or hand against the wall as a stabilizer.

_____ He/she appears to get dizzy far too easily.

_____ He/she appears to never get dizzy.

_____ He/she fears or avoids activities or games that involve movement.

_____ He/she excessively craves, seeks out, or invents movement activities.

_____ He/she flops down onto chairs or onto the floor, instead of using a fluid and natural movement in his/her change of position.

_____ He/she feels vulnerable and unsteady when walking on uneven ground or uneven surfaces.

_____ He/she feels dizzy or disoriented after turning quickly or after bending over forward or backward.

_____ He/she consistently rocks, sways his/her body, or jumps up and down.

Red Flags of Proprioceptive Dysfunction

_____ He/she is not reaching motor milestones on schedule.

_____ His/her grip is very loose or weak.

_____ He/she continues to consistently walk on his/her toes.

_____ His/her movements are clumsy, stiff, robotic, or floppy.

_____ He/she consistently breaks crayons or pencils from using too much pressure when trying to write.

_____ He/she has great difficulty copying your movements or following instructions for physical movement.

_____ He/she consistently spills when carrying or pouring drinks.

_____ He/she looks at his/her body (uses visual cues) to make position adjustments.

_____ He/she has difficulty turning doorknobs and opening doors.

_____ He/she appears to consistently exaggerate movements.

_____ He/she very frequently drops objects he/she holds in his/her arms or hands.

_____ He/she feels fear, embarrassment, or apprehension about participation in movement activities and tries to avoid sports activities, and even birthday parties where activities may involve movement.

_____ He/she is extremely accident-prone, always falling, stubbing, or banging different parts of his/her body.

What You Can Do Now: Exercises to Help Stimulate Sensory Processing

For Your Baby

Touch and tactile stimulation, along with vestibular and early proprioception experiences, are extremely important for your baby's healthy development. Here are some suggestions to help your baby experience, tolerate, and integrate sensory input. Remember, helping your child to engage early is truly advantageous for your child.

Massage is one way to bond with your baby while you give her tactile input. Most babies enjoy a calming massage with a bit of pressure, over the feel of tickles or feathery light touches. A massage once or twice a day may help your baby with digestion, and though it is hard to believe, you will actually be stimulating neurological development as you gently rub your baby's skin.

Babies, especially newborn infants, also enjoy skin-to-skin contact when held or resting. Being held against the skin of your chest, shoulder, breast, or stomach is calming for babies and can help them maintain their body temperature.

Let your baby feel the textures of different toys and objects. Gently take your baby's hand and pat the stuffed dog or rub the soft, but slightly prickly baby hairbrush over your baby's hands, arms, and legs. Have several teething toys at hand that are varied in texture.

Many parents, without even realizing it, give their babies a healthy dose of vestibular stimulation every day. To make sure your baby is experiencing vestibular input, rock your baby in your arms and also in a rocking chair. Lift her up above your eye level, and then bring her down to you. Take your baby for stroller or carriage rides where she will experience forward, and at times, backward motion, along with the many bumps, jolts, and different "feels" of the different surfaces walked upon. When your baby has good head and neck control, gently swing her in a baby swing, or help her safely slide down a small slide.

Little songs and games that have movements are great for proprioception stimulation. Songs like "Patty-cake" that include hand and arm movements that you perform as you sing can stimulate your baby to try to imitate your movements. You can help him make movements with you initially in a gentle hand over hand fashion. After repeated play, he may make some earnest attempts to participate in the movements all by himself.

For Your Child

Encourage your child to participate in active activities that touch upon many different sensory systems. Games that require spinning or jumping, and activities that may require petting animals, finger painting, or copying dance or sports movements, are helpful for sensory processing development and practice.

More specifically, if you feel your child needs to exercise distinct sensory processing skills due to perceived weaknesses, suggestions are listed below.

For children who have tactile hypersensitivity
(are tactile defensive):

- Have your child use her finger to taste cookie dough or have
  her "lick the bowl" using her fingers when making brownies or a
  cake.

- Put a mystery little toy into a large lump of playdough, and have
  your child try to find the toy.

- Buy a plastic tub or container and make a small sandbox by filling
  the container with sand. (This is less threatening than a typically
  sized sandbox.) Add some toys and model the fun activities your
  child can do.

- Have your child try out an electric toothbrush, which may feel
  more comfortable against his teeth and gums. Some children enjoy
  the vibration.

- Fill a shoebox with enough salt or sparkles to cover the bottom of
  the box completely. Have your child draw pictures or letters with
  her fingers.

- Pour shampoo into a large zip-close plastic bag. Seal the closure
  with packing tape and give this squishy bag to your child to feel
  and play with.

- Finger paint with shaving cream on a hard, flat surface.

- Encourage your child to go barefoot in the house, and whenever
  possible, barefoot in the grass.

For children who have tactile hyposensitivity:

- Establish regular "bathroom breaks" where your child must "go" as
  well as check the bathroom mirror for food or debris on his face,
  neck or in his hair.

- Teach your child about appropriate and inappropriate touch. Longer stretches of appropriate tactile behavior with family and peers can be complimented and rewarded.

- Have some activities, objects, and toys that will give your child some needed tactile stimulation. Fuzzy area rugs, ball pits, large stuffed animals, and bean bag chairs are all good choices.

For children who have tactile hypersensitivity inside their mouths (oral defensiveness):

- Offer your child beverages that are different temperatures and different thicknesses, and even offer her soda so that she can feel the fizz inside of her mouth.

- Offer your child foods with different textures, from crackers to puddings, to hard-to-chew bites of meat.

- Massage your child's mouth and gums with an oral massager. Oral massagers can be bought at many drugstores or pharmacies.

For children who are hypersensitive to vestibular sensations, or who have gravitational insecurity:

- Have your child sit on a swing with his feet on the ground. Tell him that he does not have to swing, to just sit and feel the slight rocking of the swing.

- Place a large box on the floor that your child can climb in and out of.

- Put a little plastic slide or gym in your child's bedroom or playroom, so that he can attempt movements or experiment in ways he would not at the playground.

- Have your child sit in a hammock or gently rock with you in a rocking chair. Maybe she would try a rocking horse.

- Have your child imagine what it would be like if the ceiling were the floor, and the floor the ceiling. Have him lie down on the floor on his back and scoot his head back a little, as he looks up at the ceiling. Tell him to imagine walking on the ceiling.

- Encourage your child to sit on a low scooter board and use his legs to wheel around.

- Encourage your child to try a trampoline, sitting down if necessary.

- Have your child sit on and play on large therapy balls or hoppity toys.

- Take your child on short "hikes" where she will experience walking upon varied surfaces.

For children who have vestibular hyposensitivity:

- Place pillows on the floor and allow your child to somersault back and forth along the pillows.

- Establish rules of safety before any activity or game begins, and do the same before you let your child run free at a playground. Enforce your safety rules by frequently repeating them, and by carrying out consequences for dangerous decisions or behaviors.

- Allow your child to swing or jump on a trampoline for a period before she must contain her sensation seeking, for instance, before you must attend a special event or before company arrives. If your child is unable to go outside, use a sit-and-spin toy or mini trampoline.

- Clearly tell your child your expectations and establish rules of conduct before every event. Possibly allow him to slip away from the dinner table to use his sit-and-spin toy before the dessert is served. Your child's "sensory fix" will help him to remain more organized and in control of himself.

For children who have bilateral integration difficulties:

- Play clapping games with your child. Tell stories where she has to clap to make a genie appear or a dog talk. Or clap with her as you listen to music or sing songs.

- Play balloon volleyball, where your child must help to keep a balloon in the air by using a two-handed "hit."

- Play one-handed "pass the bean bag" where your child must sit next to you and pass the beanbag to you using his arm and hand on the far side. Play in both directions.

- Encourage running and jumping, and help your child to learn to swim.

- Blow bubbles in a direction and way that encourages your child to run and jump while trying to pop them.

- Teach your child to make angels in the snow. If the season is a warm one, teach her to make the snow angel movements on the floor of your home.

- Have your child rub lotion on his body. Encourage him to try to reach "hard to reach" places.

- Play "wheel barrel" with your child. Hold her legs up, while she walks on her hands.

For children who have difficulties with proprioception:

- Have your child carry some heavy objects or books. Or have him pull or push a load of toys or groceries in a wagon or cart.

- Take frequent walks with your child.

- Encourage your child to engage in beach play, such as filling pails with water or sand, or digging in the sand.

- Play a game where your child must close his eyes and touch different parts of his body without looking. Ask him to touch his pinky toe on his right foot or his belly button.

- Fill a small pitcher with your child's favorite drink and encourage her to independently pour.

- With supervision, have your child walk your dog with a leash.

- Give your child piggyback rides, where she must hang on by holding tightly with her arms and legs.

- Keep crayons, pencils, and paper available for your child to use.

- Take the stuffing out of one of your child's stuffed toys, and restuff it with beans or birdseed, making for a weightier friend.

PART III

Taking Action and Getting Help

EIGHT

Getting Your Child an Evaluation

"My husband and I are very confused about where to get help for our two-year-old son. I've heard that children can get help early. But from where?"

Many parents feel tense and anxious as they contemplate whether to have their child evaluated for a disability or disorder. Yet most of us who have weathered this stressful period find the knowledge gained from an evaluation to be helpful and informative. Parents frequently state that the information they learned from their child's "eval" was essential in making their decision about how to proceed. If you are ready to get some help and guidance so that your child can move forward, this chapter is for you. Moving forward with new knowledge in hand from this book or from an evaluation can be a liberating experience. It can also be a crossroad of great magnitude for you and your family. Many parents find themselves hesitating to make that first phone call, even though they fully intend to help their child in every way possible. Many parents do not yet trust themselves to make the right decisions when faced with different options or differing opinions. So it is with great respect for you and the important decisions you will make on behalf of your child that I present the paths to progress that I have come to know over the years.

Ask for Help, Accept Help

So you think your child may have some potential problems that should possibly be assessed? There are a few different avenues you can take to start this assessment process. We will discuss each one of these avenues separately and in more detail. No matter which avenue you choose, help for your child is out there.

The very same day my children's pediatrician told me to not let my profession make me paranoid, I dialed up our local school district and let them know I was concerned about my child. I made an appointment, right then and there, to start the evaluation process. Some parents choose to have their child evaluated by a child development clinic or a private professional. In these cases, for insurance reasons, parents may need or want a doctor's referral to have their child's symptoms evaluated and investigated.

With my own son, I was definitely tense and did not initially have the trust needed to comfortably "hand him over" to professionals and therapists (be it for a half hour at a time . . .). I did develop comfort and trust over time, after getting to know the personalities of different therapists. I also began to see the therapists were getting to know my son and were positive and encouraging with him. My initial anxiousness faded and transformed into companionship and support for my child and his helpers. I like to tell parents a "swimming story," a little experience that I had that helped me to get over my discomfort when first stepping into the world of early intervention and special services.

My oldest son was very fearful of water. At the beach, he would stand at the edge of the water. When I took him into the pool with me, to try to begin to teach him to swim, he clung to me so tightly, we really did not achieve anything together, other than overall moods of frustration. I tried to show him that other children were swimming, including little kids that were younger than him, but that did not seem to help at all in the motivation department. After receiving a flier in the mail from our local recreation center, I enrolled him in a swimming class at a local pool. On the day of the first lesson, he was very anxious. But I witnessed the swimming teacher somehow getting my fearful son to try things that he never attempted with me, no matter how hard I tried to get him to. I was amazed. I saw him, in the presence of his peers, push through some of his fear and really try to accomplish what he saw other children doing. I learned that sometimes strangers who are focusing on getting your children to learn certain skills can get your children to try and learn things that they would not attempt readily with their moms, dads, and caregivers, because they are less likely to seek protection, comfort, or openly oppose the adults they meet in a friendly working environment. My son was also encouraged by his peers, who were also working and struggling to swim, just like him.

Many of us find it a little hard to let go, even for very short periods of time, especially when we feel our child is in some way more vulnerable than others. We worry about whether child professionals or therapists will like our child, or whether they will understand or be kind to our child. We also envision our child feeling scared or overwhelmed when faced with new tasks in the presence of adults who are strangers. Through my personal and professional experiences, I have seen a lot of caring and truly gifted child professionals. Most adults who devote their life's work to helping children really care about and relate well to them. Most children getting special help like their teachers and therapists and work hard for them. Of course, there are teachers and therapists you may not see eye to eye with. If you feel uncomfortable about how a teacher or therapist may be working with or treating your child, seek out another professional you can trust.

Many parents also worry about having to disclose personal information that they would rather others not know. It is a common concern that you or your family may be judged by the adults who are evaluating or working with your child. This issue alone, at times, stops parents from giving their children opportunities for progress. If you begin your own journey into the world of child special help, understand that developmental delays and disabilities really do exist in families of all different styles, backgrounds, and financial statuses. Many child professionals and therapists have worked with all kinds of children from diverse situations, and with diverse issues. There is no "way of life" that can completely eliminate child medical issues or developmental issues. Sometimes things happen, and most child professionals and therapists understand this. If you do find yourself in a situation where you feel judged, kindly state your discomfort and ask for the name of another professional that you may speak with.

Many parents frequently express a complaint about their doctor's lack of concern for their child. Like all professionals, no two doctors are alike. Many doctors attend to a large number of children in the course of their day, and time constraints may appear as an insensitivity to developmental inquiries and concerns. Regardless, alert your child's physician about your concerns and ask for guidance in the matter. Some physicians are very knowledgeable and observant when it comes to development. If you are lucky enough to see one of these physicians, you will be met with great support and will receive excellent advice. If your doctor does not take your concerns as seriously as you would wish, your visit will still be productive, for your concerns will be noted. In this case, a second opinion may be beneficial, and this should be with a **developmental pediatrician**, who is specially trained in childhood developmental issues and syndromes.

Most physicians try hard to make accurate judgments about children's development with the information they have from your child's records, from you, and by examining and observing your child in the short time period of your child's visit. Letting parents know that their child will grow out of certain behavioral characteristics can in many cases be an accurate assessment. But for one-in-three to one-in-four children, a shortsighted assessment can cause a delay in getting the important early help the child needs, during important windows of opportunity for developmental skills. Many parents of developmentally delayed and disabled children describe in retrospect moments where their concerns were "passed over" or ignored. And unfortunately, there are some pediatricians and family physicians who are not skilled at investigating concerns, or who truly do have a belief or an all-encompassing philosophy that children grow at their own rates, or that they should be allowed to progress without interference. Some doctors believe that many developmental problems or learning difficulties should not be, or cannot be assessed until a child enters elementary school. A doctor's "wait and see" attitude can unfortunately have detrimental consequences for a child who truly does need some special help.

This is why it is so important to express your concerns clearly, and in a knowledgeable way. Pediatricians and family physicians take notice when a parent expresses a concern using words that show some knowledge of the subject of development. When parents tell a doctor exactly what they are seeing, and they give the doctor important information about how long their child's behavior has been occurring, as well as their observations about their child alongside same-age peers (it *is* okay to compare your child), doctors will frequently make a much more careful and focused assessment of the situation. They may possibly even ask the parents to make a special appointment where the issue could be investigated even further. If needed, pediatricians and family physicians can conduct a **developmental screening** of your child to get a general picture of where your child is with his developmental milestones. It is truly helpful to doctors when parents make a concerted effort to paint a detailed picture of their concern. As parents, this extra effort will get your child the attention and help she needs and deserves.

Many parents also mention that they wish they had felt more comfortable about standing up to certain doctors' opinions. Many of us recognize doctors as authorities, and challenging their opinions, even when it pertains to our children, can seem inappropriate and even frightening. If you do not agree with your doctor's assessment of your child or feel your doctor is not "seeing" the behaviors or characteristics of concern, seriously consider getting a second opinion.

If your pediatrician sees reason for concern, he or she may also recommend that you see a specialist or make an appointment with a child development clinic. Many will recommend that you call your local school system.

Getting Your Child Evaluated

Children are evaluated for several different reasons. Parents frequently want accurate information and answers as to why their child is developing differently or displaying concerning behaviors. Parents also want to know whether their child's symptoms indicate a particular disorder, and what that might mean for their child's future. Parents need to know whether their child will be eligible for services, and if found eligible, what the services might be. By having their child evaluated, parents will learn a lot about their child's strengths, weaknesses, and how their child learns best.

When a child is born with a known or obvious disability, special therapeutic help is accessible from the moment the child takes his first breath. When atypical behaviors and symptoms lead parents to suspect that something might be wrong, help is accessible for that child if testing reveals that there is a developmental problem in one or more areas.

To have your child evaluated for developmental concerns, you can call:

- Your local school system.

- A child development clinic at a hospital center or major university.

- A private child professional who evaluates children.

Your local school system will evaluate your child at no cost to you. Your child does not have to be school-age, and you do not have to already have a child attending school. You only need to live within the public school district.

Your pediatrician may also give you a referral for an evaluation at a development clinic, or recommend an evaluation with a particular child professional or specialist. You, of course, are welcome to call development clinics and private child professionals on your own. Your insurance may cover a portion of the cost of these evaluations.

THE INDIVIDUALS WITH DISABILITIES EDUCATION ACT

A law called the Individuals with Disabilities Education Act (IDEA) gives children with delays and disabilities the right to get help from the moment they are identified as having a delay or disability. Because this law protects all children in our country, the evaluations, when given through a public domain or state service (and at times a private service, when hired by the state or county), are free. Services are also frequently free. This law helps and protects children who have special needs regardless of their family's financial situation. Through each state's programs, children who qualify can receive early intervention if they are younger than six, or special education and related services. Each state sets up its own policies and procedures, but most avenues to early intervention and specialized programming are similar.

Will Your Child Qualify for Special Help and Services? The Evaluation Process

The evaluation process begins with a letter or phone call. You can write to or directly call your doctor or local school system, or you can call a nearby child development clinic or private specialist.

The evaluation begins with an initial meeting. At this meeting, you present your concerns to a team of child professionals. The child professionals and therapists frequently take notes at this meeting and ask questions that only you can answer. This meeting, which occurs before any actual evaluating of your child takes place, is a wonderful opportunity for you to get to see the different faces and personalities that your child may possibly work with during testing sessions and therapy. Here, you can express concerns about testing; for instance, many parents feel their child will not separate from them easily. Child professionals and therapists frequently invite parents to be present during testing when this is the case.

YOUR LOCAL SCHOOL SYSTEM

If parents call or are referred to their local school systems, a coordinator from that school system will start the process for you. Call your local elementary school's principal or vice principal and find out the name of the person you should speak to or write to if you feel your child may have special needs that should be evaluated. If your child is an infant or toddler, he will be assessed to see if he qualifies for early intervention. If your child is a preschooler or older, he will be assessed to see if he qualifies for special education services, or possibly a 504 plan, which allows children to use modifications and adaptations in their regular school classes. (We will discuss what these options entail later in this chapter.) Some states will assess children for certain therapies, such as speech therapy or occupational therapy, and provide services to them even if they do not qualify for special education. Some states will allow children who are entered into special education to access special therapies if they are age three or older.

Your school system coordinator will schedule the initial meeting. In a public school setting, all attendees at the meeting are considered to be members of a "team." All must decide together, based on the information gathered, through testing, observation, and developmental history knowledge, whether the child has clear symptoms of a delay or disability. This team of adults is frequently called a multidisciplinary team. As a parent you are an important team member. You know your child best. The child professionals on the team have expertise in their fields and experience helping children in situations that may be similar to your child's. Sometimes child professionals have differing opinions; this is one reason a multidisciplinary team is necessary.

So who are these professionals that make up most multidisciplinary teams? Your multidisciplinary team may include:

- a pediatrician, medical doctor, or specialist (more commonly in early intervention)

- a psychiatrist

- a psychologist

- a special education teacher

- a preschool teacher, teacher, or caregiver

- a physical therapist

- an occupational therapist

- an audiologist

- a speech therapist

- a social worker

- a teacher of the visually or hearing impaired

- a coordinator

On average, most teams have five or six members, and on average, three child professionals or therapists may evaluate or test your child.

As a parent, you must sign a form that will give the child professionals permission to evaluate your child. Nothing will be done without your permission. Usually this form will list the different professionals and disciplines that will make up your child's complete evaluation. After this initial meeting, the different child professionals and therapists will call parents to schedule the testing sessions with your child.

THE CHILD DEVELOPMENT CLINIC

Child development clinics, especially when attached to major university or hospital centers, are top-notch places to go when you would like to have your child evaluated for developmental and behavioral difficulties. The staff at these clinics or child study centers have a lot of training and experience with testing children. But choosing to have your child evaluated at a well-known clinic may present some problems of its own. Clinics can be pricey, and insurance may only cover certain portions of the evaluation, if any at all. They may also have long wait lists. Parents must decide whether they are willing to wait to have their child evaluated. If you feel a certain child development clinic or child study center will give you a better picture of your child, then by all means put your child on the waiting list and have your child evaluated in turn. But don't wait many months or years for that initial assessment. In the meantime, have your school district or someone else assess your child's current functioning so that you do not waste precious time.

THE PRIVATE EVALUATOR

Many parents like to bring their child to private evaluators. This option may be costly as well, although many parents feel that they were able to pick someone that they feel comfortable with, and comfortable receiving advice from. When having your child evaluated at child development clinics or in your local school district, you do not get to pick the evaluation professionals. Many parents also appreciate the extra time private professionals put in. Many private child evaluators will observe the child in the home or at school. Many try to get to know "the whole child," and not only give recommendations for the child's education, but also give recommendations for what can be done at home. Child development clinics usually see children for just two or three days. Clinics and child study centers usually do not observe your child before an evaluation, or see your child in your home or at school. In situations where there are disagreements between parents and schools about how to best help a child, lawyers will, at times, recommend that parents have a private evaluation for their child, so that an expert separate from the school's experts can be put on the stand in a courtlike hearing.

If you would like to contact a child development clinic or private evaluator, do the following:

- Contact your pediatrician and ask for a referral.

- Call a private special education school in your area for a referral.

- Contact special-needs organizations and ask for referrals.

- Ask parents in your area for any recommendations or knowledge they may have about where children can be evaluated.

- Look in your local phone book under "Psychologists" for listings of those who work with and may evaluate children, and give them a call. You also may want to look under "Educational consultants."

WHAT HAPPENS DURING TESTING?

I always get a lot of questions about testing, and what kinds of things happen during testing. Many parents are concerned about their child's comfort, and even whether their children might somehow experience pain. The truth is, most children actually *enjoy* being evaluated. Most child professionals and therapists who evaluate and assess children are quite kind and engaging. And they truly try to make the testing process fun for the kids. Much of the testing will feel like play and special games. There are even toys that children get to explore and play with as part of the process. Children will at times become frustrated if they are unable to perform a certain skill, but the professionals who are evaluating will do their best to encourage the children. In a frustrating moment, an evaluator might suggest that a child try another activity instead.

Assessments Your Child Might Have

- Medical Testing

Doctors and medical staff at developmental clinics may compile a detailed developmental history, as well as a comprehensive family history of your child. They may give your child a complete physical examination. Some children will have a *neurological exam*, which may include genetic testing, MRI's, CT scans, or EEG's. Genetic testing usually involves a blood test that shows whether a child has a specific genetic syndrome or disorder. MRI's and CT scans are used to get a picture of the child's physical brain. EEG's show the electrical activity of a child's brain and are used to check for any seizure activity. Children frequently nap through an EEG test.

- A Psychological Evaluation

Psychologists administer several different types of tests that give valuable information about a child's learning style. An IQ test is usually included in a psychological evaluation. Not all "psych evals" are the same, though. The psychologist's opinion and judgment will affect the number of tests your child receives and the comprehensiveness of the psychological evaluation.

- Behavioral Observations

Behavioral observations are noted observations of your child in typical daily settings. Behavioral observations give clues to the "whys" behind atypical behaviors. Observers can record what took place directly before a behavior and how the behavior was handled. Behavioral observations help to make sense of your child's actions.

- Behavioral Rating Scales

Behavioral rating scales assess a child's ability to attend, level of activity, impulsivity, and behavioral choices. They are usually filled out by two or more adults who spend time with the child on a daily or frequent basis. We most often hear of their usage when trying to discern whether a child may or may not have ADHD. There are also ratings scales for autistic-like behavior.

- A Speech and Language Evaluation

Speech and language evaluations assess how a child communicates, and whether the child understands what is said to her. They assess a child's processing of language, language production, the child's ability to produce sounds, and the way she uses her mouth and surrounding areas. A child's knowledge of certain concepts, ability to follow directions, and memory are also assessed.

- An Educational Evaluation

The educational evaluation will assess your child's cognitive, pre-academic, and academic skills. Parents and team members will discover the child's learning approach and style, his ability to problem solve, and his performance level as compared to same-age peers. Educational evaluations frequently include an assessment of the child's ability to perform *activities of daily living* (ADLs), which are tasks such as dressing, independently using the toilet, and using tools such as forks, spoons, toothbrushes, and combs.

- Gross and Fine Motor Assessments

Gross and fine motor assessments give a detailed picture of a child's overall motor performance and strength. Since many motor skills develop in a predictable pattern, motor testing gives information as to whether a child is behind in reaching motor milestones. Fine motor testing is very valuable because a child needs adequate fine motor ability to be able to perform everyday, typical pre-academic and academic tasks. Motor testing also helps to give a picture of the child's tone and stamina.

- Sensory Integration and Sensory Processing Checklists

When sensory issues are suspected, some child professionals ask parents to fill out sensory integration or sensory processing checklists. These checklists help define the sensory discomforts and atypical sensory habits a child may have, and whether the child is overregistering or underregistering sensory stimuli.

A child who is being evaluated may see a professional or therapist between two and four times, each session lasting a half hour to an hour and a half. The whole process may take a few weeks or a couple months, depending on how elaborate the testing must be. The coordinator, usually by phone, lets you know when the results are in.

When the Results Are In

When the results are in, you will be notified, and a meeting will be scheduled so that all of the results of the testing can be shared. Remember, you, as a parent, are considered to be a team member. Let your team members know whether what you are hearing makes sense to you. Sometimes professionals use lingo and words that you may not be familiar with. Kindly speak up in these cases. Most child professionals simply forget that most adults are not exposed to the same words and terms that they use daily. Most are happy to explain things further. Many parents find that they learn a lot at these meetings. They learn about ways their child learns best, and weaknesses may become more defined and clearer than before the evaluations.

Each child professional and therapist who evaluated your child will get a chance to "report out" to the team their results, findings, and recommendations. Here are some examples of the types of skills multidisciplinary team members, or private child professionals and therapists, may report out on:

- The pediatrician may report out relevant developmental screening results, assessment results, or any health information that may be important to know.

- The psychiatrist may report out results from neuropsychological testing and observations. Information about a child's history on medications may also be reported out to the team.

- The psychologist may report out results from observations and IQ testing results. Many psychologists perform and report out on ADHD checklists, as well as screening tools for other various disorders.

- The special education teacher may report out the results of cognitive testing or educational testing in specific academic subject areas. The special education teacher may also report out on observations, as well as strategies and interventions that have helped the child.

- The physical therapist may report out the results of gross motor testing, as well as observations of the child's use of his gross motor skills.

- The occupational therapist may report out the results of fine motor testing, visual-motor testing, and possibly sensory integration or sensory processing checklists, as well as observations of the child's use of his fine motor skills.

- The audiologist may report out the results of the child's hearing tests, as well as observations of the child's use of her hearing.

- The speech therapist may report out results of speech tests and tests that evaluate a child's use of language, and how she uses language.

- The social worker may report out notes from meetings and observations, and may report out any information observed or learned about the child or child's situation that may affect the evaluation process.

When my son's results were reported, I learned of some cognitive and language strengths I had no idea he had. There were concerns about my son, and some weak test results, but I had already been concerned about these particular areas, so testing weakly in those areas came as no surprise.

But for some parents, actually hearing that their child is not performing nearly as well as same-age peers in several areas is devastating. Somehow, seeing test results makes the concerns suddenly seem more real, and the emotions can be potent. Strong feelings and reactions can sometimes sneak up on you, even when you vowed you would remain calm and in control. Again, most child professionals will be supportive if you become emotional. You will find that many child professionals and therapists have lived the experience from your side of the table, as a parent or other family member. And the test results are truly to be used as a tool to decide how to proceed from this point on. It is up to the entire team, which includes you, to decide how it will be best to proceed. Possibly, the team will report your child is not far from target and may need just a little extra focused work at home. Whichever direction your situation seems to point toward, it is the team's decision, not just the decision of one professional or the coordinator of the meeting. If you ever feel overwhelmed, as if you are too much in "shell shock" to participate in the decision of how to proceed, just let the other members of the team know. Take the test results home and look over them when you feel more calm. Another meeting can be scheduled if needed.

Most parents are thankful for the new wealth of information about their child, and when children do qualify for services, many parents are eager to start right away.

Labeling a Child

To begin special services, a child must be diagnosed or "labeled" as having a developmental delay or disability. Your child may be diagnosed by a medical doctor, but when she qualifies for early intervention services, she is usually labeled as "developmentally delayed." This is done in part to protect a child's right and ability to "grow out of" her difficulties and early diagnosis. As a child enters elementary school or turns six (in some states, eight) years old, and is still in need of services, she is no longer allowed to carry the label of "developmentally delayed" and must be labeled with a more specific disability. This means that a child will be officially labeled as having a disability.

Doctors diagnose a multitude of medical and genetic syndromes, as well as various learning disorders and psychological disorders. But when a child is evaluated by a school system, the resulting label a child receives is usually one of a set of federally approved labels. For instance, a child may be labeled as having:

- autism

- specific learning disability

- deafness

- hearing impairment

- speech or language impairment

- mental retardation

- deaf-blindness

- emotional disturbance

- multiple disabilities

- severe disability

- visual impairment

- orthopedic impairment

- other health impairment

- traumatic brain injury

Some parents view diagnosing or labeling their child as an expected and welcome step to getting help and services. Others find this process a bitter pill to swallow. Remember, having a label does not take away the normal and typical qualities in your child, nor does it mean you should give up your hopes and dreams. In certain cases, though, we do realize we must adjust the dreams we had for our kids. I, personally, see a label as a tool to get the help needed to bring weak areas of performance up into "normal" or "typical" range. But I am aware of the stigmas and attitudes toward certain labels, so I, like many other child professionals, understand the difficulties and hesitancies that surface when labeling a child.

Some parents pay little attention to their child's "label" and truly focus on their child's progress, and self-esteem. Others find that the label their child carries actually affects how they themselves view their child, and many parents are concerned about how others will view their child, if the label were to become known.

For this reason, there has been a movement to just call children "different" or "quirky," so that children's differences would not have to be highlighted. Regardless, label or no label, adults and children notice differences. As children with special needs enter school, they usually gain an awareness of their own differences and become aware of their difficulties. This is why many children find having a label or diagnosis a relief. When children know that they have a special need or a disability that makes something extra difficult for them in comparison to most kids, they have a reason, an explanation for their hardship. They tend not to blame themselves and wonder "what is wrong with them" anymore.

An Early Help Checklist

Check one of the following:

_____ I have concerns about my child's development, so I have made an appointment with his pediatrician.

_____ I have concerns about my child's development, so I have called my school district or local elementary school to find out the name of the person I should talk to about my concerns.

_____ I have concerns about my child's development, so I have called a local child development clinic, or an independent child evaluator.

Check off all of the following as each is completed:

_____ I have requested in writing or over the phone (which may require a follow-up letter in writing) that my child be evaluated. My letter or explanation included the areas of her development that concern me.

_____ I have met with the child professionals who will be evaluating my child. I have the names and phone numbers of each one.

_____ I have written down or noted in some way, some goals that I would love for my child to achieve in the course of about a year. These goals would help him, and probably help our whole family.

_____ I am seeking out extra support and knowledge by asking child professionals if they know of parent groups in my area, or by asking friends for their support and knowledge about developmental issues. I will speak to other parents who have experienced similar issues with their children.

_____ I will not forget to take care of myself, or lose touch with the other members of my family. My child is one member of a family whose members each have different and unique needs.

Reaching out to child professionals and getting your child an evaluation is a huge step toward finding the right, specialized treatment that will help your distinctly individual child progress.

NINE

Getting the Right Treatment

"When my daughter was labeled and put into a special class, I felt like I had just done something horrible to her by making her 'a special ed. child.' Now, I've seen the progress she's made and how much it helps her and our family. I would say I'm now a fan of special education and very thankful that help like this exists."

After evaluation results have been reported, some parents go home relieved and elated that their child's overall performance was within normal range. Other parents will experience the at-times uncomfortable process of their child being labeled with a developmental delay or disability. Parents do fear stigma and wonder "why them?" and "why their child?" But often, mixed with the discomfort is a rapidly growing sense of relief. Parents know that having their child labeled is a first step toward getting help.

Once a child is labeled, discussions usually begin for a plan of action that will help to address and remediate the child's weaknesses. Discussing possibilities for treatment with child professionals and therapists can be both motivating and uplifting. Your child's age and disability will affect the type of help and "plan of action" she will receive. There are a few different types of plans, and in this chapter you will be introduced to them, as well as learn about what child professionals and therapists do to help children progress, during treatment and therapy.

Programs and Plans

EARLY INTERVENTION
AND THE INDIVIDUALIZED FAMILY SERVICE PLAN (IFSP)

Early intervention is specialized help for your baby, toddler, or young child. This help usually begins very soon after your child receives a diagnosis and may even begin soon after your child's birth. Professionals called **infant and family specialists** will work with your child to stimulate developmental growth and help him to become a full, participating member of his family.

Infant and family specialists are trained in child development and the typical progression of developmental milestones. Some specialists oversee a team of child professionals that are working to remediate your child. Each member of an early intervention team takes on a specific role and function to help your child progress, from the time of his birth up until he is about three years old.

Visits to your home are often a part of early intervention services. Home visits, though welcomed by many, can cause some parents to feel anxiety or embarrassment. If you feel yourself hesitating or feeling uneasy about scheduling regular home visits, take heart. Your job as a parent does not include having a perfect home, perfect family members, or brand-new, state-of-the-art baby items or clothing. Your job is to help your child be the best she can be. Help your child take advantage of all the possibilities and help that are available for her. You will feel good knowing that you are helping your child to progress and succeed. Parent involvement, and a willingness to receive help, are considered to be critical factors for the success of early intervention.

During home visits, your child learns how to participate and understand his own environment, including the people in his environment. And the people in your child's environment need to learn how to best communicate with and support your child. By getting to know a child's family and community, which may include a child's day-care environment, infant and family specialists can help parents formulate goals for their child that would not only help their child, but the child's entire family. They can help parents to make decisions about their priorities for their child, as well as decisions about the ways early intervention services may work best in their particular and individual family situation. Specialists help to introduce families to other sources of support such as support groups, parenting groups, or to other area parents who have experienced similar events with their children. Infant and family specialists can teach parents ways to stimulate development in their child by modeling games and activities, and by suggesting (or allowing parents to borrow) certain toys, apparatus, or equipment that may be helpful for the child.

Infant and family specialists can advocate for the entire family and help to make sure that the needs of the entire family are considered, in addition to the specific needs of the child. This will be helpful when the Individual Family Services Plan (IFSP) is written up at a meeting of the multidisciplinary team.

The Individual Family Services Plan (IFSP)

An IFSP is written up for every child entered into early intervention. It is a unique plan for treatment, in that there is a focus on delivering treatment and services in a child's "natural environment" or community. The plan is also considered to be "family centered" or "family oriented." Knowing the daily routines and priorities of a family is an important key to making an IFSP plan its most effective.

The IFSP plan is written up at a planning meeting of the multidisciplinary team assigned to your child. Remember, you are an important member of the team and know your child better than any other at the meeting table. There are ways you can prepare for this IFSP planning meeting so that you will be comfortable taking an active role, and speaking up on behalf of your child and your family. Try to do the following before you attend the planning meeting:

- Speak candidly with your infant and family specialist about what will be taking place at the planning meeting or the format of the planning meeting.

- Try to find and speak with other parents in your area who have attended early intervention planning meetings and ask them if they have any advice or whether they would do anything differently knowing what they know now.

- Do some research on your child's disability, online or at a nearby library.

- Write down questions you may have and plan to bring them to the meeting.

- Plan ahead and let your infant and family specialist know if you might need transportation to the meeting or an interpreter at the meeting.

- Write down goals that you and your family members believe will be important for your child and your family.

Specific goals and objectives are listed in an IFSP plan as well as how progress will be measured over time. Each child professional who will be working directly with your child will list goals and objectives. These goals and objectives will give you an idea of the skills your child will be working on during treatment or therapy. An IFSP will also include:

- A description of your child's current developmental level.

- A description of your family's resources and skill priorities.

- Information about expected outcomes and how progress will be measured.

- A clear list of the interventions and services that will be provided, who the service providers will be, and in what settings the services will be provided in.

- Clear information about how often each service will be provided, and the length of time each service session will be.

- The name of the professional who will be your child's service coordinator.

Remember, no matter what type of developmental delay or disability your child may have, your child will be growing, developing, and changing over time. Your child's IFSP plan will need to be adjusted frequently to accommodate your child's changing needs. Some families find themselves revising their IFSP plan after three months, while others may revise their plan after six months.

SPECIAL EDUCATION
AND THE INDIVIDUALIZED EDUCATION PLAN (IEP)

If your child is age three or above and newly diagnosed as having a developmental delay or disability, you may be given the opportunity to enter your child into special education. Special education is a little bit different than early intervention. To receive special education and special services, at no cost to you from your public school district, your child's disability must impact his ability to learn or access learning in a typical educational environment. Not all children with disabilities participate in or need special education. An example of this would be a child with a hearing impairment whose hearing is acute enough, with the use of hearing aids, to perform well in regular education. Another example would be a child who lost a limb in an accident, but who sufficiently uses a prosthetic limb. Some children with disabilities do not need specialized instruction and do not need to be removed from typical classes for learning or therapy.

If you and your multidisciplinary team decide that specialized instruction and/or therapy is needed for your child, then together your team will begin to formulate an individualized educational plan, called an IEP.

An IEP has many similarities to an IFSP, although there are some distinct differences. An IFSP is a family-based plan, while an IEP is a purely child-based plan. Home visits are much more rare when a child enters special education, for service usually takes place within schools and programs for special-needs children. School districts use information from their own professional testing or testing from clinical or private sources to formulate goals and objectives for your child. Here, parents are, again, important members of the team. To help you communicate your thoughts about possible goals and objectives for your child, it will be helpful for you to do the following before your child's IEP planning meeting:

- Make sure you have a copy of your child's evaluation results, and read the evaluation in its entirety. If possible, use a highlighting pen to mark areas that strike you, or sections you have questions about.

- Separate from the evaluation, think about the types of difficulties your child has daily and how they may play out in a class or school setting. Do you think your child will have difficulty making friends or working among other children? Do you think your child will have difficulty indicating when she might need to use the bathroom? Will she have difficulty feeding herself at snack time? Jot down your thoughts, so you can inform the team about some important skills your child may need to learn or work on.

- Seek out friends, family, or other parents who have knowledge of or experience with special education and IEP meetings. The more you learn about the process, the less anxious you will be.

- Invest in a notebook or sturdy folder, and mark it as your child's "special education information." In this notebook, you can keep any information given to you, and your own personal notes. You will be receiving material and jotting notes frequently. Keep it all in one place.

- Think about whom you may want at your child's IEP meeting in addition to the multidisciplinary team members. Some parents like to bring a doctor, private therapist, or caregiver whose opinions may be an asset for all involved in the IEP process.

- Let a member of the multidisciplinary team know if you may need transportation or an interpreter.

While at your child's IEP meeting, you may experience many different feelings, from exhilaration to discomfort. If the professionals propose working on skills you hadn't really thought of as priorities, this would be the perfect time for you to begin to advocate for your child. You really are an expert on your child, so it is important that you speak up on behalf of your child and express your thoughts. Speaking up and being an advocate is new and uncomfortable for many parents. You will realize that special education will not only be a learning and growing experience for your child, but a learning and growing experience for you.

An IEP includes many different sections:

The Present Level of Educational Performance

The present level of educational performance is a description of your child's current levels of functioning. The purpose of this description is to paint a picture of your child's abilities and difficulties at that date in time.

Goals and Objectives

Each child professional or therapist who will be working with your child will write specific goals and objectives that should help to remediate your child's difficulties. Clear statements as to how progress will be measured are written directly on the IEP.

Information on the Use of Assistive Technology

Assistive technology is the use of special tools that are not typically used by regular education students. Your multidisciplinary team must consider and note on your child's IEP whether your child will require assistive technology tools or devices.

Information on Extended School Year

If the severity of your child's disability, or the tendency to regress affects your child's ability to retain skills during the summer vacation, your multidisciplinary team must consider and note on the IEP whether your child qualifies for free summer services.

Details about Service

Details about your child's service must be noted on the IEP, including how long and how often service will be provided, and by whom, in what setting service will take place, and the dates service will begin and end.

Modifications and Adaptations

If your child will be included for most of, or a portion of his day, with typical peers, modifications and adaptations may be listed on your child's IEP. Modifications and adaptations are special things that can be done in a regular classroom setting to help learning be more accessible and more comfortable for your child. These might include shortened assignments, special seating, or extra time on tests.

An IEP also includes the name of who will be the coordinator, supervisor, or monitor of your child's special education program. You may, at any time, call a meeting to review your child's progress and IEP. The multidisciplinary team must meet and write a new IEP for your child each year.

HEALTH AND PHYSICAL DISABILITIES AND THE 504 PLAN

Some children have health conditions and disabilities that affect their everyday functions to such an extent that special accommodations must be put in place to help them succeed in their educational settings. This is accomplished through a 504 plan.

The 504 plan gets its name from the provisions under section 504 in the Rehabilitation Act of 1973. The 504 plan is not a special education plan. It is a plan to help assist children with health conditions or disabilities who receive their educations in regular education classrooms. Yet, like early intervention and special education, a child must qualify for a 504 plan. A child must be found to have a condition or disability that restricts at least one major life activity.

There is often confusion regarding what is a major life activity and what is not, for there is no distinct or complete list of all of life's major functions. Such a list would be almost impossible to complete. Child professionals find that they must consider each 504 case independently. Here are a few examples of what may be considered "major life activities":

- being ambulatory or walking

- breathing

- hearing

- seeing

- caring for oneself

- learning

- communicating

- eating

- maintaining stability of physical or mental health

Children with medical conditions or genetic syndromes may be intellectually intact and not need special instruction or special education, though they may indeed need a 504 plan for special accommodations to assist them in "regular ed" settings. Some children with conditions such as diabetes or hypoglycemia may need to leave class for a snack, medication, or a blood sugar check. Children with physical abnormalities or disabilities may need to leave class early to start walking to their next class, or they may need to leave school a couple minutes earlier than others to board a special bus or to avoid the difficulty of navigating among a crowd. Children with ADHD or asthma may need to leave class at certain times for medication or a break if symptoms disrupt their learning.

These important "allowances" that must be part of many kids' days are called *accommodations*. Some schools do all they can to accommodate students even without a formal plan. But a 504 plan can be a very important plan to have, in that, legally, the school must make sure that the accommodations listed are implemented. In other words, no matter whether the administrators or teachers change, or whether your child changes public schools, the accommodations listed on your child's 504 plan must be in place, must be known, and must be implemented.

A 504 plan is put into place in a very similar way to how an IEP is put into place. A child is usually brought to the attention of an administrator or professional in the child's school as being in need of special accommodations. Often, a parent, teacher, school psychologist, or physician refers a child for a 504. An initial meeting is then scheduled to review whether assessments will be needed or whether documentation of the child's condition or disability (that restricts one or more major life activity) is sufficient. Having a medical diagnosis does not automatically qualify a child for a 504 plan. Team members at the meeting must show that there is a record of the child's condition or disability, and that the child had been "known" and "considered" to have the condition or disability before being referred for a 504 plan. A 504 plan can be reviewed and revised at any time upon request, and is commonly relooked at every year.

Now that you are aware of the different plans of action that may help your child get on her way to a successful home and school life, let's take a look at what therapy and treatment may be like for your child.

A Look Inside Therapy and Treatment for Children with Developmental Delays and Disorders

When the meetings are over and the plans are in place, therapy and treatment begin with high expectations and a focused resolution that progress will be made. Your child will be entering a world of hard work, fun, and new experiences that she may wholeheartedly embrace or initially reject. Your support and encouragement will be important for your child, and your attitude toward the therapy and treatment will be your child's model as to how he should feel about it all. For this reason, you should take a minute or two and examine your own feelings about your child's need for special services, and your disposition when speaking about it and dealing with it, especially in front of your child. Many parents are not even sure what to think about special services because they don't really know what happens in a special class or therapy session. To increase your knowledge of treatment and therapy, let's take a look inside the different types of therapy sessions and classes that children attend and participate in.

INSIDE A SPEECH AND LANGUAGE THERAPY SESSION

Speech and language therapy may be provided by your public schools or by a private provider. In public schools, to receive speech and language therapy, a child's deficits must negatively impact the child's ability to understand, respond, learn, or relate to peers. Speech and language therapy is not the same for every child. Treatment is planned and individualized for each child's unique difficulties and level of severity.

Derek was evaluated when he was four and was found to have a speech and language delay. He started to go to speech and language therapy twice a week at the local elementary school. Because of his developmental delay, we got our district to send over a SEIT (a Special Education Itinerant Teacher) twice a week to assist his preschool teacher. He was considered to be "included" and in a "least restrictive environment" and the speech therapist would visit him at his preschool every other week.

Derek always goes willingly into the speech office, and upon entering the room, the therapist gives him a couple directions to follow (he has to remember a sequence of two directions). She says something like, "Derek, get me the red paper on the table, and get me the blue crayon from the crayon box." Next, the therapist and Derek sit together at a table, and she tells him a short story. The therapist shows Derek pictures that go with the story, and he has to put the pictures in order: what happened first, next, and last. After this, Derek tries to answer questions about the use of several household objects. The therapist asks, "What do we use a stove for?" or "What do we use soap for?" and Derek must, using his words, tell what the objects are used for. Derek knows most of these, but when he answers, his wording is a little off, so the therapist models for him the correct way, and he repeats it. He used to motion a lot with his hands and try to act out his answers. Now, Derek uses his words much more to communicate.

Derek also works on language concepts. These are words like in, out, on, in front of, behind, high, low, fast, and slow. Derek has to show the therapist that he understands these words. They also work on *wh* questions. *Wh* questions are questions that begin with the words: *where, when, who,* and *why. Why* questions are the hardest and are still hard for Derek to answer.

Derek takes a "speech and language homework book" home with him after every session. This book has exercises for him to practice, at home with his mom or dad. The book also serves as a communication tool between parents and therapist.

Gemma, a five-year-old girl, goes to speech therapy for a different reason. Gemma is very hard to understand and tends to drool. An evaluation showed that she was significantly behind in her sounds. Gemma gets speech therapy twice a week during her kindergarten school day, with each speech session being thirty minutes long.

The speech therapist uses a mirror that she sets in front of Gemma at a table. The therapist then shows Gemma how to place her tongue and move her lips when trying to make sounds. The therapist uses little flavored toothettes to help Gemma lift her tongue.

To help Gemma exercise her mouth and tongue, the therapist has her blow bubbles and lick lollipops and blow into a variety of little whistles and horns to make them make sounds. They also use Cheerios in a game where Gemma has to use her tongue to move a Cheerio over her gum line from one side to the other.

The speech therapist gives Gemma "peanut butter homework," which she always enjoys. Gemma's mom puts peanut butter along Gemma's top lip, and Gemma has to use her tongue to lick it off. Gemma told the therapist just this past session that she wanted "chocolate pudding homework."

Kids practice new speech and language skills within the confines of the therapy room, and then begin to generalize them into their communications and habits with others.

INSIDE AN OCCUPATIONAL THERAPY SESSION

Occupational therapy helps children develop their trunk strength and fine motor skills. It also helps children tolerate and remediate their sensory processing issues. Children who undergo medical interventions or who are victims of accidents may need occupational therapy to help them relearn or restore motor skills and daily living skills.

Tristan, four, sees an occupational therapist twice a week. Each session is about forty minutes. His therapist usually starts a session by putting Tristan on a couple different types of swings (for vestibular stimulation). The occupational therapy room is set up like a large special gym with several different swings and mats. There are jungle gyms and ramps. Tristan gets excited, though he is very hesitant to try anything. Tristan is very sensitive to movement, so the therapist first puts him on a low hanging platform and gently swings him back and forth. Then she swings him from side to side (linear) and then in a round motion without spinning him at all (orbital).

Next, the therapist takes Tristan over to a ramp on gym mats. She has him walk up the ramp (for a lot of deep pressure into the muscles and proprioceptive system) and then run down the ramp into a pile of pillows. The therapist calls this "crash and bump." This helps Tristan get input into his muscles and his joints, which then gives his brain input. Crash-and-bump activities help him organize himself and focus better.

After working on full-body activities, the therapist has Tristan sit down with her at a table. She makes sure his sitting position and posture are all right, and then she gives Tristan a container or plastic tub filled with something to touch. Tristan, when he first started, wanted no part of this, because he would have to use his hands to find hidden treasures within the stuff in the tub. After time and much encouragement though, he got much better at tolerating, holding, and feeling different textures. One week it was a tub full of beans and another week, a tub full of rice. He's also had to find little plastic frogs hidden in shaving cream. These tactile activities help Tristan focus better. Earlier in therapy, the therapist had to use a weighted vest (for deep pressure) to calm Tristan enough so that he would be able to sit down and participate at the table. Giving Tristan this weighted feeling helped him to learn more about his body and helped him to sit and pay attention for a few minutes while at the table. In the beginning he really would not sit at all.

Tristan works on fine motor and visual motor skills at the table. The therapist has Tristan do a puzzle, or a sorting activity, or she sometimes has him do some snipping with scissors, coloring with crayons, or putting pegs into a pegboard. The therapist helps Tristan develop skills that he needs for school.

Note: Vestibular and rotational input are very important for healthy vestibular development. Spinning is also a way of getting input, but should be done only by a therapist if your child shows sensitivities to movement. Spinning a child whose system is not ready to process this level of input can cause the child to become physically sick or to display physical symptoms that may require medical assistance.

Occupational therapists can tell by a child's movement that a child is having trouble, but they are not able to tell right away what the brain is picking up. One of the ways occupational therapists gain information about a child's ability to process information about movement is through observing reflexes. When a person spins around, the vestibular system kicks in and tries to adjust and adapt to the rotational movement. If the person suddenly stops spinning, the adjustment back to a typical still and even stance is not immediate. If you look into the eyes of a person who just stopped spinning, you will see his eyes horizontally darting from side to side in a reflexive motion. This is called a *nystagmus*, and by measuring the reflexive movements after spinning, occupational therapists can determine whether a child's brain is developmentally typical in handling vestibular input. If the nystagmus is not as long as it should be, the child is probably not registering the vestibular input and may have a sensory processing problem.

Remember, spinning a child to bring forth a nystagmus should only be done by a therapist. Some children, developmentally, cannot handle rotational spinning and will have unusual and powerful reactions because their systems are underdeveloped. Some children crave spinning, and they will spin and spin without ever getting dizzy. Occupational therapists will frequently work with these children, as well as children who are underresponsive, until they display a relatively normal response.

Occupational therapists may also give children *sensory diets*. Sensory diets may include a brushing program, where parents may be asked to brush their child's skin with surgical hand brushes several times a day (this provides tactile deep pressure, which develops the child's ability to tolerate tactile stimuli and reduces tactile defensiveness), or a self-regulation program where parents may be asked to give their child heavy input or heavy work activities (that can provide proprioceptive deep pressure). Here, children may be asked to carry heavy books, or photo albums, even heavy books of wallpaper samples to help develop better proprioception and self control.

Occupational therapy in a school setting may only address what affects a child's academic performance. Traditionally, this would mean a child receiving OT would only receive help for fine motor, visual motor, or postural difficulties. More and more, though, schools are finding that sensory issues are affecting children's performances in the classroom. Many therapists do now try to implement some sensory activities with the cooperation of the child's teacher.

INSIDE A PHYSICAL THERAPY SESSION

Physical therapy helps children with all kinds of motor and mobility difficulties. The techniques that physical therapists use help children gain strength, skills, and independence.

Like occupational therapy, there are two types of physical therapy services that a young child may receive. They are medically based physical therapy and educationally based physical therapy. To receive medically based physical therapy from a private provider or clinic, a child needs a prescription from his doctor. To receive educationally based physical therapy free of cost from a child's school district, not only does a child need a prescription from his doctor, there also needs to be evidence that the child's physical difficulties adversely affect his ability to receive an education. This can cause a lot of confusion for parents, for if a pediatrician recommends physical therapy for a child, the child will not automatically get physical therapy services from his school district. For instance, if Jane has a weak thigh muscle that makes her gait awkward and noticeably atypical, she may receive physical therapy at any clinic to strengthen her muscles. But if Jane is able to get around her school independently and play on her preschool playground without a lot of difficulty, it is unlikely she will receive educational physical therapy. Educational physical therapy is a service for children who need physical therapy to access their educational environments.

Landon, who is four, has been receiving physical therapy at his full-day preschool. Landon was evaluated, and found to have delays in several areas, gross motor being one of them. Landon works on his motor weaknesses in class, and then one-on-one with the physical therapist in a different room. In class, he participates with the other kids in specially planned motor centers. The physical therapist works with a few kids at a time at the center. There may be a ball activity or a little flight of steps.

On Tuesdays and Thursdays, Landon goes to a room down the hall for physical therapy. The physical therapist begins by showing Landon picture communication cards. These help Landon understand what they will be doing together during the session. He likes knowing what will be happening beforehand. Next they usually work with balls. Landon might have to step up onto a step and throw a ball in a bin, or step up onto a step and put a sticker on a picture on the wall. When he does a good job, the physical therapist has Landon high-five her. He works on balance skills after this and has to stand on his tiptoes to reach a plush monkey or to reach a swinging spider toy. Landon also walks (with help) on a balance beam and tries to balance on one foot.

The latter part of Landon's session is usually devoted to running games, jumping games, or stair work. Recently, the therapist was having

Landon go up and down one of the regular stairways in the school. They were practicing for when the kids go to and from the playground (because they regularly go up and down that stairway).

INSIDE A COUNSELING SESSION

Counseling or psychological services for young children share few similarities to the therapy sessions that adults experience. Counseling for children involves support in learning appropriate play and socialization skills. Psychologists can help children understand right from wrong and help them learn about feelings: their own feelings as well as the feelings of others.

Graham began counseling at four years old. A psychologist became involved when Graham's preschool wanted him to leave because of behavioral problems. Graham was kicking, pushing, and biting other children. His parents asked the local system for a meeting so that Graham could receive the additional help that he needed.

Graham began to see the psychologist twice a week, once in a one-on-one session at the local elementary school and once at preschool in his classroom. The psychologist helped formulate a behavior plan to use in the classroom every day, where Graham would get to swing on the tire swing on the playground for ten minutes after twenty minutes of appropriate behavior. (The psychologist and teacher were later able to change this to ten minutes of swinging time for forty minutes of appropriate behavior.) In the beginning, during those twenty minutes when he was supposed to behave appropriately, Graham would receive a sticker on top of a cone (like putting scoops on an ice cream cone) every five minutes, and if he got four scoops, he got to go out on the tire swing. If he did not get all four scoops (stickers), he would be praised for the scoops he did get and would be encouraged to try again the next half hour. Graham really loved that swing, and he craved swinging, so this worked well for him.

The psychologist also helped Graham (the speech and language therapist got involved with this, too) to learn some appropriate phrases to use with adults and peers when he wanted something, or wanted someone to stop doing something. They also taught him phrases he could use when he needed help. Graham learned that people will help you if you let them know in "this" appropriate way, or "that" appropriate way. He needed to be taught socially appropriate behavior in one little lesson at a time.

The psychologist would also discuss emotions with Graham and would have him look at different kids' expressions to try to determine what they were feeling. Graham later had to try to determine and name what he was feeling, but he learned to communicate better, and his frustration and inappropriate behavior decreased.

Children like Graham, who display some questionable behaviors, often need specialized help to learn socially appropriate skills. With the help of a skilled psychologist, who is willing to help the child (and at times, the child's parents) implement new skills, more successful and appropriate relating is truly possible.

INSIDE AN EARLY INTERVENTION HOME VISIT

Home visits are an important part of early help for babies, toddlers, and small children. Infant and family specialists work with children in their own natural environments, respecting the children's family dynamics, cultures, and priorities.

Alexandra is a little girl, born with cerebral palsy, and her mother describes an early home visit:

"Alexandra was a little infant when a specialist came to our house to work with us. The specialist was very kind, and she asked me questions about how feeding was going and whether we were getting any sleep. I told her about the trouble I was having bathing Alexandra and how she would scream uncontrollably. The specialist said that she would devote one of her visits to helping me figure out a way to make bathing less stressful for Alexandra. That first day, the specialist showed me how to massage Alexandra, and move her slowly when picking her up and setting her down. She showed me how to use a couple rolled-up towels to support Alexandra on the changing table and in her bassinet. She gave me a lot of information about what to encourage with Alexandra, and she showed me how to put her on her stomach on a quilt on the floor for a little while. She even got down on the floor with Alexandra and tried to get Alexandra to make eye contact with her. She sang a few little songs, and then asked me to get down where she was and try to get Alexandra's attention. I started doing this every day, and I did see her get stronger in her neck. She soon could lift her head to look at me. We talked about my desire for my husband and son to feel comfortable handling Alexandra, and she scheduled some sessions when we would all be present together. We talked about some safety issues and made a plan for emergencies. I felt like she did care about us, and she was wonderful with Alexandra. She gave me a lot of ideas that I know have helped."

Knowing how to stimulate development early, no matter if your child's difficulties are subtle or severe, can make a big difference, in your child's progress, in your own confidence, and in your outlook on the future.

INSIDE A SPECIAL EDUCATION CLASS

Special education classes give children specialized instruction that begins at the level your child is at. Depending on your child's learning style, different approaches are used to use your child's strengths to help remediate areas of weakness. Special educators will work on specific goals and objectives with your child, and they will try many strategies to help your child learn. A child may join a special education class as early as three (two and a half in some states). Here is an observation of a typical day at a special education preschool:

When the children enter the room, the special education teacher, speech therapist, and aides meet the kids and encourage them to hang up their coats and put their backpacks in their cubbies. They want them to do it independently, but if they can't do it, they get a little bit of help. Then the children sit down at the tables in the room for "table toys." Table toys are different choices of toys that help to improve the children's fine motor skills. There were about twenty different choices, like beading to making pin flowers for clothes, to little race cars with tiny tracks. During this time, both the special education teacher and the speech therapist try to engage the children in conversation and they model what the children can say back to them if they are not sure how to respond.

After this, the children are called over to a rug area for circle time. The special education teacher works with the children on calendar activities, and then works with them on recognizing their names and the first letter of their names. Then she and the speech therapist switch, and the speech therapist takes over the circle, reading a book, asking questions, and having the children blow on a magic wand. They have to blow and blow to make something happen in the story. (Blowing is good for articulation.) Then both the speech therapist and special education teacher lead the children in a sequencing activity that had pictures from the story that has been read. The children have to figure out what happened at the beginning, in the middle, and then what happened at the end.

After that, the special education teacher has the children pick a center to go to by picking index cards with pictures of the different centers. She explains that everyone will get to do all of the activities in turn. One activity is a large motor climbing activity. One activity is painting on easels. One activity is a rhyme-and-sound activity with the speech therapist, and the last one is a big, bigger, biggest activity with the teacher. The kids rotate through all four activities.

During this center time, the occupational therapist comes in to work with two of the children, and the physical therapist comes in to take one of the children with her to work in a therapy room.

Next, the class has to wash their hands and sit down for snack. The children have to pass out napkins, cups, and even serve crackers and juice. They have these little pitchers that the children have to pour from. All of the adults walk around and speak with the children during this time. They also encourage the childen to socialize with the children sitting next to them. As the children finish, they are encouraged to use the toilet if needed or sit quietly looking at a book on the rug for a few minutes.

Then, the children have to put jackets on themselves, but the special education teacher, speech therapist, or aides help if they are really not able to do it, and they go outside to the playground. On the playground, the physical therapist takes a little group of two kids with her to the slide ladder.

After going back inside, the children are allowed to play in the "play areas" of the room, like the block area, and the house area, or they can use crayons or markers at the table. When the classroom playtime is over, the children go to the rug for a good-bye circle and say good-bye to all of the teachers and classmates.

Some children progress so rapidly in preschool programs like this one, they end up attending regular kindergarten. Some children end up attending regular kindergarten but continue receiving additional therapy. And some children move on to special education kindergarten.

INSIDE A REGULAR EDUCATION CLASS AS AN "INCLUDED STUDENT"

More and more frequently, children with delays and disabilities are being included into regular classrooms, like Joel.

Joel is in kindergarten, and he is autistic. He is in a fully inclusive classroom situation and has a full-time aide to help him with his work and daily routines. When Joel arrives at school, his aide meets him at the door with his "morning list," which is a list of Joel's morning tasks. Some of the tasks are:

Walk nicely and quietly down the hall to your room.

Say, "Good morning" to Miss Haydon.

Put your backpack and jacket in your cubby.

Sit down in your chair.

Joel does read relatively well, but they still have a Polaroid of Joel performing each task next to the sentence, which is a helpful reminder to
him. (They have lists like this for him for tasks and classes throughout
the day.)

Joel makes noises at times or flaps his hands (which actually makes
noise when he does it) and the school's special education teacher, who
monitors Joel's progress, found that simply cueing him with a card (one
of several cards) that says to quiet himself, with a "Shhh" picture, does
the trick. Joel can take a couple breaks a day in a corner of the classroom
where he can pace or flap for a few minutes and then rejoin the class
activity.

Joel does the regular work in the classroom. He's a very smart boy.
But his aide is needed for fine motor tasks. Sometimes the occupational
therapist will be in the classroom assisting him, or sometimes the aide
will assist him by having a project already cut and ready for him. He
does not like to be touched, so hand-over-hand help does not work well
with Joel.

The kindergarten teacher and special education teacher set Joel up
with two "buddies" who help Joel out at lunch and during recess. This
helps him learn to be with children (they are great role models) in typical
situations. Joel sits between these two children at lunch, and they try to involve Joel as best they can at recess.

Before the class changes activities, Joel is always shown his "day calendar" that shows him what he will be doing that day from start to finish.
Somehow having this in writing, and seeing this, helps Joel remain calm
through the day. He is always told beforehand when something different
will be taking place, or if there is a change in schedule. "Sameness" makes
Joel comfortable, while any surprises can make him very agitated.

For homework, Joel is given three copies. This is because Joel can
be messy with his work, and he gets frustrated if he makes a mistake. He

often feels he must start again. Usually, Joel does three of the same thing, and then picks the best one to turn in.

Parents of the typical children frequently ask why Joel is not in a self-contained special education class. Joel's parents wanted him to become used to dealing among children and adults in the "real world." He is already picking up better social behaviors, and he watches and sees others even though it is difficult for him to act like everyone else. Joel's intelligence is already appreciated in the school, and many of the teachers there are excited about him and like him. For Joel, and many others, inclusion is a good choice, and a positive experience.

A Word on Inclusion

Inclusion is the practice of allowing children with disabilities to learn and play side by side with children who are not disabled, with the help of necessary supports. Some believe that an inclusive environment and *mainstreaming* are one in the same, but they are not. Inclusion involves giving a child supports that can help her to succeed. Mainstreaming is the "pushing in" of special-needs children into a regular environment for a period of time without supports. Many parents and professionals steadfastly believe that children benefit greatly from being among non-disabled peers.

I have witnessed the importance of inclusion in a child's daily program. I have seen disabled students pick up age-appropriate behaviors by being with same-age "role models." I have also seen friendships form between disabled children and non-disabled peers. Non-disabled children can be very accepting, compassionate, and helpful. Even children who may initially feel discomfort with a disabled child, or joke about a child with a "difference," often learn, grow, and become more sensitive. They often later see the disabled child as just another classmate.

Inclusion does have its critics. There are parents and teachers that find inclusive environments distracting and restricting. Some view inclusive classrooms as classrooms where special-needs children are "dumped," and where teachers are expected to handle and deal with situations that they are unqualified for and not trained to deal with. Teachers who do want to include special-needs students sometimes wonder if they will be able to handle the disabled student in addition to their "regular class." Many parents of non-disabled children wonder how the presence of a disabled child in the classroom will affect their child. They wonder whether their child's teacher will be busy with the disabled child, or whether their child's work will be constantly disturbed. They wonder if everyone's attention will be diverted to the disabled child.

Luckily, most inclusive experiences work quite smoothly. Most teachers who have an inclusive classroom view the special-needs student as just another student member of the class. Most teachers who have included a special-needs student would include again, and express that they have personally grown as a result of the experience. Inclusive classrooms can be welcoming and successful environments for all children. Here are a couple of elements that, when present, make for a positive experience:

- *Open, frequent communication* between a child professional experienced in inclusion, and the teacher who will be teaching the disabled child among non-disabled peers.

- *A positive attitude* toward the disabled child. The teacher will be the model for the non-disabled children, who will follow his or her lead when interacting with the disabled child.

Public schools are not the only environments where disabled children can be included. State or local government–run agencies and organizations must include children with disabilities in their programs and activities. Parks, libraries, and recreation departments may not discriminate against a child by denying participation in its events.

Include your child in your family activities, worship, and recreation. Soon you will know and be celebrating *your child's* individual interests, and special gifts.

TEN

Moving Forward Successfully

"It was very hard for my husband and I to listen to the scenarios our doctor saw for the future of our son. He kept telling us to not get our hopes up because our son wouldn't be able to do many things. I'd look at my beautiful son and think how valuable and how loving and deserving he already was. I told our doctor that he must gain awareness of what the gift of love and support can do for a child."

There are no magical cures or quick fixes when it comes to remediating most developmental delays and disabilities, though we wish there were. Reassuring parents that their children will catch up to peers may not be appropriate in all cases. Real improvements take real work. And it is important to *not* allow your child's weaknesses to take over your daily life, your family time, or your outlook. It is helpful for many parents to take one day at a time, and to devote just a part of each day to their child's special help and work. This is, of course, easier said than done. Parents often feel that they need to be vigilant and constantly watching over their child. It is hard for many parents to even fathom being in a different room from their child, many times for fear of safety or separation issues. But with your child's progress, with the help of child professionals and with new contacts and knowledge, you can reconfigure your days, one at a time, in a way that can suit you, and in a way you can feel good about. You can have the wonderfully fulfilling life you dreamed of, it just may be a little different from what you imagined.

How Parents Can Make a Difference

As a parent, you can truly make a difference. You can be positive and strong for your child, even when you are feeling unsure. You can give your child encouragement and love, even during times you may feel discouraged. We are all only human. We are all imperfect in different ways. And it is okay to love someone who is imperfect.

One of the keys to a successful future for all children, including children with developmental differences and disabilities, is having love, encouragement, and support from parents and family. The time spent on the phone with therapists or the time spent researching new programs is not really time spent getting to know your child. Your child has likes, dislikes, preferences, and interests. Do you know them? Overseeing your child's special help can be a time-consuming and all-encompassing job. You must be careful. It is too easy—and unfortunately, very common—to begin to distance yourself from your child as the little person who needs you, while instead focusing on your child as the one who must be "fixed," and who happens to have an open day on Tuesday and could maybe use more therapy. Remember that your child is a person with feelings and not a "project in motion" to be managed.

One key to your child's success will be your devoted attention to her feelings, value, and humanity. By doing this, you will be encouraging growth far beyond what your child will learn in a special class or series of therapy sessions. Also, let your child have time to relax and have fun. Most children like to have down time to just play. Not every minute of every day has to be structured. Not every minute of every day has to be therapeutic. You, yourself, could probably use a reprieve at times, too. It can be a hard job juggling the needs of a child who receives special help and services.

TAKE CARE OF YOU

An important key to your child's success is having parents and family members who are able to be there and be loving and encouraging. A key to your child's success will be your taking care of you.

Stress, grief, anxiousness, and doubt can take their toll, while support systems of friends, family, and other parents can be very helpful in offsetting them. Having or finding someone you can honestly confide in can do wonders for your outlook, not only by helping you to see the positives in your life, and your child's life, but also by letting you know that you are not crazy, nor a bad person for feeling stressed or overly emotional at times. A trusted friend or confidant will appreciate you for who you are. You must not forget that you are also valuable and deserving of love. Though your schedule may be a little busier than you had imagined, take time to do what you like to do. Your happiness will give you a positive outlook that will no doubt help your child and family have a positive outlook, too.

Also, try your best to remain aware of your attitudes toward your child, because your attitudes and beliefs about your child will affect your child's attitudes and beliefs about himself. When one of our children is lagging behind, we may be doing all we can for him, but we may harbor hurt and anger at having been dealt a hand we feel unprepared to handle. Many of us may feel deep love and empathy one minute, and utter frustration and rage the next. I have seen many parents feeling badly about themselves and feeling extremely guilty that they even have negative thoughts about their child. Negative thoughts are normal, as is discouragement. But when we begin to express our negativities, fears, and anxieties in ways that upset or frighten our family members, we are usually in need of extra support. Parenting is demanding, and parenting a child with special needs can be at times exhausting and overwhelming. Talk with other parents who have had experiences similar to what you are experiencing. You will learn that you are not alone in your roller coaster of emotions, nor your focused resolve to help your child.

HAVE HOPE AND EXPECTATIONS

No child will stay exactly the same as she is on the day she is diagnosed. All children will grow and develop no matter whether they have a subtle difficulty or if they have a severe disability. We often hear child professionals and parent advocates declare that parents should "raise their expectations for their child." I have attended many meetings where parents wanted goals and objectives changed for their children because they wanted harder and more age-appropriate goals and objectives. Though the parents knew their children were not even close to performing the objectives they asked for, they felt that they needed to raise their expectations for their children. The parents had been told, by someone they trusted, they should do this, and subsequently felt that increasing the difficulty of their children's goals and objectives would help their children achieve maximum progress.

You *should* have hope for progress, and expectations that you will see progress as the result of your child's hard work in classes and in therapy and hard work at home. But raising expectations for your child does not mean you should be unrealistic about your child's abilities or that you should expect your child to do something he clearly cannot do. Raising expectations involves holding onto hope and not giving up, especially when you are facing and confronting opinions of your child that are discouraging. It means not giving in to common biases about what a special-needs child can achieve. Biases and negative outlooks are limiting. Give your child chances to do things and to try things, even if others try to limit your child with their own expectations. If you can, brainstorm with your child about how he might go about attempting what he wants to attempt. Ask him if he would like assistance. Ask for the assistance of others, if necessary.

Remember, it is important to be positive and supportive with your child. An encouraging parent works wonders and can help a child achieve despite a disability. A discouraging parent works wonders, too, making a disability truly disabling.

GAIN KNOWLEDGE

Some of the anxiousness that we feel when our children are in need of specialized help stems from our own self-doubt about our ability to make the proper decisions when facing education and treatment options. We also feel stressed about our ability to discern whether the professionals who work with our children are really making a difference or not, and we wonder whether the goals and objectives proposed for our child are what they should be. You will alleviate some of this stress and anxiety as to whether you are doing the right thing for your child by *knowing your child* and *knowing your child's disability*.

You should find out as much as you can, through reading books, reading information on the Internet, finding other parents or parent groups who deal with the same or a similar disability, and by talking to doctors, teachers, and therapists. The more you know the more confident you will be. And you will see that as you learn more and reach out more, you will be forming new friendships and new relationships that will not only support your child, but will support you as well.

ENGAGE YOUR CHILD EARLY

When parents educate themselves about child development, they learn how important it is to engage their child early on, which can help stimulate healthy development. The developing brain of a child, as we have learned in this book, is extremely sensitive to stimulation and persons in the child's environment. A child's growth and development can be hugely affected as a result of early experiences. This is why early vigilance is so important. Parents who know that early stimulation and good care have a positive effect on their child's growth and development focus more wholeheartedly to give their child, whether a typical or special-needs child, the best start possible.

GET THE MOST FROM YOUR CHILD'S SPECIAL HELP

To help your child and family get the most out of your child's special help, work toward honest and clear communication with the professionals and therapists who work with your child. Many professionals are under pressure to not say certain things, and they may feel at times as if they cannot openly express their opinions due to the legal implications of what might be said. Let the professionals know that you want them to be forthcoming and honest with you, and that you don't mind if they word certain opinions in a way that will protect them legally. You want to know the complete truth about how your child is doing and progressing. You want to know if they feel the path taken is truly the correct path. Also, you should find a way to participate in an ongoing mode of communication with your child's teachers and therapists. Many of us wish to meet frequently with and speak in person with the child professionals who work with our child. Don't forget, the professionals who work with your child are also working with other children who are just as valuable to their families. Try to participate in some form of *written* communication with your child's teachers and therapists. Possibly use a little notebook as a communication book, and send it back and forth with your child. Or e-mail your teacher or therapist, so that he or she can respond to you during a free moment. Many times a teacher or therapist will welcome you for an update at the very end of a school day or therapy session.

Many therapists express that they feel it is beneficial for parents to observe therapy sessions. As a parent, you should feel free to request to observe or ask if there is a way you can participate. There are some cases in which this is hard for the child. Some children feel the need to look to their parent for approval frequently, and though in many cases a parent's presence can be encouraging, sometimes it is distracting for both therapist and child.

Remember, you must remain realistic when observing your child. It is helpful to avoid the tendency to compare your child to typical children, at least for a little while, as your child works hard to improve herself.

When you do wish to observe your child on a regular basis, try to take a moment and examine your reasons for observing. If you are trying to discern what else you can do at home to help your child work on skills, or to educate yourself more about your child's disability and how it affects your child, by all means let the therapist know.

If you are observing because you feel the therapist or teacher is not living up to an expectation you have, or if you do not feel a comfortable sense of trust for how a therapist or teacher may or may not be helping your child, it may be more beneficial to call a meeting of your child's team to discuss your issues of concern. Try not to attack the teacher's or therapist's strategies when meeting, and try to listen and weigh carefully what the team members say. If a meeting and discussion does not help with your concerns, think about finding another therapist or educational setting. The stress of wondering if the help your child is receiving is the right help or whether the help your child is receiving is working can cause a negative dynamic that can possibly trickle down to your child.

SHARE THE GOODS

Make sure information about your child is shared, and that all of the professionals who work with your child, including aides, are aware of your child's delay or disability. All of the adults who work with your child should be aware of the strategies and interventions that your child's teachers and therapists successfully use on a regular basis. When adults in your child's environment feel confident with your child and feel that they know how to work with him, they will help your child to achieve some degree of success every day. Help make sure that all adults who work with your child are aware of any interventions, modifications, or special handling needs. Ask for some help from your team of teachers and therapists if you feel there are certain professionals who are not invested in being consistent with your child.

DO YOUR HOMEWORK

In addition to finding out all you can about your child and your child's disability, you must leave some time and space to focus on the small daily tasks and homework assignments given by your child's teachers and therapists. Helping your child to practice skills at home is an important key to your child's success. The little daily practices of tasks and skills will add up over time. So when a therapist sends home an assignment, or if a therapist asks that a skill be practiced at home, honor the importance of these steps, and do the assignments regularly and diligently. If a therapist gives your child a brushing program for tactile sensitivity or another type of sensory diet to be done at home, take it seriously and keep up with the program. A therapist may give your child language exercises or a special writing program to be done at home. Do them. If a certain type of assistive grip is recommended for your child, make sure your child is using the grip at home.

Doing your homework also involves watching for progress and new problems. If you notice a problem, start keeping a log of it. Even if you see a subtle change of behavior, or a subtle regression in your child, write it down and keep a log of it. Though the change may not seem like a big deal to you, one of your child's doctors, teachers, or therapists may be able to see some type of pattern emerging that you may not notice.

Discipline Your Child

Moving forward successfully requires discipline at school and at home. Parents and teachers can at times fall into a pattern of making excuses for their special-needs children, or fall into a pattern of giving in to them when trying to avoid difficult behaviors or situations. Most of us would do all we can to help our child avoid a meltdown.

Discipline can be extremely difficult for parents of children with developmental delays or disabilities, because guidance materials and advice about disciplining children generally refer to typical children at typical ages. With typical children, certain types of issues and challenges are almost predictable. It can be very hard for parents of special-needs children to know whether their child understands directions or whether their child would even have the ability to act appropriately if and when disciplined.

Though it may be difficult and challenging, disciplining your special-needs child will be important to her success. All children, special-needs children included, need the guidance, direction, and structure that discipline provides. It will be important to model and define appropriate behavior for your child and set reasonable limits that are appropriate for his stage of development. If you need assistance in setting limits that are appropriate for your child, ask for assistance at a multidisciplinary meeting, at a parent group meeting, or ask for some guidance from a psychologist in your local school district. There are many child professionals available to you that would be happy to help you with your questions. Here are some tips to help you now:

- Give your child structure by having a predictable pattern to his day. Try to have set routines he can rely on.

- Pay an enormous amount of positive attention to the behaviors of your child you want to keep, and very little attention (if possible, no attention) to behaviors you want to extinguish (unless the behaviors are dangerous in some way).

- Allow your child to experience some natural consequences. For instance, if he throws his favorite toy car at the wall, and it breaks, do not replace it.

- Try to speak and remain calm in challenging situations, even if your stomach is in a knot. Try to model calm problem solving for your child.

- Give your child a job at home that she can do successfully. Help your child feel like a valuable member of the family.

- Be consistent with your expectations and rules, and state them frequently. Praise your child when rules are heeded and when expectations are met.

- If you are in a safe environment, try to walk away from your child's tantrums. It is hard to have a tantrum when there is no audience. If he is having a tantrum in an environment that you cannot leave, try to show calm indifference or try to calmly move him to a different environment. Save your emotional reactions for his positive behaviors.

- Try to figure out what your child is communicating with his negative behaviors. Think of a replacement behavior that may work for him, and discuss it with his team of professionals.

- If a negative behavior works for a child, and she gets what she wants through screaming, kicking, or crying, expect her to use the same behaviors again. If you decide that you will not allow her to get what she wants when she screams, kicks, or cries, expect her to try to use the negative behaviors to an even larger degree in the hope of using what worked before in the face of opposition. If over time, the behaviors just don't work anymore, and she doesn't get what she wants, she will stop using them. In the meantime, calmly suggest and model the appropriate behavior you would like instead.

- If you are concerned that your child will display inappropriate behaviors in a certain environment, plan ahead. Find a way to engage him that will be incompatible with the atypical behaviors you are concerned he may engage in. For instance, if your child makes odd flapping motions with his hands or aggressively grabs others, plan an activity that will engage his hands. Maybe he could play with dough, play ball, or maybe he could play with puppets.

- Pick your battles. And pick carefully. It is easy to confront every shortcoming we feel we see in our children, especially when we, ourselves, are feeling frustrated. Really consider whether your reaction "fits the crime" when dealing with your child. And remember, accidents do happen.

- In an effort to reduce possible battles of the wills, try at times to redirect your child. Interrupt his inappropriate behavior. Offer him an attractive alternative.

- Try to speak to your child with a positive attitude so that she will more readily cooperate with you. Even when children do not understand exactly what we are telling them, our attitudes come through loud and clear.

- Help your child to feel good about himself as often as possible.

Creative Solutions

Taking atypical patterns of behavior and changing them into more typical and functional patterns is not an easy endeavor. Many teaching and therapeutic methods are implemented universally, but many parents, teachers, and therapists find that they need to think creatively in order to make lasting differences for their kids.

REPLACING BEHAVIORS

One of the ways you or a child professional can help a child to progress is by *replacing* an inappropriate behavior with a more desirable and appropriate behavior. Here is an example of what I mean:

Dennis was five years old when I began working with him. He was for the most part nonverbal and had autistic-like qualities, but he did not fit the typical autistic profile because he had dead-on, excellent eye contact. Dennis was in kindergarten at the time, and whenever the school bell would ring, which was every forty-five minutes, he would jump from his seat and, in terror, pace the perimeter of the room while flapping his arms and screaming. When his teacher had once tried to keep him from getting up, he had kicked her. Dennis's classmates feared him, as did one of the classroom aides. Whenever the bell rang, the class was disrupted, and so many of the kindergartners began to display anxious behaviors whenever they anticipated the bell ringing.

I, and my assistant, wanted to replace this reactive behavior of Dennis's with a more functional one. So we began by putting a huge piece of paper on a wall in the room and giving Dennis his own big crayon. I told him that when the bell rang, to go over and make a mark or a line on that piece of paper, and we would count them at the end of the day. This first step allowed for his familiar movement and screams. At first when he would jump up, I would have to go and put the crayon in his hand, lead him in a way to the paper, and have him, with hand-over-hand help initially, make a line as he passed the piece of paper while pacing. At first, he would actually break the crayon while making a line on the paper, and the line was usually a jagged twelve inches long. Dennis soon learned though to take the crayon with him when he jumped up and he would, with full force, make a line on the paper. When Dennis had the hang of what we were asking of him, we replaced the huge piece of paper with paper that took up half the original space. Later we moved the paper to the wall nearest his table. We kept slowly paring down the inappropriate behavior until in the end, Dennis would carry a pad in his pocket and pull it out and make a mark, instead of jumping up and scaring those around him. This process took about four months.

As you can see, we did not force Dennis to stop reacting. We simply gave him a better alternative that he adopted over time. You may be able to help your child replace certain inappropriate behaviors or even develop a tolerance for uncomfortable situations, and this will allow her to function more appropriately.

HELP WITH TRANSITIONING

I once worked with an autistic girl named Cara. Cara had transition tantrums throughout the day, making learning difficult, and movement around the school almost impossible. Transition tantrums happen when a child is unable to handle the movement from one place to another or the changing from one task to another.

Cara would have tantrums walking from the carpet to the snack table. As soon as she would walk off the carpet, she would drop to the floor, kicking, screaming, and wailing. Walking through the doorway of the classroom into the hallway would also set off a transition tantrum, as would walking into a classroom that was not her own. (Interestingly, entering our classroom did not set off a tantrum.) Needless to say, this made the school day not only difficult for Cara, but also difficult for me, as her teacher, and difficult for her therapists as well. It was very hard, everyday, to have Cara drop to the ground and have a tantrum while walking inside from the playground. It was hard to see her traumatized several times a day. Though I was told repeatedly that her "behaviors" were probably in protest to ending an activity, to me, this did not really seem to be the case. Cara would begin to get up and follow or go, and though she did not like to stop what she was doing until she was finished, she would do it. We wanted to help Cara with her transitions, so we began by taking notes on all of the locations where the transition tantrums would occur. We also took notes on the times of day they would occur. I remember tracing Cara's steps, listening carefully, looking around, and trying to feel what the difference was, and what the adjustments would be.

The points of transition and tantrums were consistently the same. So, I began to carry Cara over her points of transition. It must have looked quite strange to all of the other adults in the school, and even strange to the students, but though she would whimper, she would not lose control and have a tantrum when I carried her. At times, I would literally carry her for about five feet across a transition point. Later, I would pick her up just before the transition point and put her down a couple feet past. And even later, I began to hold Cara tightly against my side and have her walk with me across the transition point. I remember I could always feel her tense up, even when I would hardly hear a cry or sound. I believe she could not stand how it felt for some reason. After holding her tightly, we were able to simply hold her hand tightly. Those transition points always affected her. She never did not notice she was transitioning. But Cara was finally able to, while holding tightly to my hand, or a therapist's hand, cross her transition points throughout the school in a seemingly appropriate way.

Cara's transition difficulties were extreme. Many children do experience transition difficulties in much more subtle ways, and they may demonstrate irritability or resistance to stopping an activity or moving to a different location. You can help by giving your child warnings that a change will be taking place. Warn your child ten minutes before the change, then five minutes before the change, and then a minute before the change, to give your child time to begin to adjust, before stopping or moving.

SATIATION

Unique behaviors must be dealt with in unique ways. I needed to use a technique called *satiation* with one little boy I worked with, to substantially reduce an inappropriate, self-stimulating behavior that made him "un-available" for learning.

Ryder was five years old and would shred his socks every day in his classroom. He seemed to like doing this and would not stop unless his socks were taken away. When his socks were taken away, Ryder would have a tantrum and bite at his shirt sleeve. His teachers and aides had stopped trying to take his socks away and had refocused on trying to simply keep his hands away from his socks. At one point, a teacher had asked Ryder's mother to send him to school without socks, but his mother reported that she couldn't get Ryder to keep his shoes on without socks. Ryder's constant shredding made lessons at school and therapy sessions almost worthless. It was clear that if any progress was to be made with Ryder, the teachers and therapists would need to reduce this self-stimulating behavior.

We began to confront this behavior of Ryder's by appealing to the entire elementary school to donate to us as many old socks as they could spare. The school cooperated, and in about a week's time, we had five full boxes of socks. We began to give Ryder "morning work" upon his arrival every morning. His morning work was to shred a sock for us. At first, Ryder seemed thrilled. He liked the new textures of the socks and seemed to enjoy the shredding. He was not allowed to stop, though, until we felt the sock was shredded enough. We encouraged him to continue and keep going. For the first three days, Ryder actually shred all day, except during lunches and snacks. I remember it was the fourth day when he made an angry grunting noise when I told him the sock he was shredding was not shredded enough, and that he would have to keep going. On the fifth day, we gave him two socks to shred and told him to get going or he would not finish shredding both socks in time for lunch.

What we were doing was changing Ryder's self-stimulating good feelings toward the sock shredding. Shredding was no longer an activity that always gave him a good feeling. The shredding was beginning to feel like work to him and was no longer calming. He was now feeling stress while shredding, and as the days went on, Ryder clearly wanted to stop many times.

We ended up using only one box of socks with Ryder. And he did stop shredding. When a teacher or aide would see Ryder reach for his sock, they would mention that they noticed he would like to shred, and they would inquire if Ryder would shred some socks for them from the boxes in the coat room. Ryder, in response to this, would immediately remove his hands from his socks. He now apparently self-corrects and will independently stop himself from touching his socks.

Without his self-stimulating shredding behavior, Ryder began to participate in more appropriate sensory and learning experiences. This creative solution helped Ryder move forward.

Environments and Tools for Learning and Living

Can different learning environments affect a child's learning? They can indeed. Child professionals and teachers must be mindful of the stimulation levels in their environments. The "feel" or "tone" of an environment, whether calm or frenetic, can make or break a learning experience. The amount of visual stimulation, like eye-catching decorations or displays around the classroom, mixed with the auditory stimulus of the noise level and additional stimulation from the movement of classmates, can be a little too much for many special-needs children to tolerate. Finding a good environmental fit for children with special needs, or for children who have great difficulty focusing their attention, is a key to having successful learning experiences.

Knowing your child and your child's sensitivities can be very advantageous, for not only your child, but your child's teachers and therapists, too. If you can meet with your child's teacher about these issues, your child's teacher can put some time and thought into how she can make the environment more comfortable for your child. To reduce visual stimuli in the classroom, possibly the teacher could move certain displays of work or art to a hallway bulletin board. To reduce auditory stimuli, possibly the teacher can place your child's seat at a quiet table, or in close proximity to her own desk. Possibly she can seat your child along the outskirts of the classroom so that the auditory stimuli and motion will not surround your child entirely, from all sides. The teacher could also set up a quiet desk, where a set of headphones would be available for your child.

She could even help further by making times of movement consistent and predictable.

USING ASSISTIVE TECHNOLOGY

Assistive technology devices are also used to help children with developmental delays and disabilities succeed. Many parents find that not only do assistive and augmentative communication devices help their children become more independent, but they also find that the assistive devices become motivating tools. Children with developmental difficulties may shut down out of the frustration of not being able to communicate or participate in activities with others. Many children stop trying when they feel that their attempts to be understood or attempts to perform a task are hopeless.

An assistive technology tool may be as simple as a little rubber grip to help a child hold a pencil in his hand correctly, or as elaborate as a specially programmed computer system that can, on command, speak for the child in a computerized voice. Finding the right tools for your child can be a challenge. But if you find an assistive technology tool that is motivating to your child, and one that opens doors for her, it can feel like your family has won the lottery.

Assistive technology may not be for all children with developmental delays and disabilities, though. We want our children with special needs to function as typically as possible, and sometimes our very functional special-needs children are forced to use assistive tools when they are quite able to function without the use of special devices. Whether simple or elaborate, assistive technology devices can enhance the lives of children with special needs, as well as increase their participation and productivity.

Assistive tools may be used for:

- communication
- mobility
- reading
- writing

- math
- switch controls
- eating
- dressing
- bathing
- hearing
- seeing
- social interactions

Celebrate Your Child

Celebrate your child's successes, big and small. Applaud your child as he practices and gains new skills. You may find that as you do this, you establish a new sense of confidence and strength. Revel in the fact that your experiences with your child have given you an appreciation for many of the little things in life that most take for granted. Celebrate the lessons you learn about hard work, courage, and not giving up. More important, help your child feel value in his hard work. And show your child empathy and compassion when she is frustrated. It can be hard for all of us to try, when we feel like the "carrot" keeps moving farther and farther away from us. So, celebrate, encourage, and appreciate your child's efforts and tiny advances. They will add up over time. Here are a few ways you can celebrate your child every day:

- Show off a strength or positive attribute about him/her to a friend or family member.
- Relax and have fun together for a little while.
- Cheer on his/her efforts.
- Notice how beautiful her hair is or how beautiful his eyes are.

- Compliment him/her.

- Ask him/her if you may be of assistance somehow.

- Involve him/her in your favorite hobbies or interests.

- Play something he/she likes, or visit a person or place he/she enjoys.

- Invite others to ask you and him/her questions about his/her disability. Show him/her there is nothing to be ashamed of.

Here are some ways that others celebrate their children with special needs:

One way that we celebrate our child is by letting people get to know her. I used to shield our daughter from other people, including aunts and uncles, and I probably acted pretty defensive if someone wanted to ask questions, or if someone tried to give me advice. One day, it just really hit me that our daughter, despite her autism, is a really great and intelligent girl, and everyone who spends time with her ends up loving her. So outwardly enjoying my daughter was a big step for me, and now, letting others get close to her, so that they, too, can see how amazing she is, is how I celebrate her.

When we found out that our baby was deaf, the congratulatory phone calls and visits from family and friends literally stopped. The mood of almost everyone around us went from "tell me everything," to "what's happening is none of our business." My husband and I felt that we had the most beautiful son, whether he could hear or not, and we were positive that he was very smart, too, so we decided to take our situation into our own hands, and we actually threw a party for our baby son. We invited everyone we could think of to come to our home and visit and celebrate with "our family." Our son completely won everyone over. Many of our guests held him and all it took was that little smile! I am so glad we celebrated him with that party. Our family members and our close friends are all now very comfortable with our son's deafness, and they are also very supportive of our new language in the family (American Sign Language).

We have a special book for our son, who is now seven. We call it his "How I've Grown" book. We have pictures from his very first therapy sessions in the book, and we've had all of James's therapists over the years sign the book with congratulations on his progress. When we look at the book, we realize how far James has come, and we remember our time with some of the very wonderful people we've worked with over the years. I go to this book when I'm feeling a little down, and it never fails to lift my spirits and give me hope. When I look at it, I feel pride for how hard my son has worked, and feel amazed at how gracefully he has gone through some really hard times. When James feels a little discouraged, I pull the book out and we look at it and laugh together. We are always very excited to enter new pictures and notes. So this is one way I celebrate my child with others.

It is important for parents to see their child as a person, and not just see the developmental delay or disability. Be hopeful and positive if you are on a journey of getting specialized help for your child. With your commitment to finding out more, and the knowledge you have gained from this book, you are more than ready to help your child climb one small hill at a time, or race down a path to progress.

I wish for all of you, success and joy along the way.

Relevant Laws

Individuals with Disabilities Education Act (IDEA)—reauthorized 2004
Mandates that children who have disabilities have the right to a "free and appropriate education." Mandates that children will receive an individualized educational plan (IEP) with goals and measurable objectives.

No Child Left Behind Act—2001
Mandates that all states, school districts, and schools that accept Title 1 federal grants, must have qualified teachers and paraprofessionals, must report standardized test performances of all students, and must work to ensure that all children, including children with disabilities, reach a level of proficiency in reading and other academic subjects.

Assistive Technology Act—1998
Mandates that information about assistive technology will be made available, as well as funding options and loan guarantee programs.

PL 105-917 Part C—1997

Mandates that states should develop early intervention programs for children birth to age three, and that professionals should service families, not just the disabled child, individually.

Americans with Disabilities Act—1990

Mandates that persons with disabilities will not be discriminated against in any public setting.

Rehabilitation Act, Section 504—1973

Mandates that persons with disabilities will not be discriminated against in any public school.

Resources for Parents

American Occupational Therapy Association, Inc.
P.O. Box 31220, Bethesda, MD 20824-1220
1-800-668-8255
Website: *www.aota.org*

American Speech-Language-Hearing Association
10801 Rockville Pike, Rockville, MD 20852
(301) 897-5700, 1-800-638-TALK
irc@asha.org

Child Development Institute
3528 E. Ridgeway Road, Orange, CA 92867
(714) 988-8617
Website: *www.cdipage.com*

The Council for Exceptional Children
1920 Association Drive, Reston, VA 22091-1589
1-888-CEC-SPED
service@cec.sped.org

Developmental Delay Resources
4401 East-West Highway, Suite 207, Bethesda, MD 20814
(301) 652-2263
Website: *www.devdelay.org*

Federation of Families for Children's Mental Health
1021 Prince Street, Alexandria, VA 22314-2971
(703) 684-7710
Website: *www.fcmh.org*

First Signs Inc.
P.O. Box 358, Merrimac, MA 01860
(978) 346-4380
Website: *www.firstsigns.org*

Learning Disabilities Association of America
4156 Library Road, Pittsburgh, PA 15234
(412) 341-1515, 1-888-300-6710
Website: *www.ldanatl.org*

March of Dimes
1275 Mamaroneck Avenue
White Plains, NY 10605
Website: *www.marchofdimes.com*

National Center for Learning Disabilities
381 Park Avenue, Suite 1401, New York, NY 10016
(212) 545-7510
Website: *www.ncld.org*

Sensory Processing Disorder Resources
Auer Educational Services, LLC
8613 West 84th Circle, Arvada, CO 80005
(720) 480-4178
Website: *www.spdresources.com*

Zero to Three
734 15th Street, NW, Suite 1000, Washington, DC 20005-1013
(202) 638-1144, 1-800-899-4301
Website: *www.zerotothree.org*

Additional Websites:

Center on the Social and Emotional Foundation for Early Learning
csefel.uiuc.edu

Child Development Basics
www.childdevelopmentinfo.com

Council for Learning Disabilities
www.cldinternational.org

National Institute on Developmental Delays
www.nidd.org

Resources for the Sensory Processing Disorder Community—
The SPD Network
www.sinetwork.org

Schwab Foundation for Learning
www.schwablearning.org

Sensory Nation
www.sensorynation.com

APPENDIX III

Further Reading

Child Development—Parenting

Brazelton, T. Berry (1994) *Touchpoints (The Essential Reference): Your Child's Emotional and Behavioral Development*. MA: Addison-Wesley.

Eisenberg, Arlene, Murkoff, Heidi, Hathaway, Sandee (2003) *What to Expect the First Year—Second Edition*. New York: Workman Publishing Company.

Eisenberg, Arlene, Murkoff, Heidi, Hathaway, Sandee (1994) *What to Expect the Toddler Years*. New York: Workman Publishing Company.

Eliot, Lise (2000) *What's Going On In There? How the Brain and Mind Develop in the First Five Years of Life*. New York: McGraw-Hill.

Grenspan, Stanley I., Lewis, Nancy Breslau (2000) *Building Healthy Minds: The Six Experiences That Create Intelligence and Emotional Growth in Babies and Young Children*. New York: Perseus Books.

Warner, Penny (2001) *Smart Baby, Strong Baby: Your Baby's Development Week by Week During the First Year and How You Can Help*. Chicago, IL: Contemporary Books.

Special Needs—Parenting

Greenspan, Stanley I., Wieder, Serena, Simons, Robin (1998) *The Child With Special Needs: Encouraging Intellectual and Emotional Growth*. New York: Perseus Books.

Klass, Perri, Costello, Eileen (2003) *Quirky Kids: Understanding and Helping Your Child Who Doesn't Fit In—When to Worry and When Not to Worry*. New York: Ballantine Books.

Learning Disabilities (General)

Silver, Larry B. (1998) *The Misunderstood Child: Understanding and Coping with Your Child's Learning Disabilities—Third Edition*. New York: Three Rivers Press.

Smith, Corinne, Strick, Lisa (1997) *Learning Disabilities, A to Z: A Parent's Complete Guide to Learning Disabilities from Preschool to Adulthood*. New York: Fireside.

ADHD

Barkley, Russell A. (2000) *Taking Charge of ADHD: The Complete Authoritative Guide for Parents, Revised Edition*. New York: The Guilford Press.

Hallowell, Edward M., Ratey, John J. (2005) *Delivered from Distraction: Getting the Most of Life with Attention Deficit Disorder*. New York: Ballantine Books.

Hallowell, Edward M., Ratey, John J. (2005) *Driven to Distraction: Recognizing and Coping with Attention Deficit Disorder from Childhood Through Adulthood*. New York: Touchstone.

Hanos-Webb, Lara (2005) *The Gift of ADHD: How to Transform Your Child's Problems to Strengths*. Oakland, CA: New Harbinger Publications.

Heininger, Janet E., Weiss, Sharon K. (2001) *From Chaos to Calm: Effective Parenting of Challenging Children with ADHD and Other Behavioral Problems*. New York: Perigee.

Reiff, Michael I., Tippins, Sherill, LeTourneau, Anthony Alex (2004) *ADHD: A Complete and Authoritative Guide*. The American Academy of Pediatrics.

Dyslexia

Marshall, Abigail (2004) *The Everything Parent's Guide to Children With Dyslexia: All You Need to Ensure Your Child's Success (Everything: Parenting and Family)*. Holbrook, MA: Adams Media Corporation.

Shaywitz, Sally (2003) *Overcoming Dyslexia: A New and Complete Science-Based Program for Reading Problems at Any Level*. New York: Knopf, Borzoi.

Nonverbal Learning Disorder

Burger, Nancy Russell (2004) *A Special Kind of Brain: Living With Nonverbal Learning Disability*. UK: Jessica Kingsley Publishers.

Whitney, Rondalyn Varney (2002) *Bridging the Gap: Raising a Child With Nonverbal Learning Disorder*. New York: Perigee.

Sensory Integration/Sensory Processing

Biel, Lindsay, Peske, Nancy (2005) *Raising a Sensory Smart Child: The Definitive Handbook for Helping Your Child with Sensory Integration Issues*. New York: Penguin.

Heller, Sharon (2002) *Too Loud, Too Bright, Too Fast, Too Tight: What to Do If You Are Sensory Defensive in an Overstimulating World*. New York: Harper Collins.

Kranowitz, Carol Stock (1998) *The Out-of-Sync Child: Recognizing and Coping with Sensory Integration Dysfunction*. New York: Perigee.

Kranowitz, Carol Stock (2003) *The Out-of-Sync Child Has Fun: Activities for Kids with Sensory Integration Dysfunction*. New York: Perigee.

Smith, Karen A., Gouze, Karen R. (2004) *The Sensory-Sensitive Child: Practical Solutions for Out-of-Bounds Behavior*. New York: Harper Resources.

Motor Skills

Liddle, Tara Losquadro, Yorke, Laura (2003) *Why Motor Skills Matter: Improve Your Child's Physical Development to Enhance Learning and Self-Esteem*. Chicago, IL: Contemporary Books.

Speech and Language

Agin, Marilyn C., Geng, Lisa F., Nicholl, Malcolm (2004) *The Late Talker: What to Do If Your Child Isn't Talking Yet*. New York: St. Martin's Griffin.

Apel, Kenn, Masterson, Julie (2001) *Beyond Baby Talk: From Sounds to Sentences, a Parent's Complete Guide to Language in the First Three Years of Life*. New York: Three Rivers Press.

Golinkoff, Roberta Michnick, Hirsh-Pasek, Kathy (2000) *How Babies Talk: The Magic and Mystery of Language in the First Three Years of Life*. New York: Plume.

Autism Spectrum Disorders

Abrams, Philip, Henriques, Leslie (2004) *The Autistic Spectrum Parents' Daily Helper: A Workbook for You and Your Child*. Berkeley, CA: Ulysses Press.

Florance, Cheri L., Gazzaniga, Marin (2004) *Maverick Mind: A Mother's Story of Solving the Mystery of Her Unreachable, Unteachable, Silent Son*. New York: Perigee.

Ozonoff, Sally, Dawson, Geraldine, McPartland, James (2002) *A Parent's Guide to Asperger Syndrome and High Functioning Autism: How to Meet the Challenges and Help Your Child Thrive*. New York: The Guilford Press.

Sicile-Kira, Chantal (2004) *Autism Spectrum Disorders: The Complete Guide to Understanding Autism, Asperger's Syndrome, Pervasive Developmental Disorder, and Other ASDs*. New York: Perigee.

Sohn, Alan, Grayson, Cathy (2005) *Parenting Your Asperger Child: Individualized Solutions for Teaching Your Child Practical Skills*. New York: Perigee.

Stacey, Patricia (2003) *The Boy Who Loved Windows: Opening the Heart and Mind of a Child Threatened with Autism*. Cambridge, MA: Da Capo Press.

Wing, Lorna (2001) *The Autism Spectrum: A Parents' Guide to Understanding and Helping Your Child*. Berkeley, CA: Ulysses Press.

Social and Emotional Skills

Birmaher, Boris (2004) *New Hope for Children and Teens with Bipolar Disorder*. New York: Three Rivers Press.

Chansky, Tamar (2004) *Freeing Your Child From Anxiety: Powerful Practical Solutions to Overcome Your Child's Fears, Worries, and Phobias*. New York: Broadway Books.

Chansky, Tamar (2001) *Freeing Your Child from Obsessive-Compulsive Disorder: A Powerful Practical Program for Parents of Children and Adolescents*. New York: Three Rivers Press.

Goldstein, Sam, Brooks, Robert, Weiss, Sharon (2004) *Angry Children, Worried Parents: Seven Steps to Help Families Manage Anger*. New York: McGraw-Hill.

Grayson, Jonathan (2004) *Freedom from Obsessive-Compulsive Disorder: A Personalized Recovery Program for Living with Uncertainty*. New York: Berkley Publishing Group.

Greene, Ross W. (1998) *The Explosive Child: A New Approach for Understanding and Parenting Easily Frustrated, "Chronically Inflexible" Children*. New York: Harper Collins.

INDEX

About the Author

Laurie Fivozinsky LeComer, M.Ed., is an educational consultant to families, medical professionals, and child organizations on developmental and behavioral issues. She is also a special educator, program monitor, and evaluator who supports including children with special needs in regular education programs and classes. Ms. LeComer often speaks on the importance of early intervention, careful diagnosis, and ways to encourage rapid progress in young children. Ms. LeComer's background is in biopsychology (including amphetamine research) with graduate work in special education. She has been a member of the Harvard Graduate School of Education's Collaborative on Integrated School Services, and is a member of the Autism Society of America and the Council for Exceptional Children. Ms. LeComer continues to work directly with developmentally delayed, learning disabled, PDD, autistic, and multiply handicapped children in the Greenwich Public Schools in Greenwich, Connecticut.

Ms. LeComer is married, with three children, and currently resides on the coast of Connecticut. Visit her website at www.laurielecomer.com.

Also Available from Perigee Books

The Out-of-Sync Child:
Recognizing and Coping with Sensory Integration Dysfunction
by Carol Stock Kranowitz, M.A.
0-399-53165-3

The Out-of-Sync Child Has Fun:
Activities for Kids with Sensory Integration Dysfunction
by Carol Stock Kranowitz, M.A.
0-399-52843-1

Autism Spectrum Disorders:
The Complete Guide to Understanding Autism, Asperger's Syndrome,
Pervasive Developmental Disorder, and Other ASDs
by Chantal Sicile-Kira
0-399-53047-9

Parenting Your Asperger Child: Individualized Solutions for
Teaching Your Child Practical Skills
by Alan Sohn and Cathy Grayson
0-399-53070-3

Bridging the Gap:
Raising a Child with Nonverbal Learning Disorder
by Rondalyn Varney Whitney
0-399-52755-9

From Chaos to Calm: Effective Parenting for Challenging
Children with ADHD and Other Behavior Problems
by Janet E. Heininger and Sharon K. Weiss
0-399-52661-7

Maverick Mind: A Mother's Story of Solving the Mystery
of Her Unreachable, Unteachable, Silent Son
by Cheri Florance, Ph.D. with Marin Gazzaniga
0-399-53067-3

Available wherever books are sold or at penguin.com